Springer Series

FOCUS ON MEN

James Hennessy, Ph.D., Series Editor

Focus on Men provides a wide range of books on the major
psychological, medical, and social issues confronting men today.

Daniel Jay Sonkin has a Ph.D. in Counseling Psychology and is licensed by the state of California as a Marriage, Family and Child Therapist. Since 1977 he has been developing effective treatment approaches that help men stop using physical, sexual, property, and/or psychological violence in their personal relationships. He has coordinated his efforts with the San Francisco criminal justice system by assisting defense and prosecuting attorneys, judges, police, and probation officers in being more effective with domestic violence cases. Currently, he has a private practice in San Francisco and Sausalito, working with clients' problems which include domestic violence. He teaches classes on the subject at the California School of Professional Psychology in Berkeley, and is a consultant with the Family Advocacy Program at Oak Knoll Naval Hospital in Oakland, where he develops treatment services for active duty men who are domestic violence offenders. Dr. Sonkin's interest grew out of his work in examining the male role in family planning. As a pregnancy counselor for Planned Parenthood in Marin County he noticed that many women had bruises that were inflicted by their partners as a result of an argument over the pregnancy. Questioning the few men who were willing to discuss this problem led to his work on male violence against women. His first book, *Learning to Live Without Violence: A Handbook for Men*, was the first book written for men who batter.

Del Martin is the author of *Battered Wives*, a book that served as a catalyst for feminist organizing. She is a co-founder of La Casa de las Madres, the refuge for battered women and their children in San Francisco. She served on the Coalition for Justice for Battered Women, which was instrumental in developing the written protocol for the San Francisco criminal justice system that was the basis for a 1984 bill making police training on domestic violence uniform throughout the state of California. Ms. Martin was appointed by Governor Jerry Brown to the California Commission on Crime Control and Violence Prevention, which was mandated by the legislature to conduct a three-year study of the root causes of violence in our society. Her interest expanded to violence prevention, as she came to believe that the roots of violence are in the home as the basic unit of patriarchy.

Lenore E. Auerbach Walker, Ed.D., is a licensed psychologist in private practice at Walker & Associates in Denver, Colorado. She earned her degree from Rutgers, The State University of New Jersey, and received training in community psychology at Harvard University. She is a founding member and current chairperson of the Feminist Therapy Institute. Currently, her professional interests concern the intersection between psychology and law. She testifies as an expert witness in trials of abused persons who have killed their abusers in self-defense, and is developing videotape procedures to protect children from the trauma of courtroom testimony in sexual assault cases. Dr. Walker is the author of *The Battered Woman* and *The Battered Woman Syndrome*.

The Male Batterer
A Treatment Approach

Daniel Jay Sonkin, Ph.D.
Del Martin
Lenore E. Auerbach Walker, Ed.D.

Springer Publishing Company
New York

Springer Publishing Company, Inc.
536 Broadway
New York, New York 10012

86 87 88 89 / 10 9 8 7 6 5 4 3 2

Library of Congress Cataloging in Publication Data

Sonkin, Daniel Jay.
  The male batterer.
  (Springer series, focus on men ; v. 4)
  Bibliography: p. 239   Includes index.
  1. Family violence—United States. 2. Men—Counseling of—United States. 3. Family psychotherapy—United States. I. Martin, Del. II. Walker, Lenore E. III. Title. IV. Series: Springer series, focus on men ; 2. [DNLM: 1. Counseling. 2. Spouse Abuse. 3. Violence. W1 SP685K v.4 / WM 55 S698m]
  HQ809.3.U5S66 1985   362.8'2   85-12497
  ISBN 0-8261-5090-X
  ISSN 0277-3422

Printed in the United States of America

Contents

Contents

Acknowledgments

Writing this book has been one of the most difficult, but rewarding, tasks I have taken on in my life. I remember one night of panic, when, realizing what I had gotten myself into, I called Lenore Walker for reassurance and encouragement. As always, she came through with the right words and I went back to my writing pad. I realized that I had something important to say. The months that followed were equally difficult. As I wrote, I was aware that my relationships with those around me were constantly affected. My family, friends, and colleagues patiently accepted my frequent preoccupation with my subject, and my travels across the country that kept me distant, both figuratively and literally.

My male friends Robert Balkan, Michael Durphy, Andrew Lea, Wayne Murphy, Jonathan Pesner, Michael Searle, and Gerard Tomory have all been loving and supportive. Each is willing to struggle with what it is to be a man and how he can relate more fully to other men. Like myself, each is struggling for a balance of the masculine and feminine aspects of his inner self. The first feminist women I met in my life were my two aunts, Sylvia Levinson and Peggy Lipschutz. They showed me that women do not have to be like those portrayed in books, movies, and on television. I saw them being strong, assertive, intellectual, political, emotional, and compassionate. They embodied the most positive characteristics in both men and women. As an adult I have been fortunate to have similar positive encounters with women such as Pari Anvar, Angela Browne, Deanne Calhoun Bunce, Kathleen Burgy, Dorene Gould, Dianne Gerard, Mary McNeill, Julianne Searle,

Marilyn Segal, and of course, Del and Lenore. Each in her own way, these women have challenged me to examine my attitudes toward women, men, and myself. For this, I thank them. I would like to acknowledge the most important man and woman in my life: my father, Eugene, and my mother, Murna. They have been a guiding light, along with my brother, Karl, and sisters, Marlene and Janet.

I want to acknowledge the entire staff of the Family Violence Project of the San Francisco District Attorney's Office. It was working there that I grew the most in my understanding of the relationship between domestic violence and the criminal justice system. I would also like to thank the many dedicated women who work for the various violence shelter programs in the Bay Area. Likewise, I want to acknowledge the many men working with batterers in the Bay Area. Our desire to network, discuss openly our differences and similarities, and generally give each other support has been the spark that has kept me going for the last eight years. For that I thank them.

I would like to give special thanks to Susan Hanks, Jonathan Pesner, and Nancy Rothschild for their editorial comments and suggestions. Most recently, I have greatly appreciated working with Springer editors Barbara Watkins and Nina George. I acknowledge their commitment and that of Dr. Ursula Springer to this important social issue. I would also like to thank Ellen Thurston and Jo Anne Malone for their excellent preparation of the manuscript.

This book would probably not have been written were it not for the hard working, dedicated women and men of the battered women's movement, the many readers of my first book, and the people I have met in the workshops I have led across the country. Lastly, I would like to thank the many men who have found their way to my groups. They have not only helped me learn to work more effectively with men who batter, but I have also learned to work more effectively in my own relationships. May all the readers of this book learn as much from reading it as I did from writing it.

Daniel Jay Sonkin
Sausalito, California

It is impossible to acknowledge individually the many women in the battered women's movement and the network of shelters for victims and their children. I continue to marvel at the commitment, expertise, and creativity these women have shown in providing safe housing, fund raising, organizing support groups, developing children's programs, improving parenting skills of battered women, altering the response system of related agencies, and using the media for public education. I am indebted to those, too, who have researched the history of wife battering and the battered women's syndrome, and to the men who provide peer counseling to the batterers. All of them have helped me to understand how violence against women is basic to the patriarchal system. When we solve this problem we won't need a feminist movement any more—it's that basic.

Del Martin
San Francisco, California

In 1977 I was a keynote speaker with Del Martin at a conference on Love and Violence in Marin County, California. It was there that Daniel Sonkin and I first met one another. "If men shouldn't be working with battered women," he asked me, responding to remarks I made during my speech, "then how can we help eradicate men's violence toward women?" "Kind/gentle men must be the ones who work with men who abuse women," I responded. Daniel Sonkin and many other kind, gentle, nonabusive men have looked into their own hearts and souls, become professionally and personally skilled, and have begun to help fight this domestic war by counselling men who commit violence. I want to acknowledge these caring men, along with the women who have made it possible for them to understand the male batterer and help him adopt a nonviolent lifestyle.

Lenore E. Auerbach Walker
Denver, Colorado

Introduction

Michael Searle

When people hear that one in two women will experience some form of domestic violence over the course of their lives, they often ask whether violence in the home is increasing or has always occurred with such frequency and has heretofore been underreported. The difficulty in answering this question reveals the lack of public and professional knowledge regarding family violence. It is remarkable that the problem of spouse abuse or woman battering was largely unrecognized prior to the early 1970s. Most mental health professionals have received no training specific to domestic violence. Few psychology departments offer courses or training on this issue and familiarity with the problem is not yet a requirement for licensure to perform psychotherapy in any of the fifty states. With a level of incidence this high, it is safe to say that most mental health professionals have had clients who are either victims of domestic violence or offenders.

For therapists the problem of intervention in this area of family life is compounded by the family's conspiracy of silence as well as the therapist's own lack of understanding of domestic violence. Violence is, quite simply, a difficult issue to talk about. Batterers and battered women both feel shame and fear in discussing violence. Therapists often feel uncomfortable raising this issue, as they may be unfamiliar with their own feelings about violence. However, there are reasons to be hopeful. Resources are becoming increasingly available to victims and offenders, so that they can get assistance in stopping the cycle of violence. Training and educational materials are now available to therapists so that they can increase their knowledge and skills in helping with this problem. *The Male Batterer* is a valuable contribution to this effort.

Daniel Sonkin's knowledge about domestic violence comes from eight years as a psychotherapist working with men who batter women. In addition he has worked as an educator, administrator, and consultant with battered women's shelters, law enforcement agencies, military programs, criminal justice and medical personnel. He is someone who sees the need for a broad-based response to the problem of domestic violence. This is an invaluable perspective to offer not only because domestic violence cases involve responses from many social agencies and professions, but because working with this problem in whatever capacity can be very stressful. In order to optimize the possibility of successful treatment, it is essential to have good working relationships with other involved professionals. Daniel's positive approach to this problem, and his infectious belief in the ability of people to change and grow, make these working relationships a source of mutual support and encourage the kind of brainstorming of ideas and innovation that are required to effectively stop violence. This book is an example of what can come from this kind of collaboration.

Two renowned authors who have contributed chapters to this book are Del Martin and Lenore Walker. Del Martin is considered by many to be the founder of the battered women's movement, with the publication ten years ago of the internationally acclaimed *Battered Wives*. Having been read by battered women's advocates around the world, *Battered Wives* crystallized a growing awareness and spawned a movement that developed the first alternatives for women living in battering relationships. Although the focus of *The Male Batterer* is effective treatment for men, Sonkin, Martin, and Walker agree it is important to understand domestic violence within the context of a society that condones and even encourages violence as a means of resolving conflict and gaining power. Del Martin has done more than anyone to call attention to this.

Lenore Walker was the first clinician to write extensively about domestic violence from a psychological perspective. Her book, *The Battered Woman*, is considered the definitive text on counseling the victim of abuse. Her chapter in this book will help the therapist working with the batterer understand the effects of violence on the victim. This understanding is crucial to effective treatment of the batterer. All too often we hear the response from therapists or other professionals that "this woman is crazy," or "masochistic," or even "if I were married to her I'd probably hit her myself." An individual working with this problem must sensitize him/herself to the effects of being subjected to ongoing violence and learn to see "provocative" behavior as an expression of the victim's rage and helplessness, and not as behavior that deserves a violent response.

The collaboration of these three authors and their shared belief in professional networking and support mirrors an emphasis in counseling that encourages batterers and battered women to develop new support systems outside their marriage or relationship. We have found this to be a key intervention in stopping violence. Typically, batterers and battered women have few, if any, close friendships outside their primary relationship with each other. Even their respective families of origin, which are often intrusively involved, are held at bay by the couple. For the batterer, getting close is often seen as an attempt to control and dominate. He is vigilant in identifying threats to his own fragile sense of control. In this way he may perceive attempts at intimacy or offerings of help as threatening. Likewise, the battered woman has learned to limit her relationships outside the marriage because of her husband's jealousy. This results in an escalating dependency and concomitant isolation that become additional sources of stress. With few, if any, resources outside the relationship, batterers and battered women lack the essential perspective that can provide options to solving conflict and disagreement with violence. Many men and women feel as if they are the only ones who fight and experience violence as they do. They also feel as if no one understands. This intensifies already reduced self-esteem and the ensuing frustration contributes to escalating hostility.

By encouraging batterers and battered women to develop support systems outside the marriage, some of this pressure is alleviated. This is the distinct advantage that group treatment for batterers provides. Relationships develop in the group; men exchange telephone numbers and are encouraged to call each other for help; disagreements between men in the group can be worked out without violence. The result is men can see that their hostility is not only limited to their relationship. This ultimately makes it easier for them to admit that they do have a problem with anger and not explain it away as a problem caused by their partner. By encouraging men to depend on each other for support, the extreme dependency on their primary relationship is reduced, and increased options are then available during times of crisis.

The Male Batterer offers many useful techniques for dealing with the angry and violent client. However, an underlying premise of this book is that while techniques are very valuable, they must be utilized within the context of a meaningful relationship with a client, based on respect and understanding. This relationship can be as difficult for the therapist as for the client. The therapist's fear of his/her own anger, as well as the client's, makes it tempting to try to devise techniques to control anger in order to keep it at a distance. If therapists use anger management techniques to avoid confronting their own or their clients' anger it will ultimately lead to frustration for both the therapist and the client. The batterer will withdraw from treatment if he senses the therapist is trying to control him. He may already see himself as being controlled by others such as his partner, his boss, the courts, and his family. A clinician who emphasizes technique over an honest attempt to understand and respect the batterer as a person, will only confirm the batterer's fear that any relationship he enters will require abdication of his own autonomy. As with any therapeutic relationship, an atmosphere of trust and empathy is essential for success. A therapist who has examined his/her own attitudes toward anger and violence is in a much better position to bring this about.

Violence is learned in the home. Studies show that most male batterers witnessed violence between their own parents, or were themselves the victims of abuse. Violence is a learned pattern of relating, and it is handed down from generation to generation. Those who learn to accept violence as a legitimate means of resolving family disputes may see violence as acceptable in resolving community, national, and international conflict as well. This pattern of destructive family relationships can contribute to furthering cultural values that threaten us all. A person working to stop violence in the home contributes to a much needed change in cultural values.

Violence in the home can be stopped. We have found that an emphasis on relationships provides the central context for the most effective use of anger management techniques in the therapist's relationship to the client, with other professionals working in the field, and to his/her own anger. It is equally important for the client to examine his relationships to those who can offer support and encouragement, and to examine his anger for which he must find a more appropriate expression. All of these are areas that Daniel Sonkin, Del Martin, and Lenore Walker cover in depth. This book will be invaluable to those helping men to live without violence.

"...it is like you have knocked a glass of milk off the table. It has fallen onto the floor and the glass has shattered into hundreds of pieces. It has happened, there is nothing you can do about it, you cannot go back and undo it. But it is not over yet. It is not over until you have wiped up the spilled milk and have picked up the pieces of glass. I guess that is what we are doing here; we are trying to pick up the pieces ..."

A Male Batterer
1984

1

Domestic Violence: A Sociological Perspective

Del Martin

When I began to research my book *Battered Wives* in early 1975, I found that most people quickly changed the subject to child abuse, presumably a safer topic for social discourse. References to woman beating in the professional literature were rare. In usage were such terms as "domestic" violence, "marital" violence, "spouse" abuse, or "intrafamily" violence—terms that failed to identify the gender of the assailant and victim, implying that it takes two to tango or tangle. Feminists who had struggled so long to get people to use nonsexist language became frustrated when they observed the neutral term "spouse abuse" was being used to cover up the very gender-directed crime of wife beating.

Feminists had gathered more and more evidence about the prevalance of woman battering from women victims. But finding convincing statistics to back up their contention that it was a national social problem of epidemic proportions was difficult. Police did not keep records of "domestic disturbance" calls, though they admitted that these took up a good portion of their time. Incidents were lumped together with other crimes of assault, battery, aggravated assault, assault with a weapon, attempted murder, and homicide. The only police study, conducted in Kansas City, Missouri, in 1971 (Martin 1981), showed that one-third of reported aggravated assaults were due to "domestic disturbance." Police had been called previously at least once in 90 percent of the cases, and five or more times in over half of them. Also, 40 percent of the homicides were "spouse killing spouse." In 50 percent of these cases, police had been summoned five or more times within a two-year period before the murder occurred.

These statistics clearly indicated that violence unchecked escalates and can lead to serious injury and murder. Aware of the movements in Europe, Canada, and Australia to establish refuges for battered women and their children, feminists in the United States began to gather statistics in their communities in order to convince the public and officials of the need for a local refuge. Since a "needs assessment" was prerequisite to obtaining funding, women combed private and public agencies (police, hospitals, family courts, mental health, welfare, social services, and family agencies) for evidence. Mostly they received educated guesses because few kept such records. Also, many of the resources they relied upon for information were unaware that many of their clients were battered women: that injuries of "accident" victims they treated were due to battering, or that the women treated for depression were actually being battered.

From the figures the feminist network was able to gather from scattered sources around the country—actual numbers or educated estimates—common sense told me that incidents of violence perpetrated against women by the men they love and live with (whether married or nonmarried) reached into the millions. My editor argued that my data were too sketchy and unscientific to warrant such a conclusion.

Today, more research is being conducted on domestic violence, in particular the psychology of the batterer, the effectiveness of criminal justice intervention, and the extent and scope of the problem.

It is estimated that in one out of two marriages at least one incident of violence, probably more, will occur. In one out of five marriages the violence will be ongoing, with five or more incidents per year. At the extreme, episodes will happen monthly, weekly, or even more frequently. This conclusion is based primarily upon the only national "scientific" survey conducted by Murray Straus, Suzanne Steinmetz, and Richard Gelles, published in *Behind Closed Doors: Violence in the Family* (1980).

I would be remiss if I did not mention that these researchers found that wives showed a high rate of violence, suggesting to them that "spouse abuse" is not a misnomer. The announcement not only caused

tremendous controversy among professional colleagues but also resulted in a misleading media representation of the prevalence of
"husband beating."

The national survey relied upon one member of the couple recal-
ling and admitting the number of violence incidents that had occurred
during the previous year, the type of violence used, and who performed
these acts. Critics questioned the methodology because it did not take
into account the context in which the violence took place, the interaction before and after the acts, whether the woman acted in self-
defense, the actual force of the acts, and the damage sustained or the
lack of it (Fleming, 1979; Pleck, Pleck, Grossman & Bart, 1978).
Schechter, (1982) pointed out that a slap by a woman may momentar-
ily sting, but a man's slap has broken jaws. Battering men have a
tendency to minimize the extent of the force they employ and its
subsequent effects. If a period of time has elapsed, women victims may
also minimize the violence. Hilberman (1978) said the same paralyz-
ing fear and passivity that keep women from leaving their violent
husbands also prevent their striking out against them. Other critics
cited contrary statistics showing that the incidence of husband beating
is infinitesimal by comparison to wife beating (Dobash & Dobash,
1978; Fields & Kirschner, 1978).

To mollify his critics, Straus (1978) admitted that the survey's
"wife beating index" involved more severe violence than "ordinary
pushing, slapping and shoving." He estimated that almost two million
wives are beaten by their husbands in any one year and that for various
reasons this figure is probably underestimated: "It could be double
that."

The seriousness of wife beating as a social problem cannot be
diminished or denied. Quantitative methodologies provide limited insight and can be misleading. Qualitative methodologies, as we shall see
later in this chapter, are necessary to provide depth as well as breadth
to our understanding.

The Battered Women's Movement

In the 1970s, many feminists turned their attention to what they
perceived to be a systematic expression of men's violence directed
against women from childhood to old age. They set up rape crisis
centers and found that rape, or the fear of it, is the way men exercise

power over women and control their movements in society. They brought incest out of the family closet and noted that most of the sexual assaults against children are perpetrated by fathers and other males in the family circle. They exposed sexual harassment at the work place as economic rape, keeping women in low-status jobs by withholding raises or promotions unless they permitted their male supervisors "sexual favors." They started a shelter movement across the country to give battered women a safe place in which to heal their psychological and physical wounds, sort out what was happening to them, and consider their options.

In the beginning, women opened up their own homes or apartments to battered women who called rape crisis centers or sought legal services. Meanwhile, they documented "needs assessments" to convince the public and funding sources to establish community shelters. They permitted battered women and their children a longer stay in which to address the myriad associated problems. The first shelters were based upon a "women helping women" philosophy, a self-help approach run by women's collectives who recognized that the plight of battered women was not so different from the experience of all women.

Marya Grambs, one of the founders of La Casa de las Madres shelter in San Francisco, challenges women who doubt that the battered women's experience is similar to their own. She asks,

> "Did you ever back down from an argument with a man because you felt intimidated? Did you feel that if you had said anything more the situation might get out of hand? Have you ever felt threatened by a man's superior strength? Were you afraid that if he became any angrier he might strike you? Have you ever stayed in a relationship longer than you should have? Did you stay because you felt responsible for the other person? Were you afraid of loneliness? Did you stay because of the children? Did you have gnawing doubts that you could not make it on your own in the outside world? Were you fearful that you couldn't earn a decent living and manage the children by yourself?" (In Fleming, 1979, p. 9)

Whenever I give a public lecture on wife battering, I look around the audience and see the expression on women's faces as they recall buried incidents in their own lives and identify the feelings they have in common with battered women.

Like women, men must ask themselves similar questions about their tendency to intimidate and control women. They must realize that battering men are only an extreme on the continuum of being "a man" in this society. All men to one degree or another share the problems of the male batterer when they are unable to communicate their feelings, when they do not struggle toward equality in their relationships with women, when they devalue the feminine aspect of themselves or devalue the women around them.

Schechter (1982) noted that in the early days of the battered women's movement, grassroots shelters organized in different parts of the country and in isolation seemed to rely on feminist principles, insights gleaned from the victims themselves, and common sense, to learn how best to help battered women. They rejected traditional theories of cause and treatment as exacerbating the problem, not relieving it. Peer counseling, support groups, and the sense of sisterhood that "we," staff and resident alike, are in this together replaced the traditional professional–client relationship. Those who started the shelters had been "trained" and "credentialed" in the feminist movement. They had expertise as advocates for women, as rape counselors and problem solvers. A peer counselor at Project Outreach in Hayward, California, told me, "I have seventeen years of experience in a residential treatment center—my home."

Lisa Leghorn (1978) pointed out that the most refreshing and powerful aspect of a battered woman's first encounter with a shelter group is *validation*. She feels a tremendous sense of relief to find others who will listen to her and believe her and who share similar experiences. For her it is the beginning of self-empowerment.

A nonjudgmental approach as well as respect and acceptance for each individual is paramount to a successful outcome, in which the battered woman regains her self-esteem and begins to make her own decisions. For many, being free to make a decision is a new experience. One woman who had graciously offered to drive me from the shelter to a somewhat distant town for a speaking engagement told me on the way that her return trip would be the first time she had driven any distance alone. She said that each day, to strengthen her self-confidence, she tried to do something on her own that she had never done before. "You'd be amazed at what others take for granted that are monumental feats for me. But I'm tackling them one day at a time."

Today, professionals from all disciplines are becoming sensitive to the battered woman and are responding to her in this way. This change in perspective is a direct result of the education the women and men in the movement have provided in professional circles.

It should be noted that children comprise the largest population in the shelter. Special programs have been developed to meet their needs, especially the trauma they experienced from living in a violent home. Many children are relieved by getting away, some are withdrawn, and others, particularly the boys, display highly aggressive behavior. One rule that everyone in the shelter must adhere to is *no violence*—no hitting anyone else and, in many shelters, no spanking of children. Everyone, including the children, learns to deal with anger in constructive ways and to resolve conflicts without resorting to violence. Efforts are also made to repair any damage to the mother–child relationship and improve the woman's parenting skills so that she will be able to manage the children when she is on her own.

Negotiating help from existing community resources and maintaining the feminist principles of the shelter was a delicate balancing act. Sometimes it meant turning down much-needed funds because of the strings attached to their receipt. To government and foundations, a shelter had no credibility without an executive director and a board of directors, or at least having a tax-exempt nonprofit organization act as sponsor and conduit for receiving and administering the funds.

To protect the feminist ideology which views woman battery as a social problem that is linked to the oppression and liberation of all women and the collective "treatment" model which had proved so successful in helping women to alter their situation, shelters banded together in state and national coalitions. They worked together on legislation, shared in training programs, and tried to keep from competing against each other for funds.

For example, a California bill which proposed spending $280,000 on a demonstration shelter project met with opposition from the California Alliance Against Domestic Violence. Members of the coalition argued that it would be far more useful if the funds were allocated to a number of shelters rather than just one. Grants as little as $20,000 would at least guarantee the rent for existing shelters and serve as seed money to establish new shelters. Sharing instead of competing and settling for less instead of trying to get it all was an alien concept to legislators. Eventually, however, they did revise the bill to accommodate six shelters by geographic location in northern, central, and southern California, including rural as well as urban centers.

When state funding programs dried up because of budget constraints, the shelter network took the lead from Florida and persuaded legislators to raise marriage license fees to generate revenue for shelters. By 1983, 23 states had passed marriage license and/or dissolution surcharge laws (Woods, 1984). These laws have withstood challenges in Nevada and Alabama.

Attorneys in Missouri (Balsam, Ferry, & Przybeck, 1984) have suggested that another means of raising funds for shelters may be the use of the Necessaries Doctrine, which makes the husband primarily liable for food, shelter, clothing, and medical attention furnished to his wife, unless he has already adequately provided these "necessaries." Since a husband remains liable under the laws of some states even though she has left him, and he is not without fault in the couple's separation, they said that shelters could conceivably bill the husband for reimbursement of provided necessaries when the wife cannot pay. Laws vary from state to state, and shelters are urged to get legal counsel before deciding to sue if the husband refuses to pay.

If there are points in the law that affect the status of the shelter by following such a policy, I suggest that instead of acceding to them an effort be made to persuade legislators to enact exceptions to the rules. Many legislators today are more "enlightened" about domestic violence and would probably be more than happy to shift the financial burden from the state to the perpetrators of the violence.

Maintaining the shelters is one thing. Finding jobs and housing so that the women can be self-sustaining after they leave the shelter is quite another. Many shelters take advantage of federal job bill monies for training and apprenticeship programs. Others have received assistance through a Ford Foundation grant to the National Coalition Against Domestic Violence for its Employment Training/Small Business Project. Small business ventures can provide funds for the shelters and at the same time provide job training for residents who need it. Efforts to establish satellite housing are more a dream than a reality to date. But some women are renting houses and merging families to share expenses and give each other support as they seek economic self-sufficiency.

Shelters are a microcosm of the outside world. Women from every walk of life come to the shelter. They bring with them the baggage of misconceptions and prejudices to be found in society at large. Their common denominator is the desire to stop the violence. The principle of "women helping women" means making every woman welcome, learning to communicate and live with others of differing backgrounds. Task forces within the National Coalition have developed training tools and provide technical assistance to build bridges, enhance cross-racial and cross-cultural communication, and cope with sex role attitudes and homophobia among staff, boards, and residents.

Feminists who had rejected the establishment and its traditions learned how to use the system to effect change. They have become skilled lobbyists, negotiators, mediators, teachers, publicists, fund raisers, coalition builders, and entrepreneurs. The battered women's movement is a demonstration of the empowerment of women to bring about change in ourselves, in our families, and in society at large.

Feminist Research on the Battering of Women

Social scientists have a tendency to attribute a man's violence to the use of alcohol or drugs, poor impulse control, stress, unemployment, jealousy, frustration, provocation by the victim, inability to express feelings, and experiencing or witnessing violence in the home.

Susan Schechter (1982) complained that these theories provide "simultaneously helpful, confusing and contradictory insights" They list varied factors that contribute to male violence, but they do not tell us why so much violence by men is directed "toward a specific target, women, or within a specific context, their home." She pointed out that "stress" does not "cause" abuse. Many men deal with stress in other ways. "Poor impulse control" is a grossly misleading term, "since battering men know very well what they are doing." (pp. 210–211).

Indeed, battered wives report that an enraged husband does not just slap, he uses his fists and he generally aims his blows at places that do not show. He goes for the breasts, the stomach (even during pregnancy), the base of the spine, and parts of the head where bumps and bruises are hidden by hair (Martin, 1981).

Batterers exercise substantial control. Why else would some researchers speculate on what makes the difference between the man who merely wounds his wife and the man who kills her? One social scientist decided that the murderer has less experience at violence and goes too far when he loses control. Another conclusion was that alcohol could affect the judgment of the man as to the degree of battering a woman could take without dying (Gayford, 1975b).

Straus (1978) said that understanding about wife beating "is not likely to be achieved unless it is within the framework that views family violence as a whole," including practices of physical punishment and the acceptance which legitimizes violence in American society. He claimed, "In short, research focused exclusively on wife beating is too narrow an approach to produce a basic understanding of the processes that bring about wife beating" (p. 512).

I disagree with this statement. Examining violence in general obscures the very real problem of discrimination and violence against women, and it implies that wife abuse cannot be stopped until other forms of violence in society are eliminated. I am more inclined to believe that the control of women is so basic to the patriarchal structure of society that study of the origins, history, and incidence of wife beating today, together with the psychosocial dynamics of its manifestation, may lead ultimately to its solution. I also believe that confronting complexities and subtleties that underlie and reinforce the Battle of the Sexes will change the patterns of parenting that make the home the cradle of violence.

Gene Errington (1977) said, "Men beat their wives because they are permitted to do so and nobody stops them. Women are beaten because they are trained and forced and maintained into dependence and nobody helps them."

The evidence was there. Mental health professionals and criminologists embraced the "victim precipitation" theory, which blamed the victim and excused the husband's violent behavior. The police were trained to avoid arrest when the crimes of assault and battery were committed by a man against his wife. Therapists were convinced that all the woman had to do was to change *her* behavior, and the beatings would stop. No one held the batterer accountable for *his* actions. He got off scot free. Why?

In searching for answers, I found that wife beating had been an accepted practice from ancient times. Too numerous to mention here are all of the cruelties perpetrated against women over the centuries which show how deeply entrenched sexual inequality, at the least, and misogyny, at the extreme, is in human history. Wife beating has been translated into modern times as a custom, the unwritten terms of the marriage contract and the paternal hierarchical structure of the family. It is reinforced by religious doctrine, by family law, by nonenforcement of criminal law, by an economic system that keeps women dependent upon men, by service providers and therapists who reinforce sex-role stereotyping and maintain the status quo: the power of one sex (male) over the other sex (female).

The Dobashes, in their book *Violence Against Wives* (1979), reported, "It is impossible to say who first declared that wives could and should be beaten by their husbands or when this practice began; it is equally difficult to find any historical period in which there were no formulas stating the forms such beatings should take and specifying the conditions under which a wife was deserving of a good clout" (p. 31). Even in the Age of Chivalry, which romanticized "knights in shining armor saving damsels in distress," woe be unto the damsel who married her savior. A popular handbook of the day indicated that a scolding wife should be beaten and made to suffer and "let the husband have the word, and be the master" (Trevelyan, 1966, p. 260).

The first law of marriage was proclaimed by Romulus in Rome in 753 B.C. Although the law said that "A woman joined to her husband by a holy marriage should share in all his possessions and sacred rites," it went on to make it clear that "sharing" did not mean equally. Women, obliged to marry and having no other refuge in society, were "to conform themselves entirely to the temper of their husbands and the husbands to rule their wives as necessary and inseparable possessions" (O'Faolin & Martines, 1974, p. 53).

The edict that wives were to obey their husbands or suffer the consequences was incorporated, not only into man's law, but also God's law. The biblical account of creation said that woman was created after man to serve his needs. The subjugation of wives was the punishment for Eve's wrongdoing.

The male-dominated structure of the family and the ideology that supported it has continued "almost completely intact" to present times. Even today, the sacrament of marriage usually requires the bride to make the traditional vow to "love, honor, and *obey*" her husband. Many batterers still claim that they have the "right" to beat their wives if they disobey or displease them, despite the fact that laws permitting husbands to use physical force to chastize their wives were repudiated in this country a century ago.

The word *family*, derived from the Roman word *familia*, meaning "servants in a household," signifies the totality of slaves belonging to a man. The husband-owner had absolute power of life and death over the wife-slave, who belonged to him (Martin, 1982).

While "permission" to husbands to beat their wives is no longer legal, tacit permission still exists. It is embedded, not only in the male psyche, but also in the response systems of society. More recent studies of battering relationships from a feminist perspective are more useful. They provide the groundwork by which we can determine more effective methods for implementing change in behavior as well as the law, and for training of personnel in resource services to make more appropriate responses to pleas for help.

The Dobashes (1979) pointed out that the expectations of marriage by men and women are different and that "the most dramatic change that occurs is the extreme constriction of the woman's social world" (p. 76). In battering relationships the husband assumes authority and becomes more controlling and extremely possessive. He curtails his wife's freedom of movement and contact with her friends and relatives. She becomes isolated and completely dependent upon him. Even a legitimate demand, request, or complaint is viewed by the husband as nagging or an affront to his authority. Arguments center around her domestic duties (his expectations), sexual jealousy (usually without cause), and disagreements about money (which he controls).

Almost all researchers (Dobash & Dobash, 1979; Pagelow, 1981; Walker, 1979) find that the initial violent episode comes as a great shock to the wife. The cues were there, but she did not recognize them. She cannot believe this is really happening, that the man who claims to love her could treat her this way. She treats his violent outburst as an exceptional, isolated incident in which he overreacted. He promises it will not happen again. She believes him. She assumes that she must have done something wrong and tries to figure out what she did to cause her husband's reaction so there will be no reason for it to happen again.

The likelihood is that it will happen again. (1) Tension will build up over a period of time with some minor altercations, during which time she uses all of her coping skills. (2) Eventually the situation escalates to the point of no return, gets out of hand, and explodes in an acute violent episode. (3) Afterwards the husband is contrite, loving, and kind. He does not want to lose her. She wants to believe that this change in him will be permanent. This is what Lenore Walker (1979) calls the three-phase cycle of domestic violence.

The problem is that this pattern of violence will continue if something is not done about the *husband's* violent response. The experience of battered women shows that with each repetition of the cycle, the violence increases in frequency and severity. Historically, few men seek help on their own. If the wife leaves him and makes a condition of her return that he seek help, he is more likely to comply. However, once she comes back home, he will often drop out of counseling, and the cycle begins again.

With the increase in severity and frequency of the physical, sexual, and psychological violence, the battered woman loses motivation and believes that her situation is hopeless. The perception then becomes the reality—"learned helplessness" (Walker, 1979). She believes her batterer is invincible and that neither she nor anyone else can change that.

Mildred Pagelow (1981) calls the initial instance of violence *primary battering* and repeated violence *secondary battering*. She points out that not all batterers continue the behavior. Nor can we assume that all women in "stable" conjugal relationships have never been battered.

Pagelow approached her research from a social learning perspective. She tested her hypothesis: "The fewer the resources, the more negative the institutional response, and the more intense the traditional ideology of women who have been battered, the more likely they are to remain in relationships with the batterers and the less likely they are to perform acts that significantly alter the situation in a positive direction" (p. 16).

Resources are defined as material goods, capabilities, and human support systems in a woman's life sphere. Institutional response refers to the amount and type of assistance, or lack of it, available to victims from social institutions and their agents. Traditional ideology encompasses internalized beliefs that accept the "natural" order of things, including patriarchal, hierarchical social and family structure and its definition of male/female roles.

Survey respondents said that they initially turned to friends or relatives for help. Although the majority received some form of assistance (58%), some were given advice only (13%); but for many, no help was either given or received (29%). Almost all of the women had sought help from outsiders at least once, but assistance "was either not offered, was limited, or was short-lived." All the women surveyed had made prior attempts to leave. They stayed with parents or relatives (40.9%); stayed at a motel, in the car, or wandered aimlessly (24.6%); or went to a shelter (11.9%). The reason most often given by those who returned to their husbands was, "He repented, and I believed he would change." Other reasons were: "He found me and threatened more violence," "I had nowhere to go," "I found I was pregnant," or "I didn't have any money." More than half the subjects said police responded at least once. Of those who asked to have their husbands arrested (56%), only about one-fourth of these men were actually arrested, and few were brought to trial (15%). Not one out of the 350 respondents reported that her husband was found guilty or sentenced to jail.

One unexpected finding was that unemployed women or employed women with lower incomes opted out of their violent relationships sooner than women with higher status jobs and incomes. The former had less to lose. For the latter, leaving their husbands probably meant leaving their employment as well, much as they needed their jobs to support themselves and their children. Many battered women have experienced their husbands showing up at the work place, creating scenes, or even committing further violence in public.

Pagelow (1981) found that women who turned to clergy for guidance stayed longer with their abusers. And as expected, most of the battered women encountered negative responses from community agencies. The Dobashes (1979) also found that the policies and practices of agencies and case workers have influence on the cessation or continuance of violence in the particular relationship and for the more general acceptance or rejection of wife beating. These implications are not always clear, and they are often contradictory. An agency might condemn wife beating, but at the same time support the conditions that contribute to it—for example, the dominant position of the husband and the economic dependence of the wife.

Many battered women do not seek assistance from public agencies because they are not aware of available services. The woman who does find her way to a social services agency often encounters a case worker with the masochistic view of wife beating who makes the inaccurate assessment that the victim accepts the violence. In reality, she is *enduring* it because she has not been able to stop it herself and is unable to escape from it without outside help. Because of insensitivity and lack of knowledge about the dynamics of wife beating, case workers often compound the problem by making the woman feel even more hopeless.

The history of wife beating, social acceptance of men as heads of household and the abuse of power it generates, understanding of the cycle of violence and how it recurs, and inadequate responses of service agencies provide only part of the answer to Schechter's question, "Why do men beat women?"

Researchers agree that sex-role stereotyping, the socialization of boys to be dominant and girls to be subordinate, is basic. But few examine in depth how this socialization takes place, how the unnatural becomes "natural" behavior, all the subtle and blatant ways in which individuals are defined and programmed because they were born male or female.

Gender, Sex Roles, and Sexuality

One of the most important messages conveyed by the approach outlined in this book, with regard to treatment of the male batterer, is that men must change their sex-role attitudes and behaviors in order to effectively stop their violence. Service providers must understand the connection between violence and gender, sexuality, and sex roles. In doing so, this perspective may be incorporated in a treatment approach that focuses on cessation of violence.

Confusion about the relationship of gender (female or male) to sex roles (femininity and masculinity) and to sexuality exists because the dictates of patriarchal society are based on the assumption that differences in genitalia and reproductive functions (pursuit of and penetration of the female by the male) makes the sexes complementary and temperamental opposites which attract each other, and that these opposites become a unified whole when they merge in marriage.

Because the sexes are in "op-position" with the male on top in achieving coitus and pregnancy, the assumption is that males also top females in all human characteristics. Masculinity is thus defined as being strong, dominant, aggressive, logical, unemotional; femininity, being opposite, as weak, passive, submissive, intuitive, emotional.

Jean Baker Miller (1976) pointed out that dominant groups define acceptable roles for subordinates which typically involve performing services the dominant group does not wish to perform for itself. Functions the dominant group reserves for itself are carefully guarded and closed to subordinates because of "innate" defects or deficiencies of mind or body. If subordinates adopt the roles assigned to them, they are considered "well adjusted." This is the means by which the unequal relationship is obscured and legitimized, and how it is incorporated into cultural values, morality, and social structure.

Women are taught that their role in life is to marry and have children. When they take the marriage vow, their bondage is complete. Early English common law stated clearly "the husband and wife are one person in law," and that "the very being or legal existence of the woman is suspended during the marriage, or at least is incorporated and consolidated into that of the husband, under whose wing, protection, and cover she performs everything" (Blackstone, 1765/1966, p. 442).

A 1944 Florida Supreme Court decision (DeCrow, 1974) aptly described how this "oneness" has worked in our country:

> A woman's responsibilities and faculties remain intact from age of maturity until she finds her mate, whereupon incompetency seizes her and she needs protection in an extreme degree. Upon the advent of widowhood, she is reinstated with all the capabilities which have been dormant during the marriage, only to lose them again upon remarriage (p. 169).

Sigmund Freud (1905) warned that pure femininity and masculinity, either psychological or biological, is not to be found in human beings, and that every individual shows a mixture of character traits which belong to either sex. Yet mental health professionals, including Freudians, have persisted in maintaining the status quo.

The Broverman et al. study (1970), in which clinicians were asked to describe typical male and female behavior as well as "normal adult" behavior (sex unspecified) demonstrated how pervasive sexist notions are among therapists. Descriptions of typical male and female behavior matched commonly accepted stereotypes and equated characteristics of the males with what is "normal" and "adult." The message is clear. To maintain her femininity, a prerequisite to be attractive to the opposite sex, a woman must sacrifice her personhood and assume "childlike" characteristics of dependency. The woman who dares to express her selfhood and tries to act like a "normal adult" loses her femininity and her attractiveness to the opposite sex. Women are thus placed in a no-win situation.

The problem is that differences are not necessarily synonymous with opposites. Differences vary by degree. Women and men share common *human* characteristics to one degree or another. Opposites are antagonists; they are in conflict with each other. The perception that people who are different are opposites leads to hostility and discrimination against women by men and by whites against people of color—to sexism and racism. Superior/inferior roles, whether sexual or social, are learned. They are roles in "power" plays that dehumanize women and racial and sexual minorities.

If sex roles are so "natural," why the hard sell? Why must boys be trained to repress their emotions and forever be in control in order to achieve manhood? Why must girls learn to reshape or repress their personalities in order to accommodate male expectations? When both sexes are required to *repress* aspects of their psyche in order to conform to artificially imposed sex roles, it is apt to result in violence on the part of the man and depression on the part of the woman. Men are conditioned to externalize and women to internalize anger and blame.

Rev. Donald Morlan (1977) suggests that we "recognize that virtually all men are angry at women; that a man who batters is acting out in an extreme form what most men feel, at least part of the time" (p. 15). He attributes men's anger toward women to the repression of emotion in men, to limitation of intimacy to relationships with women, and to the socialization of men to be powerful.

Many men equate physical and psychological abuse of wives with sexual arousal and/or pleasure. Anthony Storr (1970) stated, "It is only when intense aggressiveness exists between two individuals that love can arise" (p. 39). He cited the Kinsey findings that anger and sexual arousal produce similar physiological changes in the body and that one response can suddenly change into the other as the reason why quarreling husbands and wives often end up in bed together. Aggression is an important component of male sexuality, he said, and "the idea of being seized and borne off by a ruthless male who will wreak his sexual will upon his helpless victim has a universal appeal to the female sex" (p. 70). To P. Evans (1973), "Violence is sexy" (p. 208). There is an "erotic shock in a good slap" applied to a recalcitrant woman whose "sensual masochism," however slight, is undeniable.

Storr also reminded women that sexual intercourse is a vital source of a man's self-esteem, that rejection can result in extreme rage from a husband or lover who feels insecure about his masculinity. A man who is not masterful and who fears women may become impotent. Rheingold (1964) said that reproach, derogatory remarks, disinterest, or exaggerated anxiety on the part of the woman in a sexual encounter may have a castrative effect on a sensitive man which could result in a lasting disturbance.

Again the woman is in a no-win situation. Her sensuality and sexuality are defined by men who conclude that because they find excitation in a "little" violence, she must, too. If a wife rejects this kind of sexual "foreplay," then she is held responsible for her husband's impotence or his rage, which in turn justifies beating her into submission.

Rape frequently occurs in a battering relationship. Research (Thyfault, 1980; Walker, 1979) indicates that 59 percent of battered women in a sample of more than 400 had been forced to have sex, and for 49 percent it happened more than once. A total of 41 percent had been forced to perform unusual sexual acts. They were tied up, threatened with a gun, beaten, or intimidated to act out sexual fantasies of their batterers. The acts included insertion of objects into their vaginas, engaging in group sex, sex with animals, bondage, and sadomasochistic activities.

By early common law a husband had "sexual title" to his wife, the absolute right to have sex with her on demand. State laws on rape have traditionally and explicitly exempted husbands on the ground that when a woman takes her marriage vows she automatically gives her "consent" to sexual intercourse with her husband whenever he desires it for the duration of the marriage. If the wife reneges, the implication is that the husband is justified in forcing her to have sex with him.

Male legislators are for the most part reluctant to remove the exemption of husbands from rape statutes on the presumption that angry wives who want to get even with their husbands will bring false charges against them. Never mind the violence, nor the fact that the burden of proof is on the complainant. Another excuse is that such a charge would bring irreparable damage to the marriage, as if that had not already happened. Male legislators and judges, of course, share the same male socialization and attitudes toward women—namely, that when a woman says no, her wishes are meant to be disregarded.

In the 1970s only six states (New Jersey, Oregon, Nebraska, Florida, California, and Delaware) had deleted the marital rape exception from their penal codes. By 1984 the number had increased to 22 (Laura X, 1984). In some states women who have formally separated from their husbands can bring charges against them for rape. Many states, however, protect the husband until the divorce is final. In these states, even though the woman has separated from her husband and has established her own domicile, technically she is still married to him and he is still entitled "access to her person."

MacKinnon (Douglas, 1983) claimed that men tend to be aroused by dominance—their own expression of it and the vicarious experience of domination by watching a woman who is subordinated, on the screen or in real life. She added that battery is sexual, not just that sexuality includes acts that are also battery.

Most research on rape shows that it is not primarily an expression of sexual desire; it is the use of sexuality to express power and anger. The "power rape," according to Nicholas Groth (1979), is the most common form. He describes the "power-assertive" rapist as using rape to express virility, mastery, and dominance. The "power-reassurance" rapist, on the other hand, rapes to resolve doubts about his sexual adequacy and masculinity. The "anger" rape is particularly brutal, and in extreme cases, may result in murder. The "anger retaliation" rapist expresses his hostility and rage toward women. His motivation is revenge, degradation, and humiliation. The "anger excitation" rapist finds pleasure, thrills, and excitement in his victim's suffering. He hurts and tortures his victim to punish her.

Groth might just as well have been describing batterers. They certainly fit the same categories: assertion of power to express dominance, or reassure his doubts about his masculinity, the expression of anger as a retaliation against women, and the sexual excitement engendered by seeing his victim suffer.

Seymour Feshback (1978) conducted an experiment in which one group of males read a sadomasochistic story and a second group a similar but nonviolent story. Then both groups read the same rape story which depicted a terrified victim who was compelled to yield at knife point. The first group (pre-exposed to violence) were more likely to be sexually aroused by the rape story, more likely to believe that the victim enjoyed the rape, and more likely to admit that they would act out their own rape fantasies if assured that they would not be punished.

As already pointed out, men in most states have only to marry their victims to gain that protection from punishment. The more intimate the relationship between the rapist and his victim, the more likely the victim will be deemed responsible for having consented to or provoked the act.

"Marriage and prostitution," Kathleen Barry (1979) stated, "are the primary institutions through which sex is conveyed and in which female slavery is practiced. Sex is purchased through prostitution, and legally acquired through marriage; in both, as outside each, it may be seized by force" (p. 230). Barry noted the parallel between the traffic of women (prostitution) and female sexual slavery in the home (wife battering, marital rape, and incest).

Feminists protest that depictions of women as victims of male violence in advertising, the media, and pornography have become more prevalent and blatant in recent years. Such groups as Women Against Violence Against Women and Women Against Violence in Pornography and the Media point out that such images of sexual violence not only appear in pornography but are also used in display advertising to sell products. They appear on billboards, in department store displays, on record albums, and book jackets sold in supermarkets. For example, a woman is shown lying on her back on an ironing board. A man is pressing an iron against her crotch. She is smiling. A cartoon in a porno magazine? No, an ad appearing in major fashion magazines.

The Bowling Proprietors Association ran a billboard campaign in which "Beat Your Wife" was spelled out in huge letters, and in small letters the message added, "Go bowling." When feminists complained, the Association president said, "We meant 'beat' in the competitive sense. It means take her up to the bowling lanes and show her who's boss." An ad by Cheeks Pants Company pictured a woman shrieking while a man paddled her "cheeks." The advertising executive explained, "We decided to develop a campaign men could really identify with. We really wanted to give it to women!"

A record album featured a bound woman with the message, "I'm 'Black and Blue' from the Rolling Stones—and I love it!" In a *Penthouse* cartoon a rape victim is calling, "Encore!" A *Hustler* cover showed a woman's body being fed into a meat grinder and coming out as so much hamburger. A magazine called *Sex Now* described "The Joy of Rape: How to, Why to, Where to" with an appendix of local maps on "How to Get Away With It."

"Such images," a flyer from Women Against Violence Against Women states, "teach us that women *are* victims in the same existential sense that grass *is* green, that women expect to be and like to be victimized, that women tolerate or accept their victimization, that women are safe, easy targets for brutal behavior, that victimized women are entertaining and amusing to contemplate, that the normal male is sexually aggressive in a brutal and demeaning way towards women."

Furthermore, the use of humor trivializes the very serious problems of rape and wife battering in our society. The extent to which this sort of "humor" goes was illustrated while I was watching the 1984 Republican Convention on television. Dan Rather, of CBS, asked Vice President George Bush in an interview, "How many debates do you plan to have with Geraldine Ferraro?" Bush squirmed a bit and finally replied, "I've not yet stopped beating my wife."

The propaganda of sex and violence, no matter how much it is trivialized, has profound effects on the erotic patterns of men and women—what Ellen Morgan (1975) calls the eroticization of dominant-submissive roles. Evidence that many women do, indeed, have rape fantasies triggered Morgan into analyzing the sexual games men and women play, the sexual signaling, and what she calls "chivalrese" and "rolese." She began to realize that women's sexuality may be "organized" by sex stereotyping that links maleness to dominance and violence. How it is organized may be different from, alien to, distressingly inconsistent with, and diametrically opposed to a woman's personal identity and values.

Morgan observed that boys and girls are taught that they are vastly different from each other and then "are trained to exhibit those supposed differences in order to be attractive to each other." In the pubertal years this training "leads straight to the connection of sex-role—instead of actual sexuality—with eroticism. Our developing female and male bodies are the real basis of the attraction we feel for each other, of course, but we are so conditioned to the notion that femaleness and maleness are essentially composed of the qualities we have been taught to regard as feminine or masculine. Only those who display 'appropriate' sex-role behavior are perceived as sexy and appealing" (pp. 13-14).

Judith Long Laws and Pepper Schwartz (1977) confirmed Morgan's observations, stating, "What is internalized through primary socialization retains much of its subjective reality, even when later learning overlays and contradicts it" (p. 9). They said, too, that the first component of sexual identity rests on "a collection of prescriptions" for femininity and masculinity that are carried over into the realm of sexual behavior: "The understanding of sexual identity requires an appreciation of both biological givens and social realities. A common error is to assume that biological facts determine social realities" (p. 27).

Another common error is the glorification of the male "sex drive" as justifying a kind of natural law of the jungle. Shere Hite (1976) claimed that available information does not support such a conclusion, that there is no *physically* demanding male sex drive that forces men to pressure and intimidate women into having intercourse when they do not want it. Lester Kirkendall (1958) verified that sex drive "seems to be very largely a psychologically conditioned component" and is more a function of desires than "needs."

Neuropsychologist James W. Prescott (1975) contended that major causes of adult violence are the deprivation of physical affection in childhood and the repression of female sexuality. He said that there is a reciprocal relationship between pleasure and violence in that the presence of one inhibits the other—that is, when the brain's pleasure circuits are on, the violent circuits are off, and vice versa. This may explain why when the ultimate moment comes, some rapists may lose their erection. Researchers have found that a surprising number of rapists are impotent.

In determining influences of violent behavior, Prescott said we should not overlook religious value systems which determine the morality of physical sensory pleasure. He made a cross-cultural study of child-rearing practices, sexual behaviors, and physical violence. He found that societies that lavished affection upon infants had low religious activity and less violence among adults. On the other hand, societies with low infant indulgence were more likely to practice slavery and polygamy and fear of an aggressive God. Societies which punished premarital or extramarital sex were likely to engage in wife purchasing, worship an authoritarian God, practice slavery, and have a high rate of violence. The dualism in Judeo-Christian theology of body–soul relationships equating men with spirit and women with body (sex, evil), Prescott pointed out, has had a deep and negative influence. The United States is a sex-repressive society and statistically one of the most violent nations in the world.

So much of male ideology of sex has to do with implied "female consent." Female sexuality is not immune to the social and political forces (family, media, religion, public education) which shape other dimensions and power imbalances in women's lives. Because of these compelling influences and social structures over which we have no control, Karen Rian (1982) said, "We *all* 'consent' to sexual desires and activities which are alienating to at least some degree. However, there's a vast difference between consent and self-determination. . . . In other words, self-determination requires that consent be both in-formed and self-formed." Rian concludes that "sexual liberation in-volves the freedom to redefine and reconstruct our sexuality, which in turn reshapes our sexual desires" (p. 49).

Marge Piercy (1984) further explains the woman's perspective of liberated sex: "To be afraid of a partner, unable to speak my mind or lose my temper or express my will, would dampen my sexuality. Under the gross inequality that has existed between almost all men and women, I think few women can flourish sexually. To be defined as a sexual receptacle for someone else means to be negated as the one who desires. . . . In good sex, my partner opens to me his full vulnerability, his capacity for pleasure, tenderness, and passion" (p. 48).

When male and female sexuality become so dichotomized the effect on the individuals may be evident in their misunderstanding, fear, distrust, anger, and/or hatred toward members of the "opposite" sex. For men this may mean the drive to become more of a "man." Homosexuality is something to be feared, even more than women.

Lehne (1976) stated that the male role is predominantly maintained by men themselves. They use homophobia to enforce appropriate male behavior and define the limits of "acceptable" masculinity. "Given the nature of homosexuality, the proof of 'manhood' must be continuous; no diploma, or marriage license, is possible to demonstrate once and for all that a man is not a latent homosexual" (p. 78).

Most mothers are apt to treat their daughters and sons as "children." Fathers are the ones who usually insist upon enforcing differential boy/girl roles. Fathers who are so afraid that their sons may become "sissies" or "faggots" recoil from father–son displays of physical affection and hold their sons—even toddlers—at arm's length with a male handshake. Such fathers indulge in rough and tumble play, show approval by a pat on the back or buttocks, but reject father–son hugging and kissing.

Letty Cottin Pogrebin (1980) pointed out that a small boy's relationship to his mother is usually one of warmth and loving acceptance. But all too soon the boy learns that he must identify with the father or another male figure if he is to achieve his manhood. He learns that such qualities as tenderness and loving kindness are "feminine" and that he must take on aggression as the symbol of his male identity. Mothers are warned not to coddle their sons lest they make "sissies" of them.

Boys are not only taught to be dominant and aggressive; they are taught to avoid behavior that could in any way be construed as womanly. An effeminate man is assumed to be homosexual and is held up to scorn. In this conditioning process, however, the message is anti-woman. Boys learn to glorify masculinity and despise all things female.

On the other hand, girls are not discouraged from adopting

"tomboy" behavior. In them it's "cute"—up to a point, that is. At puberty they soon learn to repress characteristics or interests that are male prerogatives in order to be attractive to boys. The message is abundantly clear that nonconformity or autonomous woman means lesbian.

Since women are supposed to be emotional, boys are told that they must not cry. They must control their emotions, hide their feelings, and maintain the aura of invulnerability. The repression of emotion, as mental health specialists can attest, has devastating psychological effects.

In the following chapter the characteristics of men who batter will be discussed. One of these characteristics is the tendency to deny the expression of their emotional selves. The effects of this may include the man's intolerance of his partner's emotions, his inability to communicate his emotions, and his devaluation of women in general and his partner in particular.

Beverly Harrison (1981) connected the dualism of Christian body/mind and male/female concepts with homophobia and misogyny in Western culture. "The depth of the revulsion toward women is clearly reflected in the projection of the female stigma onto males who do not fit the dominant norms of 'real manhood'" (p. 9).

Male supremacy and compulsory motherhood are the raw essentials of a patriarchal system (Pogrebin, 1980). But sex-role training, instead of enhancing the quality of life for heterosexuals, actually conditions boys "against heterosexuality because society is so relentlessly *for* 'masculinity'" (p. 298). It polarizes the sexes, makes it more difficult for men to love the other sex, and may encourage rather than discourage homosexuality, among men at least, despite the taboo against it.

While homophobia cannot prevent homosexuality, Pogrebin continued, it can destroy male sensitivity. "Real men," who feel they must maintain the pretense of invulnerability, cannot express their feelings and fear intimacy.

Denial permeates many men's lives: denial of the father's physical affection, self-imposed denial of the mother's affection because that is "sissy" stuff; denial and inability to express feelings in friendships with other boys or men; denial and fear of intimacy with women. This is a vicious circle that often leads to feelings of sexual inadequacy and violence—and further denial.

The power dynamics in patriarchal society promote heterosexuality and at the same time create a male aggressor/female victim adversary relationship which defeats its purpose. Until we recognize how detrimental homophobia and arbitrary sex-power roles are to marriage and the family, violence or the threat of violence will continue in millions of American homes.

Domestic Violence Is a Crime

In the early days of the battered women's movement we found that police had a nonarrest policy when crimes of violence occurred in the home. Except for felonies, involving serious injury that could not be ignored, police were taught "dispute" intervention techniques to prevent "a breach of the peace." Officers were warned that police action could aggravate the situation and endanger themselves. They were taught to separate and calm the parties, mediate the dispute, and make referrals where the couple could receive help in resolving their conflicts. Battered women were actively discouraged from seeking relief or protection from the criminal justice system. Police explained that the process was costly and time-consuming and could mean a loss of family income. The husband, if arrested, would be released on bail or his own recognizance in a matter of hours and would come home angrier than ever and give the wife a worse beating. When an arrest was made, few cases reached the court. District attorneys assumed that the wife would drop the charges or refuse to testify against her husband, and so it was not worth the effort to prosecute. If a case did come to trial, the judge, too, tended to minimize the violence and regard the situation as a marital dispute.

Because the police department is the only public agency on call 24 hours a day, it was crucial that officers receive training about domestic violence and more appropriate ways to respond. Police were invited to be speakers on law enforcement panels at family violence conferences. They spoke the party line and left. They seldom attended other workshops to learn more about the dynamics of wife beating or suggestions which might improve police response. Only once in my experience did a law enforcement agent stay for the entire conference. He was the police chief of a small town in Kansas. The fact that a local battered woman had been murdered recently no doubt prompted his concern and willingness to learn. The folklore of disputes and disturbances desensitizes law enforcement officers. The word *violence* in the phrase *domestic violence* has no impact upon them until it is too late.

Advocates for battered women appealed to police administrations to change their policies, to give notice to battering men that their violent acts are crimes, and to effect arrests even for misdemeanors. Some police chiefs permitted these advocates to make presentations at the police academy. But recruits soon learned from old-line officers in field training that "those women do-gooders don't know what they're talking about. They aren't the ones who go out on these calls." But these officers did not know what happened after they left the scene of the crime. By taking no action, they conveyed to the batterer that he could get away with beating his wife. He might be violent again because she had called the police. Detaining the offending husband would give the victim a chance to escape, to find a safe place to stay. Instead, she became convinced that no help was available and that she was trapped in a violent home.

Legal advocates for battered women decided that the only way to get police to respond appropriately was to sue. Class action suits were brought in federal courts against the police departments of New York City and Oakland, California, citing discrimination and unequal protection under the law. Through consent decrees, new procedures were drawn up for police training and for treating domestic violence as a crime like any other crime of violence. Bolstered by this success, feminists began to negotiate in earnest for change in other jurisdictions.

In San Francisco we had the Family Violence Project in the District Attorney's office. It was originally established by funding from the Law Enforcement Assistance Administration to develop a systems approach to domestic violence, to coordinate training and networking of all public and private agencies in the city which have any contact with violent families. By the time the LEAA went out of existence and federal funding was dropped, the Project had been so successful that it was comparatively easy to convince the city and other funding agencies to pick up the tab.

The Coalition for Justice for Battered Women (an ad hoc group composed of feminist attorneys, law students, and service providers) was satisfied with the Family Violence Project's performance and its unit established within the Hall of Justice to counsel victims whose cases had entered the criminal justice sytem. Police response, however, was still a problem. The number of cases the Project saw were few by comparison to the number of domestic violence calls received by police communications.

With the backing of Mayor Dianne Feinstein, who instructed her newly appointed Police Chief, Cornelius Murphy, to work with the Coalition to improve police response to domestic violence, we established a new written protocol. For nine months the Coalition negotiated and argued, sometimes vehemently, with Deputy Chief James Shannon and other police administrators. The outcome was a new general order. Shannon later became an ardent supporter, always on the alert for loopholes in the system.

Provisions in the new general order included the following:

1. Officers shall treat all domestic violence as criminal conduct.
2. Mediation shall not be used as a substitute for appropriate criminal proceedings.
3. The officer's course of action is *not* to be influenced by marital status, regardless of whether the suspect lives on the premises with the complainant, the existence or lack of a temporary restraining or stay away order, the potential financial consequences of arrest, the complainant's history of prior complaints, verbal assurances that the violence will cease, the complainant's emotional state, whether injuries are visible, the location of the incident, or speculation that the complainant may not follow through with the criminal justice process or that the arrest may not lead to a conviction.
4. When a felony is committed, the officer shall make an arrest, whether or not the victim endorses this action.

In misdemeanor cases, officers shall evaluate the likelihood of a "continuing offense" (a California statutory condition under which arrest rather than a citation is required): whether the suspect has a prior history of arrests or citations involving domestic violence and/or a prior history of assaultive behavior; whether the suspect had previously violated temporary restraining or stay away orders; statements from the complainant that the suspect had a history of physical abuse toward the complainant or that the victim expresses fear of retaliation or further violence should the suspect be released.

Officers shall inform complainants of their right to make a citizen's arrest in misdemeanor cases and shall not dissuade the complainant from exercising that right. In all incidents of domestic violence, officers shall write an incident report and give the victim the incident report number for follow-up.

Once a restraining order has been verified and there is reasonable cause to believe the order has been violated, the officer shall effect an arrest. The same applies to a stay away order, issued in a criminal case where the probability of victim intimidation exists. Attempts to prevent or dissuade a victim from attending or giving testimony at any proceeding are misdemeanors. The use of force, or the expressed or implied threat of force or violence related to the procedure, is a felony. The restraining order is issued for a maximum of 90 days, but the stay away order remains in force throughout the criminal proceedings, including sentence or probationary period.

When an officer verifies that a restraining order exists but cannot verify proof of service that the subject has been notified, the officer shall inform the suspect of that fact and the terms and admonish the suspect that the order is in effect and that continued violation of the order will result in arrest. The officer's incident report stating he has informed the suspect shall be proof of service.

A second general order noted that a "domestic violence" box had been placed on the first line of the Incident Report form and that officers shall circle yes or no on all incident reports. Whenever the genesis of the crime (whether assault, trespassing, destruction of property, or violation of a court order) is related to domestic violence, the officer shall circle yes.

Domestic violence is defined as harmful physical contact or threat thereof involving spouses, cohabitants, boyfriends/girlfriends, adult family members, separated/divorced couples, persons of the same sex in an intimate and/or sexual relationship, and any two individuals who have or previously have had a sexual relationship.

A basic key to changing police attitudes is to place domestic violence training at the police academy under "crimes against persons" instead of "intervention techniques." Right away there is a difference in perspective.

Within months after the new regulations went into effect, the arrest rate in domestic violence cases increased 60 percent. This increase is significant since a Minneapolis police study (Wurr, 1983) showed that arrest has a sobering effect on offenders and does reduce recidivism, even though they are released within 24 hours. Abusers who committed "moderate" (misdemeanor) offenses and were ordered out of the home by police for a period of at least eight hours had a

24 percent recidivism rate; in instances where officers tried to mediate and/or made referrals, the rate was 17 percent; for those arrested, it was only 10 percent.

Like police, district attorneys have avoided prosecution of domestic violence cases. They have a history of assigning such cases to the least experienced attorneys in the office, often with the goals of getting the parties together, mediating, and making referrals. They assume the victim will want to drop the charges or will change her story at trial, resulting in an acquittal.

The Coalition for Justice for Battered Women challenged San Francisco's district attorney: "If you took more cases to trial, you might learn how to win some." Two attorneys were assigned to oversee domestic violence cases, one for felonies and the other for misdemeanors. The Coalition was also permitted to do some in-service training. It was not long before we received a copy of the letter from an assistant district attorney praising the thorough investigation by the police that helped her to win her case.

The importance of having special domestic violence felony attorneys is the ability to provide vertical prosecution, that is, one attorney following the case from beginning to end. Otherwise, the file can be handled by a different attorney at any point in the proceedings. Since victims are so ambivalent about bringing criminal charges against their husbands, they need someone to relate to who will reassure them and keep them informed of the process.

Early and consistent contact with the victim and referral to appropriate support service agencies is crucial to protect the case. It is important for the attorney to gain the trust and confidence of the victim/witness while gathering evidence. The victim should be personally served with a subpoena at the earliest possible time, preferably in the privacy of the prosecutor's office. The explanation that she is just a witness and that her appearance is required by the court can help to relieve her feelings of guilt. The prosecutor should object to unnecessary continuances. The victim is more likely to follow through when a case is pursued in a timely manner. At the defendant's first appearance, arraignment, or preliminary hearing, a written stay away order should be requested to protect the victim and to discourage the defendant from threatening or dissuading her from testifying.

Following these procedures protects the case and encourages the victim to cooperate. Nonetheless, despite all efforts, some victims are reluctant witnesses, in which case the district attorney has two choices:

to request a dismissal requiring the victim to testify at the hearing on the motion that she is freely and voluntarily declining to cooperate, or to request she be charged with contempt. If the victim is found to be in contempt of court, the district attorney should request that the disposition meet her needs, such as required counseling or participation in a battered women's support group.

Nancy Sieh, of the Santa Barbara District Attorney's Family Violence Unit, explained that "successful" prosecutions in domestic violence cases should not be measured by numbers of convictions. The point is that holding batterers criminally accountable for their conduct often motivates them to alter it. Prosecutorial intervention, though short of conviction, has had a deterrent effect upon the behavior of many defendants and has demonstrated a remarkable reduction in recidivism. Better results are also noted in the process which brings a victim/witness to a greater point of awareness, enabling her to follow through on a present or future incident. The knowledge that a concerned prosecutor is available and willing to assist her can help to break the cycle of hopelessness in her life and gain her cooperation in the court process.

At the request of the American Judges Foundation and the American Judges Association, the National Center on State Courts is developing a domestic violence training curriculum and a list of judges willing to participate in regional trainings. Judges need to be more familiar with the dynamics of domestic violence in order to interpret the evidence presented: the batterer's propensity to deny or minimize his actions and the influence of fear on the victim's testimony. She, too, may minimize the history and severity of the violence. Judges should press for conclusive documentation of past incidents of violence and the severity of the victim's injuries, which are often not visible and therefore easily minimized.

Another approach is the use of expert testimony on the battered woman's syndrome (Sonkin and Fazio, in preparation; Walker, 1984). Expert witnesses are crucial in defending a battered woman who finally kills her husband out of desperation and fear for her own safety (Thyfault, 1984). Judges and juries who cannot comprehend why a woman would stay in a battering relationship or why a victim might be afraid to testify need information. Testimony of an expert witness would give them the means by which to interpret and evaluate the evidence presented to them. Expert testimony need not be limited to homicide cases; it can be useful in lesser offenses.

The judge, when faced with a reluctant witness, should be sure that she understands that there are options to incarceration as the outcome of the trial, such as diversion or probation, before dismissing a case or finding the witness in contempt.

As with criminal cases, civil cases involving child custody are affected by the presence of woman battering. Currently, most courts will not admit testimony on spousal violence when custody or visitation issues are being determined. This practice does not take into account several factors. Most shelter, mental health, and law enforcement personnel will report that the violence risk increases at the time of separation or divorce. When violence erupts, children may witness such acts and/or may be at risk for injury. Frequently, men will use the children to "get back at their partner" if she is not readily available. Even in the absence of these factors, the question remains, How does growing up in a violent family affect child development? The court does have a responsibility to assure that both parents will not act in ways that may be detrimental to the child's healthy development. The authors of this book strongly believe that men who batter must be held accountable for their violent behavior. This may mean loss of custody and/or visitation, third-party visitation, and/or court-mandated counseling as a condition of custody or visitation.

Domestic Violence Diversion Programs

By California law offenders may, upon meeting certain requirements, be eligible for Domestic Violence Diversion Programs. Most victims just want their husbands to get help so that they will stop their violent behavior, and knowledge that the goal of the criminal justice system is not necessarily incarceration and that the court can mandate counseling is an incentive to them to cooperate. Referral by the court may be the only way to get her batterer into a program, since most batterers do not seek help voluntarily.

Diversion does not apply to serious felony offenses; it is an option only in misdemeanor cases. An offender may qualify if there are no convictions involving violence within the previous seven years, if his record shows he has not failed to comply with previous probation or parole requirements, if he has not been diverted within the past five years, if the victim did not sustain severe injuries, or if the attack did not involve the use of a deadly weapon or force likely to produce great bodily injury even though the victim's injuries may not be so severe.

The diversion program can last from six months to two years. The model described in this text recommends treatment for the duration of diversion (one to two years). The success of a diversion program depends upon the attitude and cooperation of the offender and the cessation of his violence. When an offender is diverted before trial, his arrest record is erased upon completion of the program.

In some cases the prosecutor may prefer to go for probation, which could still mean court-required counseling for the offender. The offense, however, will become part of his record—a record that may be useful should there be a future offense. If the offender commits another violent act while in a diversion program, he will be returned to court for trial or revocation of probation. Domestic violence training is also vital for probation officers so that they will be more effective in determining eligibility for and evaluation of diversion programs.

Most diversion programs are based upon the model described in the following chapters. Treatment programs, to be the most effective, must be specifically designed to reflect the characteristics of batterers and have but one goal in mind: to stop *his* violence. Attention is focused on his violent behavior rather than the relationship. Marital therapy gives the false impression that both partners share responsibility for the violence. Researchers have found that most batterers had previous relationships in which violence occurred (this text). Stopping the violence depends upon the batterer's taking responsibility for his own actions and recognizing that violence is learned behavior which can be corrected by learning new and less destructive behaviors.

Chapter 8 discusses the development of treatment programs for male batterers. Such programs have been developed within battered women's shelters, community mental health agencies, social services agencies, criminal justice agencies, and men's collectives and with private service providers. The growth of these programs has paralleled the increase in men who are beginning to respond to woman battering. In a safe group environment, batterers can explore the roots of their violent behavior with other men (and sometimes with women) who have been struggling to overcome the same social conditioning. The men gain a sense of solidarity as they help each other apply new experiences to their lives, new ways of resolving conflict and exposing their feelings.

Jail time and a lengthy probationary period may be necessary where the offender has a chronic pattern of abuse that has resulted in a substantial assault, the offender shows little remorse or interest in addressing his behavior, the offender does not observe restraining or stay away orders, or the offender refuses or is unable to control his aggression. Courts are reluctant to sentence offenders to state prisons but will do so, however, if the offender's abuse is severe and chronic and has a high degree of lethality.

In the past 10 years the issue of woman battering has come out from behind closed doors. The women and men of the battered women's movement have confronted every institution that affects battered women. Law enforcement, mental health, social service, medical, and governmental institutions have changed their policies and procedures in responding to woman battering. Legislation has been enacted on the city, state, and federal level. We have shown that with persistence and dedication, it is possible to change personal attitudes and institutional response to woman battering.

The task ahead is to change individual response patterns—patterns of personal behavior that have resulted from the socialization of men to be aggressors and women to be victims. In recent years many men have struggled to open their minds and hearts to the issue of male violence against women and to the issues that have alienated men from women. As they have come to terms with their own response patterns and attitudes toward women, they have become effective as counselors in helping battering men change their destructive behavior. Some skills which can make this change possible are offered in the chapters that follow.

2
The Male Batterer:
An Overview

To date few formal studies have been conducted on the male batterer; much of what we know comes from clinical observation. Although traditionally this type of data are generally unreliable, communications with batterers' programs across the county have corroborated much of the information you are about to read. In addition, many studies that have inquired into battered women's perceptions of their batterers' history and behavior have also confirmed clinical observations (Fagan, Stewart, & Hansen, 1983; Pollack, 1980; Star, Clark, Goetz, & O'Hara, 1979; Steinmetz & Straus, 1974; Walker, 1979).

Deliberate treatment of the male batterer is a relatively new field (Ptacek, 1984). I say deliberate, because male batterers have frequented therapy for many years but instead have been treated for depression, marital problems, and alcohol or drug abuse. The violence in their lives has essentially gone unnoticed. Because this area of counseling has been described only in the past five years, most clinicians have received little or no formal training in identification and treatment of the male batterer. The programs that have been developed during this time have utilized other behavior change models, such as alcohol/drug treatment, to develop their particular approach to counseling male batterers. Not all of these programs were developed by trained professionals. Many of the first programs for male batterers grew out of the men's movement, where paraprofessional counselors helped men examine their attitudes toward women and other men, as well as learn specific techniques for stopping violent behavior. On the other hand, persons trained theoretically in helping people with their problems were either overlooking the violence in their clients' lives, attributing blame to the victim or not believing her altogether, and/or utilizing traditional psychotherapeutic techniques that were either ineffective, or in some instances, exacerbated the violence.

Both professional and paraprofessional persons counseling male batterers have had to rely mostly on common sense and intuition in developing a treatment approach that effectively stopped violence. Although the psychological literature is replete with articles on violence, only a few actually addressed the issue of *domestic* violence prior to 1974. For many, the behavioral work with substance abusers served as a model for helping men stop their violent behavior. For others, consciousness raising seemed the appropriate direction to work toward. Today, a combination of the two seems to be the most effective.

No formal studies have been conducted to determine the most effective method of treatment; however, many programs have conducted informal evaluations of their success with their particular client population. Some programs estimate 50 to 80 percent effectiveness while the man is in treatment. Such variances may be attributed to differing definitions of effectiveness, as well as different program models and goals. In either case, it is apparent that more research is needed to accurately determine the most appropriate treatment approach for the male batterer. At a recent domestic violence research conference, the researchers present agreed that formal studies—both descriptive studies as well as treatment outcome studies—need to be conducted on the male batterer. As service providers we need to bridge the gap between direct services and research. In planning programs, we can incorporate the types of assessment tools and procedures that will help us document the characteristics of the male batterer as well as measure the success or failure of a particular treatment approach.

Historically, much of what we know about the extent of the problem and the characteristics of the victim comes from the staff and residents of shelters for battered women (Martin, 1981; Roberts, 1981). Researchers have now substantiated many of the characteristics of battered women originally described by shelter staff, as well as clarified the extent of the problem. An epidemiological study, composed of a random sample from the general population, generated an estimate of 13 million couples a year who experience some form of domestic violence (Straus, Gelles, & Steinmetz, 1980). A study conducted by the San Francisco Family Violence Project found that 39 percent of those assaults reported to the police, 33 percent of the attempted murders, and 29 percent of the murders were perpetrated against family members (San Francisco Family Violence Project, 1982). Walker and Associates found that 59 percent of their population studied reported being sexually assaulted by their batterer (Walker, 1980).

A preliminary analysis of our intake/assessment data of the last 42 men we have treated has indicated the following trends:

21% were physically abused as children

7% were sexually abused as children

45% saw their mother being abused by their father

50% either saw their mother being abused or were themselves abused

83% received physical punishment as a child

24% have attacked one of their parents

93% have battered a previous partner

42 men committed a total of 153 acts of physical violence in the year previous to their entering treatment

4.82 years was the average length of their relationship

68% of the men who have children state that those children have viewed the violence

57% of the men who have children use physical punishment on those children

62% were under the influence of alcohol or other drugs at the last battering incident

43% have been violent both while under the influence and while not under the influence

29% have been violent only when not under the influence

29% have been violent only when under the influence

46% scored on an alcohol screening test as having an alcohol problem

36% have a family history of suicide (attempts and completed), wives being most frequent, self and mother being second most frequent

50% were currently involved with the criminal justice system

38% have been involved with the criminal justice system in the past

45% have been violent with others not in their family, outside their home

81% were employed

In any type of social/psychological research one may encounter problems inherent in the subject matter that may make it difficult to collect accurate data. Two potentially problematic factors in researching domestic violence are related to sampling and definition of violence.

The Family Violence Project of the San Francisco District Attorney's Office was developed in 1980 to document accurately the existence and extent of domestic violence, woman battering in particular, in the City and County of San Francisco. One problem which surfaced immediately was that the statistics varied depending on the sources one queried for data.

Court records revealing dispositional data indicated very few cases each month which led to a guilty plea or disposition. An analysis of police reports indicated that as many as 250 reports are written each month on spouse abuse cases. In the analysis of police dispatch calls, it was found that more than twice as many calls were received than were actually written up in a report, in that domestic violence cases accounted for 41 percent of all assault calls (San Francisco Family Violence Project, 1982). According to these statistics, perhaps 500 cases of domestic violence occur in San Francisco each month for which police assistance is required. Research studies indicate that many more cases go unreported because less than one half of the cases are actually reported to the police (Durbin & Letko, 1977; Prescott, 1975).

What Is Domestic Violence?

Definitions of violence may affect the outcome of an evaluation for a particular treatment program or approach. A program may report an 85 percent success rate in stopping violence, but if this were to include psychological violence, the success rate would most likely be lower. It is our experience as well as others' (Walker, 1979) that psychological violence is much more difficult to stop than physical violence.

In order to effectively stop violent behavior we need to adapt the latest research information to our treatment approach, while at the same time, our clinical experience can provide valuable insight into what aspects of battering need to be studied and documented further. No matter what the exact rate of occurrence, the problem of domestic violence appears to be so widespread that a significant percentage of any mental health professional's caseload will either include this problem currently, has done so in the past, or may in the future.

Understanding the definitions, psycho/behavioral and social dynamics of woman battering is an important first step in providing effective treatment services to male batterers. Battering is defined as physically, sexually, and/or psychologically assaultive behavior between adults in an intimate, sexual, theoretically equal relationship. This includes homosexual as well as heterosexual relationships. This couple may or may not be legally married; they may or may not be living together; and they may or may not be currently in a relationship.

The word "domestic" is somewhat misleading in that it implies a common home and/or marriage. This is not always the case. Although this book will not delve specifically into the other forms of domestic violence, which include child abuse, child sexual abuse, elderly abuse, the abuse of parents by children (in particular, adolescent sons toward single mothers), and abuse between siblings, many of the issues and treatment techniques may be utilized with these other forms of domestic violence.

Probably the most important definition to clarify with your clients is that of violence. In our program we see four types of violence: physical, sexual, property, and psychological. This breakdown into specific areas has been commonly accepted by programs around the country (Ganley & Harris, 1978; Roberts, 1982; Walker, 1979).

Physical violence is defined as the use of physical force to intimidate, control, or force another person to do something against their will. This may include grabbing, pushing, holding, slapping, choking, punching, sitting or standing on, kicking, hitting with objects, and assaults with knives or firearms.

A common statement that we hear from men in our program is: "I was just holding her by the arms to make her listen to me; do you call that violence?" The response is: "Yes, if she wanted to stand next to you while you were screaming in her face, she would not need to be forced by you."

The more subtle forms of violence such as this are the most difficult to detect because most people do not associate that kind of behavior with violence. Especially in relationships where more serious violence has occurred, the victim and offender are somewhat desensitized to lesser forms of violence. Specific techniques for assessing these types of violence will be discussed in subsequent chapters.

Sexual violence (Gelles, 1979; Walker, 1979; Walker, 1984) is the forcing of another person to engage in any sexual activity through the use of intimidation and the explicit or implicit threat of further violence if one's advances are refused. For many men sexual violence occurs as a result of sexual jealousy (Dobash & Dobash, 1979; Gelles, 1977–78; Hilberman & Munson, 1978; Walker, 1979).

Although frequently occurring in relationships, as described by Walker (1983), this information is often difficult to extract from the batterer, as well as from the victim. As with other sexual assault victims, the embarrassment, guilt, and shame lead these women be to extremely reticent about discussing this aspect of their relationships.

Property violence usually occurs in a fit of rage and/or as a means to scare or to intimidate. It includes the breaking of property, sometimes her personal property or gifts he has given her, sometimes his property (then she gets blamed for his rage and the eventual destruction of that property); having fits of pounding on the table; putting a fist or foot through the wall; breaking down a door; throwing food; and breaking dishes.

Often people do not think of breaking property as violence. The question is asked, "Isn't it better to break a dish than to hit someone?" This is probably true, but accidents do happen, and children as well as adults can get in the way of flying objects. Additionally, property violence has similar psychological effects, as does physical or sexual violence, in that it becomes a way of controlling or intimidating another person to do something against her/his will.

Psychological violence, like property violence, is usually underplayed by both victims and offenders, as well as by professionals. Psychological violence includes several subcategories:

1. *Explicit threats of violence*, such as "If you say another word I'm going to take my gun and blow you away."
2. *Implicit threats of violence*, such as "If you say another word I

don't know what I'm going to do." This is coupled with the body language of making a fist and perhaps stepping toward the woman in an aggressive manner.

3. *Extreme controlling type of behavior*, such as picking her up at work; dropping her off at school; telling her who she can bring to the house, which of her friends she can go out with, when she can go out, when she has to stay home. Essentially, controlling her whereabouts, companions, and life's activities inside and outside the house.

4. *Pathological jealousy*, which was originally described by Walker (1979), and which has been found to be quite common with men who batter. This jealousy takes the form of frequent questioning of whom she has been with or where she has been; accusations of her attraction to other men; and suspiciousness that she is going out with or being sexual with another man.

5. *Mental degradation* in the form of continual name calling; telling her she is no good, she cannot survive without him, she is a terrible mother, she needs him, she is not good enough. On a daily or even weekly basis this behavior has a profound effect on one's self-esteem.

6. *Isolating behavior*, although a part of extreme controlling type of behavior, is a type of psychological violence that warrants a separate discussion. Isolation is a common characteristic of both batterers and battered women (Searle, 1982). A batterer, because of his dependency, jealousy, and fear that others may find out about his problem, will often put strict limitations on whom his partner can see and when she can see those people. She becomes isolated and mutually dependent on him. She is also likely to submit to him because of her low self-esteem, embarrassment, and guilt about the violence. Some men are physically isolated in that they have no close friends or even people with whom they work; essentially all batterers are emotionally isolated in that they frequently have no close friends with whom they can talk about their feelings and problems. The more isolation one feels, the more dependent one gets on one's partner, the less flexible one becomes, and, eventually, the more stress one experiences. Additional stress can facilitate conflict. A person who has a history of violent behavior is therefore at greater risk as isolation increases.

These four forms of violence have several things in common.

1. They are all ways of controlling, dominating, and intimidating another person.
2. They all have potentially serious physical and psychological consequences.
3. They are all against the law.

Below is a breakdown of each form of violence and the corresponding California State Penal Code Sections

Section	Description
	Physical Violence
187	Homicide
240	Assault
242	Battery
245a	Assault with a deadly weapon or with intent to commit great bodily injury
273.5	Corporal injury to spouse or cohabitant
278	Felony child stealing
	Sexual Violence
220	Assault with intent to commit mayhem, rape, sodomy or oral copulation
261	Rape
262	Spousal rape
266a	Forcible prostitution
266b	Forcible cohabitation
266h-i	Pimping and pandering
286	Sodomy (forcible)
288a	Oral copulation (forcible)
289	Penetration with foreign object
	Property Violence
240	Assault
415(2)	Disturbing the peace
594	Malicious mischief
603	Vandalism

Section	Description
459	Burglary
602.5	Entry without consent
	Psychological Violence
240	Assault
245a	Assault with a deadly weapon or with intent to commit great bodily injury (no physical contact)
417	Brandishing a firearm or other weapon
422	Threat to commit a crime which will result in death or great bodily injury, with intent to terrorize
653m	Annoying telephone communications
273.6	Violation of court order to prevent domestic violence or disturbance of the peace

One of the finest jobs the San Francisco Family Violence Project (1982) did was to bring this point to the forefront: domestic violence is a crime.

Men who batter must get the message that violence is only one way to deal with anger, conflict, stress, and frustration, that it is in fact the most destructive way to deal with these feelings. There are other ways which are constructive and that can even facilitate closeness, intimacy, trust, and communication (Sonkin & Durphy, 1982).

Characteristics of Male Batterers

As mentioned previously, the characteristics of male batterers are described from clinical observations of men, discussions with battered women, and research on battered women (Fagan, Stewart, & Hansen, 1983; Pollack, 1980; Star et al., 1979; Straus et al., 1974). These characteristics are in no way an attempt to develop a profile, but instead are a means to describe patterns of behavior in male batterers and to imply certain directions in treatment.

Men who batter come from all socioeconomic backgrounds, races, religions, and walks of life (Giles-Sims, 1983; Star et al., 1979; Straus, Gelles and Steinmetz, 1980; Walker, 1979; Walker, 1984). Although race and socioeconomic factors present unique stresses on an individual, studies to date have not clearly indicated the effects these factors have on violence rates. It is known that those in lower socioeconomic groups are more likely to turn to the criminal justice system, hospital emergency rooms, and social service programs where this problem is less likely to be hidden and therefore more likely to be documented, whereas people of higher socioeconomic status are more able to turn to the private clinician for assistance, where identification or documentation is less likely to occur.

Minimization and Denial

Battering men are likely to minimize and deny their violent behavior (Ganley, 1981; Sonkin & Durphy, 1982; Walker, 1979). This is partly a result of their embarrassment, guilt, and shame about their behavior. On a deep level they usually know that their behavior is hurtful and ineffective. Another reason men will minimize or deny the violence is because it is often in their best interest to do so, particularly if they are facing criminal charges. As with other types of problems, people will tend to ignore the problem of violence if they feel ineffective in trying to solve it.

Some clinicians believe that this tendency to minimize and deny is in part related to the batterer's loss of memory during rage (Elliot, 1977). It is believed that women are more accurate in describing the violence because it is in their interest to watch out for punches, flying objects, and the like so as to minimize injury (Walker, 1983). Battering men tend to externalize in an attempt to explain behavior which seems to be out of their control. They blame others for unfortunate, as well as sometimes fortunate, circumstances they experience. A common occurrence in counseling is that when asked about an episode of violence, the batterer will proceed to describe everything "she" did to cause the problem.

These men will often see the woman as the cause of their violence. "If she had only done this or not done that, then I wouldn't have been violent." It is in part from these statements that women have been viewed as provoking violence in men. Certainly women can and do provoke an argument, just as men do. However, the response to such conflict or anger is each person's own responsibility, and it is chosen by that person at that particular moment as a way of responding to the situation.

Dependency and Jealousy

Men who batter are usually very dependent on their partners as the sole source of love, support, intimacy, and problem solving (Coleman, 1980; Elbow, 1977; Falk, 1977; Ganley, 1981; Hilberman & Munson, 1978; Symonds, 1978; Walker, 1979). This dependence is in part a result of the physical and emotional isolation and alienation which many men feel. Traditionally the family has been seen as a place where most of our needs for control, intimacy, love, and friendship are met. Undoubtedly for many, whether they experience domestic violence or not, this is a fact of life. However, couples and families which experience violence feel this isolation and alienation to a much greater degree as a result of the increased level of stress the violence produces. Searle (1982) discusses isolation in terms of family systems. Isolation promotes dependency and vice versa, such that a cycle of isolation and dependency ultimately causes a system to become closed. Closed systems are rigid, and rigid systems experience the most stress.

Jealousy is a natural outgrowth of a closed system. Outsiders are seen as intruders, and there is a desire to bond even closer. However, when this feeling is not mutual, anger erupts and there ensues an increased risk of violence (Coleman, 1980; Hilberman & Munson, 1978; Roy, 1982; Scott, 1974; Star et al., 1979; Walker, 1979). Another characteristic related to the male batterer's dependency and jealousy is his extreme suspiciousness. This characteristic may be as extreme as paranoia (Elbow, 1977; Falk, 1977; Walker, 1979). Violent episodes frequently will stem from his accusing her of infidelity. Her dependence on him is as important as his control of her in avoiding loss of the relationship (Elbow, 1977). Battered women often respond to the batterer's dependency and jealousy by withdrawing as a way to avoid subsequent violence. Hence, battered women's dependency becomes functional in that it is self-protective. Although both men and women are dependent, given equal support systems, women will cope better after leaving the relationship in spite of the dangers and social obstacles to doing so (Walker, 1984), whereas men are more likely to fall apart emotionally.

In Rosewater's (1982a,b), studies of battered women she found that, although most women describe themselves as passive, they are aware of responding to social pressures from the offender to act this way. Although economic and emotional dependency on the batterer, as well as fear of him, present very real obstacles to women in leaving battering relationships, they are able to muster a great deal more psychological strength once they make the break than their battering counterparts.

Low Self-Esteem

Battering men are unassertive (Rosenbaum & O'Leary, 1981a,b), in that while they can intimidate and bully their partners into giving them what they want, they lack the skills and self-confidence to ask affirmatively for what they want in a nonthreatening manner (Falk, 1977). Men also have an equally difficult time in saying no to their partners (Sonkin & Durphy, 1982). Some men have stated that this is a function of the guilt they feel as a result of the violence. They cannot say no, even though this pattern only leads to further resentment and anger. One therapist who works with male batterers describes this lack of an ability to say no, as it is seen by men, as a separation. To say no is to say we disagree, we are different, we are separate. This separation process is anxiety-provoking for many men (Dennis Dolan, personal communication).

Many of the dynamics described thus far are likely to produce feelings of low self-esteem (Elbow, 1977; Ganley, 1981; Walker, 1979). Many men who batter have had childhood experiences that led to development of poor self-image, such as child abuse or witnessing spouse abuse. In addition, men growing up in a society such as ours who experience unrealistic expectations of what it means to be a man are likely to feel some blow to their ego if they are unable to attain such levels of success. Although unsuccessful at living up to the traditional male stereotype, many men who batter do hold the stereotype as a standard in their lives (Carrillo, 1983; Ganley, 1981; Walker, 1979). Along with this standard of behavior, men lack the skills necessary to communicate in the emotional realm (Sonkin & Durphy, 1982). The socialization process men experience usually does not include learning communication skills functional in an intimate relationship. Many men develop those skills necessary in a business setting: rational acuity, strategizing, arguing facts and figures. These skills do have a place in an emotional relationship; however, if they are the only skills he has for communication, problems may arise when the emotional stakes far exceed those in business.

Childhood Abuse

Many batterers who were physically or sexually abused as children, or who lived with a father who abused their mother, grow up experiencing a great deal of anger toward the abusing parent. Frequently the non-abusing parent may also be the recipient of the anger for not protecting the child from the abuse. As a result, many of these men have a great deal of anger which they project onto other relationships. Their distrust of men is evident in their lack of close male companions and their tendency to withdraw from the men's group during times of stress. These men's lack of trust toward a particular woman is evident in their intolerance of her differences, their extreme sensitivities to rejection and/or criticism, and ultimately their abusiveness and violence. Although reconciliation of these issues is a part of the long term therapy process, bringing these issues rapidly to the forefront will raise the consciousness of the client so that he can begin to see his partner for who she is as opposed to how he perceives her.

The Batterer's Profile

Qualitative descriptions of men who batter are extremely helpful when designing a treatment approach that will address the violence as well as the behavioral characteristics described earlier. However, observable or descriptive behaviors may not always provide the clinician with an in-depth understanding of the client that is necessary to form an appropriate treatment plan and treatment interventions.

We now administer the MMPI (Hathaway & Meehl, 1951) to each client to corroborate our clinical observations and to provide us with valuable information about the man's personality structure. A preliminary examination of the data we have collected thus far tells us that batterers tend to be angry and depressed, and more than half are feeling quite anxious about these intense feelings. Their profiles are descriptive of persons with problems in impulse control and chronic acting out. A number of profiles have clearly shown denial and intellectualization as defense mechanisms, whereas others may use hostility, withdrawal and/or substance abuse as a defense in reaction to their vulnerability. Few of the clients see themselves in a positive light and many may be characterized as having low ego strength, experiencing extreme stress and feeling out of control of their lives. This test has been helpful in screening out those high risk clients, by testing for suicide, acting out, psychosis and organicity.

In addition to the MMPI, our use of the Hostility Toward Women Scale (Check & Malamuth, 1983) has been helpful as a facilitator of treatment. Knowing that high hostility toward women is an issue for a particular client will help us focus on treatment of that issue as a possible mediator of violent behavior. In addition, this scale is being utilized to determine individual differences in predicting severity of violence, frequency of violence and/or treatment outcome. In addition to these dysfunctional characteristics, men who batter have positive attributes as well (Martin, 1981; Walker, 1979). They have the capacity to be loving, caring, and gentle partners. Many times they are excellent parents. They can be charming, humorous, sensitive, and emotional people. And because they have these characteristics as well as the more negative ones, they are capable of change. The counselor must appreciate these positive traits as a way to form a meaningful connection with his/her client so that change is ultimately possible. However, a counselor should not let appreciation of these positive traits lessen his/her belief in the existence and the seriousness of the batterer's violent behavior.

Causes of Woman Battering

The causes of battering are as numerous as explanations for any human behavior. Studies to date have shown a high correlation of battering with a history of violence in childhood (Straus et al., 1980; Walker, 1979; San Francisco Family Violence Project, 1982; Carrillo, 1983; Star, 1978; Rosenbaum, 1979).

In our particular treatment program, Learning to Live Without Violence, 70 percent of the men came from homes where they and/or a sibling were victims of physical or sexual child abuse or where their mother was abused by their father (or another intimate male figure). These findings suggested that violence is a learned behavior for many of these men, and as such, a social learning model may be indicated for treatment. Early studies on social learning (Bandura, 1973; Bandura et al., 1963) have suggested that learning may occur by trial and error and by observation of others. The degree to which the modeler's behavior has an effect on the observer is a function of the power or influence the modeler has over the observer. A parent's behavior would perhaps have more influence over a child than a next door neighbor's (unless that neighbor has a parenting role with the child).

Another factor relevant to whether or not a behavior is accepted is the length of exposure. For example, a child is more likely to accept as proper behavior that which is observed from a parent over a period of 18 years than behavior by a relative seen once or for a shorter period of time. This phenomenon is not black and white and is further complicated by many mitigating factors. However, based on these statistics, it is safe to say that persons who come from homes where violence is used are likely to grow up to use violence or other dysfunctional behaviors as a way of coping with conflict, anger, stress, and/or anxiety (Straus et al., 1980).

Although modeling has a powerful impact on a child's behavior in adulthood, trial and error learning can have an equally powerful impact on an adult for future behaviors. Many of the men who never experienced violence in their childhood described the violence in their relationships with women as "something I just got into and found myself using a lot."

Through trial and error, men experience positive reinforcement for violence in several ways. First, the reduction of bodily tension makes the violence a means to reduce stress or anxiety, which is self-reinforcing. Second, violence does put a temporary end to an uncomfortable situation, even though the long-term consequences continue to propagate the discomfort. Third, the violence will often create an immobility in the woman which can be viewed by the batterer as complicity. The violence becomes a way of controlling and incapacitating his partner to the extent that he is less threatened by her independence and her possibly leaving him. In these ways the batterer sees his violence as functional. One of the goals of counseling is to have him see that violence is dysfunctional as well as against the law.

Much has been written in the past few years on sex-role stereotyping, sexism, and domestic violence (Martin, 1981; Walker, 1979; Straus et al., 1980; Sonkin & Durphy, 1982). The focus of the domestic violence movement has served to describe how violence against women has resulted from the rigid roles with which men and women are saddled from birth. Boys are taught to devalue all that is feminine in them, which ultimately leads to devaluing female figures in their lives. Women, on the other hand, are taught not only to devalue the female, but to idolize the male as well, something they can never achieve. These values are supported by every conceivable major institution. Although the women's movement has made considerable strides in educating people and changing laws and institutional policy, the fact remains that these traditional attitudes are being promoted on every level in society to this day.

The media of television and movies, some of the most influential forces in changing society, still cater to the predominant view that women act and look one way and men look and act another way. Violence in the media is still glorified and can be considered a justifiable means to a noble end.

Studies of children's cartoons show a considerable amount of violence being portrayed (Baker & Ball, 1969). There are studies showing how the observation of violence can actually support violent behavior (Bandura et al., 1963; Malamuth & Check, 1983a, b; Tannenbaum & Zillman, 1975).

Many studies and discussions of violence have centered around the issue of nature versus nurture. Is aggression innate or learned? Is violence a learned behavior or an instinct? Although some studies have shown that men are predisposed to aggression because of the effect of androgen on fetal development (Money & Erhardt, 1975), other studies have shown that social conditioning plays a significant mitigating role in the expression of violence (Macoby & Jacklin, 1974). Aggressive impulses are not necessarily unhealthy, whether innate or learned; however, violence is just one expression of aggression. Unfortunately, we live in a society which has learned to associate these two phenomena, even though they are not necessarily mutually inclusive. Thus, whether aggression is genetic or learned is not the question to ask. Instead, we should ask whether aggression can be channeled in ways which are constructive rather than destructive or violent.

The presence of alcohol and/or drugs in combination with domestic violence has been shown consistently in studies to date (Gelles, 1974; Straus et al., 1981; Walker, 1979; Walker, 1982; Rosenbaum, 1979; Coleman, 1980). Our clinical studies have shown that alcohol or other drugs were involved in the latest violent episode in over 80 percent of the cases. While this may be indicative of a causal factor, when carefully questioned, the majority of these men state that they have also been violent in the past while not under the influence of alcohol or drugs. Other clinicians corroborate these findings (Ganley, 1981). Although to date no studies have shown conclusively that alcohol or other drugs cause violence via physiological processes, it has been demonstrated that alcohol and other drugs do produce psychological behaviors which may predispose a person to violent behavior.

Alcohol is well known for its disinhibiting effect on behavior; people are likely to say or do things while under its influence that they might not ordinarily do (Ewing, 1972; Ritchie, 1965). This disinhibiting effect can easily cause a person to express anger or rage that under sober conditions they have an easier time controlling. Just as violence is self-reinforcing by means of tension release, alcohol can serve as a facilitator of the process.

For example, a person begins to feel the tension build; he turns to alcohol as a means to release that tension, which is then further released through an argument and eventual violence. In this way alcohol does not ensure violence, but rather mediates its expression. We have observed that the most serious episodes of violence occur when the offender is under the influence of alcohol or other drugs (Coleman, 1980). Therefore, as will be discussed in a later chapter, substance abuse is frequently correlated with lethality.

In the Bay Area, as in other parts of the country, cocaine use and abuse are more frequently seen by the clinician today than in the past. Domestic violence programs are no different in this aspect. Heavy cocaine use has been known to cause paranoid ideation (Ewing, 1972; Post, 1975), possibly leading one to be more irritable or verbally combative. For a person who already has a history of violent behavior, this can be a deadly combination. Frequently men who use cocaine with their partners describe arguments about who spent more money that month for drugs. Paranoid ideation of one person thinking the other is holding out on him/her is a common area of conflict. There are also increased arguments regarding finances in general, due to the amount of money spent on drugs each month. Cocaine, like alcohol, becomes a mediator in the process of a person's attempt to deal with anger, frustration, stress, and/or anxiety.

A similar argument could be made with respect to other drugs. We have treated men who act violently only while under the influence of alcohol and drugs and were less likely to reoffend when given the appropriate treatment. However, our experience also shows that the majority of clients batter whether or not they are under the influence. In both situations it is important not only to control or stop the substance use or abuse, but also to help the individual learn anger management and stress coping skills to enable him to avoid other destructive behavior patterns which may harm himself or others.

Domestic Violence and the Military

Recent attention has been given to domestic violence and military personnel (West, Turner, & Dunwoody, 1981). Although military men are subjected to similar childhood experiences of violence and sex-role stereotyping as civilians, the military indoctrination process presents dilemmas most civilians do not necessarily confront; that is, specific training in the use of violence (Raihan, 1982). Additionally, military families experience stresses unique to their particular situation which are worth discussion (Bowen, 1983a, b).

Enlisted personnel, who comprise the majority of military personnel, are taught in basic training to develop skills on the use of violence to be used during war or quasi-war situations. The purpose of this discussion will not be to weigh the advantages and disadvantages of the military and defense systems. Instead, it will be to examine how men and women are indoctrinated into the system and how that process of indoctrination possibly effects the occurrence of domestic violence in military families.

The life of an enlisted person is not an easy one; long hours, low pay, low rank and status, little or no power, and in some situations, humiliation. In adition to these stresses, one becomes proficient in the manly art of war. One is trained in hand-to-hand combat, the use of firearms, use of and/or familiarity with large weapons, survival in the wilderness, prisoner-of-war survival, and war strategy, and one develops a good healthy paranoia of the enemy. All these skills are necessary for a good soldier. What about when the conflict is at home and not on the battlefield? If a person's repertoire includes only these combat skills and these skills are most frequently used on a day-to-day basis, it is not hard to understand how violence occurs in military families.

In conducting workshops for the military, I propose that specific attention be paid to this deficit in the indoctrination process of military personnel. Classes on communication skills, stress reduction, and anger management are likely to improve the domestic situations of military personnel, which would ultimately improve on-the-job performance. Many bases across the country are implementing domestic violence programs to meet the needs of victims and offenders currently in crisis (West, et al., 1981). However, programs focusing on healthy survival at home need to be implemented as a preventive measure for further crisis situations.

In addition to this indoctrination process, as already suggested, military families experience numerous other stresses which increase the risk for men who already have a proclivity for acting out their anger. These stresses include:

1. *Financial pressures.* Low pay and having dependents to support, coupled with the high cost of housing today, create a great deal of pressure in many people's lives.

2. *Family separation.* During both basic training and tours of duty, military men and women are separated from family members for extended periods of time. This separation makes an already peripheral father even less involved in the development of his children, as well as less involved in the development of a relationship with the spouse. Additionally, reunification can be as stressful as it is joyful.

3. *Geographic mobility.* Packing up your possessions and moving to another town is stressful for anyone. This often includes leaving friends behind and no longer having the support of family members. Mobility such as this also involves additional expenses, which exacerbate an already stressful situation.

4. *Isolation and communication barriers.* As discussed earlier, isolation adds considerable stress to a family. Military personnel often feel isolated from their family because of long hours and temporary separations. Further, communication barriers add to an already frustrating lack of contact with family members. During basic training and tours of duty, the isolation and communication barriers are at their greatest. Most of us take it for granted when our jobs allow us a call home during the day or the possibility of contact in case of an emergency.

5. *Cultural differences.* Many military men who have served overseas have married women from other countries, thus introducing life-style differences and creating additional barriers to communication. This usually includes lack of support from friends and family for the women, which in turn creates more dependence on the relationship.

6. *Lack of family support.* Lack of consistent contact with one's family can produce a special feeling of isolation. It can also put pressure on an individual to create his own family prematurely, which has its own unique set of problems and stresses.

7. *Living abroad.* When a family travels with the serviceman

overseas, many problems similar to those discussed above can create stress within the family: isolation, lack of support from friends and family, difficulties in acculturation, and increased dependency on a relationship.

8. *Separation of work and home.* The film "The Great Santini" illustrates this point quite well. It is the story of a Marine pilot who ran his home in the same very authoritarian and controlling manner he ran his aircraft. As indicated by the film, this manner was functional on the job but not at home, and the consequent conflict at home ultimately affected his work performance. As indicated earlier, the violent aspect of work can be separated from home as well.

9. *Lack of privacy.* Once in the military, one's activities are closely monitored by the commanding officer, as well as other personnel superior in rank. During basic training, field maneuvers, and combat situations, servicemen live and work together. One's activities are continually supervised. If there are problems at home or at work, one's commanding officer may know about them.

10. *Job pressures.* As in civilian life, one needs to live up to certain job performance expectations in the military or else promotions, raises, and/or continued employment are at risk. These pressures are easily taken home and can affect family life.

11. *Lack of supervisor/command support.* As described earlier, when members of the civilian community receive either implicit or explicit messages from the criminal justice system that say "Don't bother me with your family problems," it can create a state of confusion and alienation. Likewise in the military community, there are persons in supervisory and command positions who may intentionally or unintentionally give a similar message. When this happens, it may add to an already stressful situation, both on the job and at home. In recent years, the military system in general has seen that a well functioning family life is an important factor in both morale and readiness of military personnel. Programs serving military families are being developed across the country.

Many of the stresses described above are not necessarily unique to military personnel, but they are found frequently enough to warrant a discussion. They are also in no way an explanation of or excuse for violence in the family. They are an acknowledgment that these stresses do exist and that unless coping skills are developed, men will turn to those skills either learned in childhood or learned through on-the-job training.

Another stress commonly found in military situations is that of Post Traumatic Stress Disorder (PTSD). This condition is found in many combat veterans (Williams, 1980). It is characterized by the experience of recognizable stress, such as combat, that would evoke significant symptoms of distress in nearly everyone. The disorder includes reexperiencing the trauma through recurrent and intrusive recollections, dreams, or a sudden acting or feeling as though the traumatic event were recurring. This also includes a numbing of responsiveness to or reduced involvement in the external world, such as diminished interest in one or more significant activities, feelings of detachment or estrangement from others, or constricted affect. It also includes several symptoms such as sleep problems, impairment of concentration, guilt about surviving the trauma or about behavior required to survive, and hyperalertness or exaggerated startle response (American Psychiatric Association, 1981).

Post Traumatic Stress Disorder is frequently found, not only in combat veterans, but also in victims of natural disasters, victims of violent crimes, rape victims, and battered women. In the San Francisco Bay Area in 1982, excessive rains caused serious flooding, extensive home damage, mudslides, many injuries, and several deaths. The following fall when the light rains began, many adults and children were reexperiencing the trauma from the previous year. A special project was developed through Community Mental Health to train mental health professionals to meet the increased needs of clients seeking mental health services for a variety of related issues.

Although Post Traumatic Stress Disorder is known to most people, through the media, as being associated with violence, the majority of men suffering from this problem are not acting out violently, but they may be suffering from any one or a combination of the characteristics described above. When assessing combat veterans, it is important to determine when the violence is a function of PTSD alone and when it is a function of PTSD coupled with a proclivity for violence because of a history of violence and/or poor anger-management skills. As with substance abuse, a dual referral may be indicated in such cases.

Recent studies have also examined the relationship of past military experience and incidence of domestic violence. Rosenbaum et al.

(1981) found that 77 percent of the men interviewed had enlisted in the military, and that of these, half (50 percent) had a history of disciplinary discharges from the service. A majority of the men who suffered disciplinary discharges had a history of alcohol and/or drug abuse, violent behavior, and desertion.

In Walker's 1983 study, 58 percent of the women interviewed reported that their partners had military experience, and 37 percent of those had direct combat experience. Eisenberg and Micklow (1979) found that 90 percent of their clients studied had prior military service, and almost one third had received dishonorable discharges. While these data could be interpreted in various ways, there does appear to be a correlation between violence at home and performance in the military. Further studies need to be conducted to articulate further this interrelationship.

From this discussion on the causes of domestic violence, it is easy to see that the causes are very complex and therefore the solutions will not necessarily be any less complex. The variety of men experiencing this problem necessitates flexibility on the part of service providers and institutions responding to the problem. One reality is that many men do not seek counseling of their own volition. The Family Violence Project reported 60 percent of their referrals from the criminal justice system (San Francisco Family Violence Project, 1982), which is partly attributable to their being a criminal justice program. Domestic violence programs in the community report a slightly lower criminal justice clientele, although many of these programs coordinate closely with criminal justice programs (Battered Women's Alternatives, Concord, CA).

Domestic Violence and the Criminal Justice System

The criminal justice system has contact with more domestic violence families than any other institution because of its capacity to respond to crisis 24 hours a day, seven days a week (San Francisco Family Violence Project, 1982). As indicated by police statistics, hundreds of new cases are identified each month. Unfortunately, the response by police has been less than ideal, but domestic violence programs across the country are now working with the police to help them find effective solutions to the problem.

In the early 1970s the direction in police work was toward fewer arrests and more mediation. Police were being trained in conflict resolution, in essence, interpersonal counseling. Although this approach may have diffused the crisis at the moment, several messages were given to the couple. First, that both contributed to the violence. Both people did contribute to the argument, but the one who was violent chose to respond to the conflict in that way. There is a qualitative difference in these two statements. Second, the offender was not given the message that he broke the law, and consequently this gave him implicit permission to act violently. Third, the victim in this situation learned that the police were not going to help her. This nonresponse by the police encourages a victim's feeling of learned helplessness (Walker, 1979).

When police respond based on whether a crime has been committed, as opposed to what the original argument was about, men begin to get the message that violence is a crime inside or outside the home. Women get the message that they do not have to tolerate the assaults.

When domestic violence cases go through the criminal justice system, the onus is typically on the victim to pursue the case and prove the offender guilty, unlike many other types of crime. Additionally, victims of domestic violence are the only crime victims who often live with or have an ongoing relationship with the offender. This puts the victim into a very difficult situation. District attorney's offices in several cities are finding that they are more likely to gain the cooperation of a victim to testify if they aggressively prosecute these cases and solicit the victim's cooperation, rather than leaving it all up to her (San Francisco Family Violence Project, 1982; Santa Barbara County District Attorney, 1981). Historically as well as currently, few cases of domestic violence make it to court because of this bias against victims and/or complications with a particular case (Martin, 1981). The majority of cases are dropped, and once again the batterer gets an implicit message that there will be no consequences for his behavior.

In 1980, the California legislature created a statutory alternative to either full criminal prosecution or no action. The legislation is entitled Special Proceedings in Cases Involving Domestic Violence (Title 6, Chapter 2.6, California Penal Code §§1000.6–1000.11, inclusive), and it provides that an offender is eligible for diversion out of the criminal justice system into a counseling and/or education program for a period of not less than six months nor more than two years, when certain prerequisites are met. These are:

1. The offense charged must be a misdemeanor or have been reduced to a misdemeanor.
2. The defendant shows no conviction for any offense involving violence within seven years prior to the alleged commission of the charged divertible offense.
3. The defendant's record does not indicate that probation or parole has ever been revoked without its thereafter being completed.
4. The defendant has not been diverted pursuant to the domestic violence diversion chapter within five years prior to the charged divertible offense.

Further, the chapter defines domestic violence broadly enough to encompass situations in which no actual physical assaults have occurred ["causing or attempting to cause bodily injury to a family or household member or placing a family or household member in reasonable apprehension of imminent serious bodily injury to himself or herself or another," §10006(d)], and defines "family or household member" so as to include current or former spouses, parents, blood relatives, or any other person then residing in the offender's household or who has so resided within the preceding six months (§1000.6(e)).

The idea of diversion is to give the offender the opportunity to change his behavior with the criminal justice system monitoring his actions for a delineated period of time. Should the individual fail to perform satisfactorily (e.g., drop out), fail to benefit from the program, or reoffend during the period of supervision, diversion can be revoked and criminal proceedings reinstituted. On the other hand, if the offender successfully completes the period of supervision, the arrest is "deemed to have never occurred" (§1000.10), and the individual is free to disclaim any arrest or diversion pursuant to the chapter, with the additional incentive that:

> ... A record pertaining to an arrest resulting in successful completion of a diversion program shall not, without the divertee's consent, be used in any way which could result in the denial of any employment, benefit, license, or certificate. (Penal Code §1000.10)

After just over two years' experience with this type of diversion, we have seen a wide variety of men in treatment who, by their own admission, would never have been there had it not been for diversion. The cases least likely to succeed on diversion are those clients who have extensive criminal histories, who were arrested for the most violent assaults (originally felonies but reduced to misdemeanors), who were terminated in less than six months, and who had alcohol and/or drug problems but were not mandated for alcohol and drug treatment as a condition of diversion.

For the most serious cases and those with extensive prior criminal records, we usually recommend probation (i.e., supervision after an admission of guilt rather than before) with counseling. In this way an offender who has the potential of a jail (or prison) sentence hanging over his head may more likely be induced to change his behavior.

Diversion and probation provide a temporary check on an offender's behavior, during which time counselors can work with the individual to assure long-term change. Working with the court-mandated client presents unique dilemmas for the clinician and will be discussed in subsequent chapters.

In most counseling programs, if a client is not referred by the courts, he is probably referred by his partner. Often the man gets a message, whether clear or ambiguous, from the woman he is battering that if he does not get into counseling, she will leave the relationship.

Many of our first referrals came from battered women in shelters who had told their partners to get help or they would not be coming home. This ultimatum is effective for a short period of time, but people in crisis, such as battered women, are not as consistent with this message as are outsiders, such as the courts. Many shelters have a six-week limit for residence, and afterwards, because of a lack of resources and often because of a commitment to the relationship, the women return home, at which time the offender usually drops out of treatment. For this reason, we usually encourage the use of the criminal justice system as often as possible.

These two routes in which men seek counseling are generally consistent with people who externalize their behavior. The motivation comes from others, not from himself. One of the goals of counseling is to help him learn that he can take responsibility for his behavior so that ultimately he will be in counseling for himself, not others.

A small but significant percentage of men in counseling do come in of their own volition. They are men who feel anxious or disturbed about their behavior and want to change it for themselves. These men usually are the most motivated and account for approximately 10 percent of our referrals, a necessary population of men that provide a positive model for those men court or partner referred. The court-referred clients also provide a positive model that the criminal justice system will respond to this problem, which can be an incentive for the men marginally uncertain about whether they have a problem.

No matter how men are referred to treatment, the problem of woman battering is a potentially dangerous one facing both the victim(s), the offender, and others in proximity to the violence. For this reason, we encourage the readers to educate themselves as much as possible by viewing films, reading the abundant literature on the topic, talking to others working in the field, and trusting their own intuition and creative abilities in order to develop an approach that is effective in helping men learn to live without violence.

3

Domestic Violence Assessment and the Determination of Lethality

Treatment programs for the male batterer have come into vogue only in the last five years, and the majority of these have become operational in the last two years (Ptacek, 1984; Roberts, 1982). Because of this fact, it is difficult to assess the most effective form of treatment. Programs across the country reflect the variety of backgrounds of the people running them. Some take a more traditional psychotherapeutic approach; others are educational in nature. Some counselors use family and couples therapy (Cook & Cook, 1984; Margolin, 1979); others use individual and group counseling (Purdy & Nickle, 1981; Star, 1983). Some groups are behaviorally oriented (Deschner, 1984; Saunders, 1982); some are self-help (Goffman, 1984); others are consciousness-raising (Adams & McCormick, 1982; Garnet & Moss, 1982).

Although many of these persons may be professionally trained, few have had any formal training in this specific area. Most people have developed their approach from direct experience working with the men, as well as from talking with other counselors in the field. Our approach was developed through these means. Through trial and error we have found a style of working with male batterers that works for us. It may not work for you. What will most likely be the case is that some techniques will be useful to you, while others will not. This is not the definitive approach to working with this population; it is *an* approach. You will undoubtedly take some of these ideas and use them in *your* way, which will then make them uniquely yours.

Talking about Violence

It is an important first step for anyone who wants to work in the area of domestic violence to become more aware of his/her own attitudes toward violence. Is violence justified in any situation? Does anyone, or do women in particular, provoke violence? What is violence? Is slapping or grabbing violence? Is it all right to slap a partner? These questions and others need to be addressed before and during your work in this area. For it is these attitudes which will ultimately affect your particular approach to counseling and its effectiveness.

In addition to attitudes about violence, we find it important to examine your attitudes about men and women, sex roles, relationships, and anger and conflict, because these issues are the critical factors which affect the occurrence of domestic violence.

One's own upbringing vis-à-vis the above issues plays a crucial role in one's attitudes today as a person and as a counselor. We have found that almost everyone has had some personal experience with violence in their lives, either as a victim, a perpetrator, or an observer. It is these experiences which truly affect our attitudes today, and if not closely examined, not only will they come across in counseling but they also may give a message we do not mean to give. The following thought problems are meant to help you examine your attitudes about relationships, anger, and violence. We encourage you to discuss your answers with friends, family, and co-workers, to explore this issue so as to bring those attitudes to awareness and within your control. The goal is not necessarily to change them, so much as it is to make them conscious so you can be more effective in counseling.

Thought Problems:
Values and Beliefs Concerning Interpersonal Violence[1]

The purpose of Thought Problems: Values and Beliefs Concerning Interpersonal Violence is to help workshop participants clarify their

[1]Copyright 1983, Susan E. Hanks, L.C.S.W., 3155 College Avenue, Berkeley, California 94705.

personal values about violence in relationships and explore how their attitudes may reflect commonly held myths about family violence.

Please indicate whether you agree or disagree with the following statements.

Agree   Disagree

_____   _____   If a child hits your child, your child should hit back.

_____   _____   Women see being hit as a sign that men care about them.

_____   _____   Teachers should be allowed to physically discipline children who are disruptive in school.

_____   _____   Children do not really know that their father hits their mother unless they witness the fight.

_____   _____   Battered women sometimes provoke their husbands into hitting them.

_____   _____   Nobody should tell a man/woman how to handle his/her own family unless asked.

_____   _____   If women really tried, they could prevent their partners from becoming violent.

_____   _____   A slap across the face is OK.

_____   _____   It is OK to hit a child on the bottom.

_____   _____   Batterers hate the women they batter.

_____   _____   Most batterers feel justified about their violent behavior.

_____   _____   Most batterers feel ashamed and guilty about their violent behavior.

_____   _____   What happens in the privacy of your own home is nobody's business.

_____   _____   A woman who stays with a batterer must have a serious psychological problem.

_____   _____   What happens inside a family is nobody's business.

_____   _____   If a woman has money, it is easier to leave a violent relationship.

Agree   Disagree

_____   _____   A man who would batter a woman is usually someone who is involved in other types of crime or violence.

_____   _____   "Spare the rod, spoil the child."

_____   _____   Men who batter their wives when intoxicated will stop being violent if they stop drinking.

_____   _____   Few battered women actually die from their injuries.

_____   _____   If women would not nag their husbands so much, maybe they would not get hit.

_____   _____   The fact that women often do not call the police when being beaten proves that they want to protect their batterer.

_____   _____   Most batterers are "losers" and unsuccessful in life.

_____   _____   Men are born more aggressive than women.

_____   _____   Women often injure their husbands.

_____   _____   When your neighbors are fighting, it is your responsibility to intervene.

_____   _____   Since many women go to shelters, or temporarily leave the batterer, but eventually return to him, it means that they must not object to the violence very much.

_____   _____   In order to go to a shelter, a woman has to be willing to divorce her husband.

_____   _____   Police are very good at protecting battered women.

_____   _____   It is always a crime for a husband to hit his wife.

_____   _____   The fact that many battered women marry more than one batterer proves that they are somehow seeking out a violent person.

_____   _____   If you know a woman who is battered by her husband, the best thing to do would be to talk with the husband.

_____   _____   It is OK to throw a shoe at somebody.

_____   _____   It is OK to throw a knife at somebody.

Agree   Disagree

_____   _____   The more professionally successful and the more wealthy a man is, the less likely he is to batter his wife.

_____   _____   It is really easy to know when a man you work with is a batterer.

_____   _____   Women often batter their husbands.

_____   _____   Police feel most effective responding to a domestic disturbance call because it is only a "family fight."

_____   _____   Men who batter are seriously psychologically disturbed and often do not know what they are doing.

_____   _____   Battered women must be "prone to violence" because they often batter their children.

_____   _____   Battered women feel safest when they are pregnant because men rarely hit pregnant women.

_____   _____   Violence directed primarily toward the wife has minimal detrimental impact on the children.

_____   _____   Batterers love the women they batter.

When confronting our own attitudes, we need to address our feelings about violence: when it is all right and when it is not. Are there no times when it is permissible? What behaviors constitute violence from your point of view? Is slapping and grabbing violence? Or must there be injuries for behaviors to constitute violence? What about psychological violence? Do you consider this violence at all? The question that comes up for many counselors is: Do I have a right to tell people how to treat each other? Who am I to tell people it is dangerous or illegal? To what extent will I go to protect people and intervene? These are just a few questions you must ask yourself as you begin to work in the area of domestic violence.

Along with examination of attitudes, we have found it necessary to develop a vocabulary conducive to working with domestic violence clients. Words descriptive of violent acts are often not a part of our normal vocabulary, and when spoken or heard usually bring up uncomfortable associations or memories. This is reminiscent of sex therapists learning to use words to describe parts of the reproductive anatomy without sounding embarrassed, yet not sounding too clinical or detached. Hopefully, this balance will also be achieved with domestic violence clients.

Just as it is important to be sensitive to our own levels of comfort in discussing violence, it is important to be sensitive to our clients' levels of comfort as well. I have found that men are usually uncomfortable discussing their own violence, for obvious reasons: embarrassment, guilt, shame, and fear of getting into trouble, to name a few. For these reasons we believe that it becomes the responsibility of the counselor to create an atmosphere of comfort for the client. This comfort can be facilitated in a number of ways. First, it is important to be able to distinguish when to be directly confrontational, when to be indirectly confrontational, and when to be supportive. The following transcript gives an example of each approach with a client who is referred by the court for counseling.

COUNSELOR: Can you tell me something about the reason you were referred for counseling? [Indirectly confrontative]

CLIENT: I got into a fight with my wife and she called the police on me.

COUNSELOR: And you got arrested? [Directly confrontative]

CLIENT: Yes.

COUNSELOR: Were you taken to jail? [Directly confrontative]

CLIENT: Yes, I stayed there over night and my brother came the next day and bailed me out.

COUNSELOR: Have you ever been in jail before? [Directly confrontative]

CLIENT: Never, it was a real drag.

COUNSELOR: I imagine it was awful, locked up, feeling helpless. [Supportive]

CLIENT: You bet.

COUNSELOR: About this fight: from my experience, people don't get arrested for having a fight with their wives unless there is some kind of violence. [Indirectly confrontative]

CLIENT: Well, I did beat her up.

COUNSELOR: Did you punch her? [Directly confrontative]

CLIENT: Yes.

When hearing stories of violence, you may begin to feel an urgency to act quickly and your tendency will be to get all the information at once, make him look at his behavior, and get him to stop. However, unless you have a meaningful relationship with this person, he may not hear what you have to say.

The men whom you will be counseling tend to be quite rigid in their approach to life (Carrillo, 1983), which is one reason why they react violently. They have not incorporated a flexible repertoire of behaviors to use when in a conflict or other stressful situation. As counselors we are role models for our clients, and we must demonstrate flexibility in how we react to people.

You may have noticed two types of questions in the previous dialogue: open-ended and closed or yes/no questions. Along with being flexible with regard to confrontation, one must be flexible in how questions are asked. As mentioned earlier, men who batter tend to minimize and deny the violence. Although it is debatable whether this is a conscious or unconscious process, it appears from experience that when asking open-ended questions, minimizing and denying are manifested in the answers. Therefore, we have found that a style of questioning which combines these two forms is the most successful for collecting information, providing less opportunity to minimize and deny, and creating a greater possibility to confront the client with his own behavior problems. The following could be a continuing segment of the intake begun above.

COUNSELOR: How many times did you punch her? [Closed]

CLIENT: Twice.

COUNSELOR: In the face, arms, chest? Where did you punch her? [Closed]

CLIENT: In the side of the head.

COUNSELOR: What happened then? [Open]

CLIENT: Well, she tried to get away, and I pushed her onto the floor and held her down.

COUNSELOR: How did you get her on the floor? [Open]

CLIENT: By pushing her.

COUNSELOR: Did you push her on the chest? [Closed]

CLIENT: Yes.

COUNSELOR: Once? Twice? How many times? [Closed]

CLIENT: I think twice.

COUNSELOR: Might it have been more? [Closed]

CLIENT: No. I think, I mean, I'm pretty sure it was twice.

COUNSELOR: What happened next? [Open]

We have found that a style of questioning which incorporates several different approaches (i.e., direct and indirect confrontation, support, open-ended and closed questions) is most likely to create an atmosphere conducive to collecting accurate information, developing trust, and creating a potential for change. Additionally, the modeling of flexibility by the counselor becomes a potent facilitator for bringing about internal and behavioral changes with the client.

Stages of Treatment

It is helpful, when discussing treatment, to divide the process from beginning to end into stages to make such a discussion more logical. The treatment process can be divided into four distinct stages or phases:

1.   Identification
2.   Intake/Assessment
3.   Treatment
4.   Follow-up/Evaluation.

Although each of these phases has its own particular goals and purposes, each may not be so clearly delineated. In other words, you may be working in several stages at any one time. Identification and intake/assesement will be discussed in this chapter, treatment in the following chapter, and follow-up/evaluation will be discussed in the chapter on program development. You may find such a breakdown in the stages of treatment difficult to apply in actual client contact, however, it is useful methodologically for the purpose of teaching people how to counsel men who batter.

Identification

It is still unknown exactly how many persons experience the problem of domestic violence (Straus, Gelles, & Steinmetz, 1980) because of

inadequate sampling techniques. Many people find it difficult to believe that the frequency of occurrence is as high as 30 percent (Gelles,
1974). We find that when counselors are taught the skills necessary to
elicit this information in a session, they are often amazed at how many
of their clients experience or have experienced domestic violence. As a
prerequisite to identification of domestic violence clients, we have
found that counselors should be aware of several factors which can
affect this process.

   One of the first goals a counselor should have when facing a client
is to determine whether or not domestic violence is a problem in his
life. If properly assisted by the counselor through careful questioning, a
client presenting any problem can focus on this aspect of his life. A
typical first step in doing this is to enquire about the status of a client's
relationship. What can follow once this is done is illustrated very
clearly by the excerpt from a transcript of a man referred to us for
depression, set forth below.

COUNSELOR:	Are you married or in a relationship?
CLIENT:	I'm married.
COUNSELOR:	For how long and do you have any children?
CLIENT:	We've been married 14 years; we have two kids, one 10-year-old boy and a 12-year-old girl.
COUNSELOR:	How are things going in your relationship?
CLIENT:	I guess OK, but when I get depressed, I tend to get a lot of flack from my wife.
COUNSELOR:	Do you sometimes find yourself getting into arguments?
CLIENT:	Yes, we do.
COUNSELOR:	You know, people in relationships tend to argue over specific things, like money, kids, housecleaning, and so on. What kinds of things do you and your wife argue about?
CLIENT:	Mostly money, sometimes the kids.
COUNSELOR:	What usually happens when you argue about, let's say, money?
CLIENT:	I usually tell her she is spending too much, and she tells me she's not or that she will cut down on her spending.

COUNSELOR: Do you ever yell at her?

CLIENT: Sometimes.

COUNSELOR: What do you do at other times?

CLIENT: Sometimes I give up and just leave.

COUNSELOR: Sometimes when people get angry they may pound their fists on the table or grab or push the other person. Have you ever done that?

CLIENT: I've grabbed her a couple of times to listen to me.

COUNSELOR: Have you ever slapped her?

CLIENT: A couple of times.

COUNSELOR: How many times?

CLIENT: Four or five times.

COUNSELOR: When did you get the most angry with her?

CLIENT: Last year when she overcharged our credit card.

COUNSELOR: What happened?

CLIENT: We got into a big fight. She ended up calling the police.

COUNSELOR: Did you hit her?

CLIENT: Yes, I guess so.

COUNSELOR: How so? Did you punch her?

CLIENT: I punched her in the jaw, and it began to bleed. I tried to make up at this point, but it was too late.

COUNSELOR: And so she called the police?

CLIENT: Yes.

COUNSELOR: You felt pretty bad about that, I imagine?

CLIENT: Of course.

You can see that several things have become clear to the therapist. First, that domestic violence is occurring in this relationship, and that the depression may or may not be directly related to that. Second, there seems to be some tendency to minimize the violence, but the client is cooperative with the counselor's attempt to elicit information. Third, some remorse on the client's part is evident, which will be useful in helping to effect change.

At this point in the interview, the counselor needs to elicit from the client a willingness to recognize his violent behavior as a problem in his life, and a desire to change such behavior. This may be done simply by asking.

COUNSELOR: I imagine you felt bad about this incident. How have you felt about other incidents of violence in your relationship?

CLIENT: Well, it's not like I want to do it, I just don't feel like I can do anything else at the moment.

COUNSELOR: Are you curious to know whether there are other ways of dealing with your anger?

CLIENT: I suppose I am.

COUNSELOR: Did you ever find yourself getting depressed after a violent episode?

CLIENT: Yes, all the time.

COUNSELOR: Maybe the two are related.

CLIENT: Could be.

COUNSELOR: Even if they are not directly tied together, if the violence is stopped, you'll have many fewer times when you'll be depressed. That's a start.

CLIENT: That would be great if you can do that.

In this case the depression was used to motivate the client to look at his violent behavior toward his wife. It seemed relatively successful. There will be clients who will deny that the violence is a problem for them. They may also refuse to work on changing that problem. At that point, it becomes an ethical issue for the counselor of whether or not, knowing about the violence, you are willing to work with a client on other issues. I have seen counselors face this situation in several ways.

1. Work with the client on the issue he wants to work on, with the intention in the back of your mind of being able to move in the direction of the violence.
2. Tell the client you will work only on the violence with him, and if he is unwilling to do so, you will gladly refer him to a colleague.
3. Tell the client you will work on what he has come in for, with the understanding that you will also work concurrently on the violence.

4. Work with the client with the first goal being to identify the violence as a problem in his life.

This is a difficult issue to face in that you may run the risk of losing your client if you push the point too hard; on the other hand, you do not want to collude with your client by minimizing the seriousness of the reported violence.

When the client is identified as a domestic violence client, either through your questioning or through the nature of the referral itself, the next step is to conduct an intake and assessment interview.

Assessment

The assessment process essentially begins once the case is identified. Its goals include

1. Assessing the lethality.
2. Assessing for motivation for change.
3. Determining the appropriate form of counseling/treatment plan.

Assessment may vary from one hour to four or five hours in length. It may include sessions with other family members, relatives, probation officers, police and attorneys, and examination of records, reports, and photographs. It may also include consultation with other therapists involved in the case and with other service providers, such as shelter workers. Obviously, the more information you receive, the better your assessment, and ultimately, the more effective the potential treatment plan.

As discussed earlier, if the primary goal of treatment is to stop the violence or lessen lethality, then a clear picture of the lethality or dangerousness of a particular situation is essential. It is our policy to speak with as many people as possible involved in a case. Our first two interviews will be with the batterer and then with his partner. A separate assessment for lethality is conducted with each person. We usually find that we get differing impressions when talking with each partner. This is consistent with the findings of other clinicians (Ganley & Harris, 1979; Walker, 1979; Walker, 1980).

Our assumption is that the woman's description is closer to the truth, for two reasons. First, her memory is likely to be more accurate because it is in her best interest to stay aware during the violence to protect herself. She is not usually the one in a rage, in which there is likely to be some memory loss. Second, the men are more likely to minimize and deny the violence out of guilt, shame, and a desire to stay out of trouble, particularly if they are court referred. Women also minimize and deny the violence out of guilt and shame and as a coping mechanism to avoid facing the reality of their situation (Walker, 1980). Thus, we assume that the violence is usually worse than either one of them cares to describe.

These differences in reports can be handled in several ways in counseling. The counselor can use these differences as a way of pointing out to the client his tendency to minimize and deny his problem. It may be used, as in the case of a substance abuser, to demonstrate the effect the drug has on his recall. If the differences are minor, you may not want to bring them up at all. If the stories are totally different, you can use that fact alone as evidence of a high potential for lethality in their situation.

On the other hand, you may wish to focus primarily on the similarities in their stories as a way to bolster motivation for change and to emphasize their recognition of the lethality of their situation. In some cases you may find it less important to reconcile differences in perceptions about the past than to focus exclusively on the present level of danger and on some immediate ways of avoiding future violence.

In addition to interviews with the offender and the victim, children and other adults living in the home often can present valuable information. Friends and other family members who have seen and/or talked with the victim or offender after a violent episode can offer valuable information as well as a different perspective. When working with court-mandated clients, we get police reports, probation reports, and rap sheets, to determine the details of violent incidents that were reported. Because of the intricacies of the criminal justice process, it is important for counselors to be aware of the fact that the final charges filed may not be descriptive of what actually occurred during a domestic violence episode. As indicated earlier, the best policy is to talk with as many people as possible, with the client's permission, in order to make a clear determination of potential lethality.

There may be clients who do not give you permission to talk with anyone else, including their partner. Your response to this situation, as with clients who do not acknowledge a problem with violence, may vary depending on the client and/or your own style of working. It is our policy to work only with clients who give us permission to contact their family members, other therapists, and other significant persons involved in their situation. If an individual is reluctant to do so, this may be an attempt to cover up important information which ultimately increases your liability and the victim's risk for future danger.

Determination of Lethality

In working with domestic violence cases one quickly becomes aware of how many violent incidents result in serious injury. Studies describing populations of battered women show a high incidence of beatings requiring medical care and/or hospitalization (San Francisco Family Violence Project, 1982; Rounsaville & Weissman, 1977; Straus et al., 1980).

According to the FBI statistics in 1979, 4.8 percent of all murders were committed by women who killed their husbands in self-defense (Bende, 1980). A study conducted in San Francisco (San Francisco Family Violence Project, 1982) revealed that 29 percent of all homicides were a result of domestic violence. All the studies to date point to a high probability of injury or death in domestic violence situations.

Most mental health professionals will agree that the prediction of a particular client's dangerousness or proclivity toward violence is at best difficult and at worst impossible. Although some professionals will say that the best predictor of future behavior is past behavior, studies have yet to statistically correlate past and future (Monahan, 1981).

The majority of studies on violent individuals have either focused on psychotic hospitalized patients (Werner, Rose, & Yesavage, 1983) or criminal populations incarcerated for violent crimes (Wolfgang, 1958, 1967, 1978; Barnard, Vera, Vera, & Newman, 1982). No studies have been conducted on noncriminal nonpsychotic populations because ordinarily they are not thought of as violent. Their violence has typically been perpetrated behind closed doors.

Domestic homicide is not a new phenomenon. Studies examining homicides have indicated that in most cases a history of physical abuse preceded these final acts of violence (Bourdouris, 1971; Browne, 1984; Thyfault, 1984). Women who kill are more likely to kill in self-defense than men who kill (Walker, 1984; Wolfgang, 1967). However, women are more likely to be found guilty of more serious offenses, and when found guilty of the same offense as men will be given a harsher sentence (Schneider & Jordan, 1981).

A recent study of domestic violence homicide cases has shown that an apparent relationship does exist between lethality and a number of factors common in battering relationships (Browne, 1984). In comparing domestic violence homicides and abuse-only cases, Dr. Browne found a number of factors that distinguished these two subject populations:

1. Frequency of violent incidents;
2. Severity of injuries;
3. Man's threats to kill;
4. Woman's suicide threats;
5. Man's drug use;
6. Man's frequency of intoxication;
7. Forced/threatened sexual acts.

Although this study does not give definitive answers as to our ability to predict time and place with regard to violence, it does shed light on our ability to predict who may be at risk for committing lethal violence.

In this chapter we will discuss factors which may contribute to lethality risk in domestic violence situations. Not enough research has been conducted to date which fully delineates the relationship between social, behavioral, and psychological factors and inevitable violence. However, it would be worthwhile for a counselor to assess for these factors, if only to get a better picture of the degree to which violence is occurring in a relationship. These factors may also shed light on the types of stresses which ultimately may contribute to further episodes of conflict and/or subsequent violence. Intervention techniques will be discussed in the following chapters.

The following sections describe 14 categories or content areas that may have some relationship to violence potential or lethality to one degree or another. They all have an impact on the occurrence of stress and/or conflict in a relationship, and they can affect the nature of the interaction between the two persons (Straus, 1980). To assess for each of these factors may be useful for the counselor in conducting a thorough assessment of an individual or family. A summary of these content areas follows.

Homicide Risk

In a study of homicide and aggravated assault in Kansas City, police had gone to the victim's home in 85 percent of the cases at least once, and in 54 percent of the cases had gone five times or more. Domestic violence accounted for 34 percent of the homicides and 32 percent of the assaults in this study (Stephens, 1977). These statistics, as well as those already mentioned (San Francisco Family Violence Project, 1982), clearly demonstrate that domestic violence can and does lead to serious injuries and death.

In assessing for this risk, you are essentially looking at the most serious or life-threatening violence which has occurred in the relationship. How often has it reached serious injury of a life-threatening nature? How long ago did the incident(s) occur? What happened as a result of these incidents? Have there ever been weapons used, such as firearms or knives? What objects have been used as weapons? Are there weapons in the home? Have there ever been threats with weapons? Have there ever been threats to kill? If so, how many?

It is our contention that if a threat to kill is made, given the right circumstances the threat could be carried out. Browne's study (1983) found threats to kill to be a significant factor in homicide cases. If there are weapons in the home, we will make removal of those weapons a condition of treatment. We also take threats with weapons seriously. Frequently we hear of incidents where an unloaded firearm is pointed at the victim, or where a gun is discharged in another direction away from the intended victim. Violence which has reached this point is considered highly lethal in that it does not take much more anger to load the gun or point it in the direction of the victim.

Suicide Risk

We routinely assess for history of suicide in the family of origin, history of suicide attempts, threats of suicide, and contemplation of suicide. We have found that men are a high risk for suicide after an acute battering incident (Walker, 1979) when the woman has left the relationship.

The contrition state can easily evolve into a depressive state with frequent suicidal ideation subsequent to separation. Women often consider suicide as a means of leaving a violent relationship (Walker, 1984). It is important for clinicians to differentiate between attempted suicide, planned suicide, and contemplation of suicide for both victim and offender. In Browne's study (1984) of domestic homicide, the battered woman's contemplation of suicide appeared to be one of the distinguishing characteristics of the homicide cases in which battered women killed their batterers.

Cycle/Frequency of Violence

This aspect of the interview includes a complete history of violence. We enquire as to when physical, sexual, property, and psychological violence began; how frequent each form of violence was early in the relationship, later on, and currently. An inventory of all four types of violence and their forms of expression is made. A sample intake form is included in the Appendix so that you can see how this information is collected. The interview may include a detailed discussion of four episodes of violence: the first episode, the worst episode, a typical episode, and the last episode. Questions are asked regarding the circumstances surrounding the episodes; use of weapons, alcohol, and other drugs; injuries sustained; medical attention sought; outside interventions (police, family, neighbors, etc.); and an inventory of actual violence perpetrated during each act.

History of Violence

A thorough history will include violence in the family of origin in the form of child physical abuse, child sexual abuse, psychological abuse, and observation of abuse between parents or other significant adult figures. Male children of violent parents have been shown to have 100 percent greater chance of being woman batterers than men who were not exposed to violence in their family of origin. In addition, persons who experienced the most punishment as teenagers were four times as likely to batter a spouse than teens who were not hit by their parents (Straus et al., 1980). A strong relationship does exist between exposure to violence in the family of origin and current violent behaviors toward a spouse or significant other (Coleman, 1980; Rosenbaum, 1979; Star, 1978; Walker, 1979).

Information about violence in previous adult or adolescent relationships is helpful in determining the history of current patterns of behavior. To point out that a previous partner has left him because of the violence can be an effective means of engendering motivation for change. The seriousness of violence in prior relationships can give you an indication of possible violence in the future.

Substance Use/Abuse

The literature is replete with studies documenting the association of alcohol and violent behavior (Guttmacher, 1960; Wolfgang, 1967). The domestic violence literature is no different. Gelles (1974) found that alcohol accompanied violence in 48 percent of the individuals studied. Of this population, alcohol-related violence occurred in the majority of cases when the man was violent. Rosenbaum (1979) found that 40 percent of the men studied were considered alcoholic according to an alcoholism screening test.

These finding have been corroborated by other investigators (as well as Bard & Zacker, 1974; Coleman, 1980; Flanzer, 1982; Walker, 1979, 1984). Although these two phenomena appear to occur in concert, there are no studies that show a direct biological link between alcohol and violence.

Of the men with whom we have worked, 80 percent were under the influence of alcohol or another drug at the time of the latest battering incident. The vast majority of these men claim that they have also battered their partners while not under the influence of alcohol or other drugs. Frequently men will use the alcohol or drug use as a way to avoid responsibility for their violent behavior (Ganley, 1982; Ganley & Harris, 1978; Gelles, 1974). Men living with alcoholic or drug-abusing women will justify their violence as a way of controlling the women when they are out of control or under the influence. The issue of substance abuse needs to be addressed in order for any kind of counseling to be effective.

Assault on Other Family Members

Research shows an association between spouse abuse and child abuse (Hilberman & Munson, 1978; Rosenbaum 1981b; Walker, 1984). Typically, the male batterer will abuse his children and in some cases the battered wife will in turn abuse her children (Hilberman & Munson,

1978; Smith, Hanson, & O'Noble, 1973). When looking at violent acts (as opposed to abuse), Straus et al. (1980) found that 68 percent of the mothers and 58 percent of the fathers engaged in at least one violent exchange with a child, with sons being the more likely victims than daughters. This study also showed that a wife who was being abused by her husband was 122 percent more likely to batter her child than the nonabused wife. The data suggest that where there is woman battering, the children are also at considerable risk (Steele, 1978).

In addition to child abuse, elderly abuse can occur in families experiencing woman battering (San Francisco Family Violence Project, 1980). Assessments should include abuse toward elderly and children; violence perpetrated against parents by children; and violence between siblings. Besides deliberate violence, children frequently are the victims of violence when they attempt to intervene in violent altercations between their parents (Snell, Rosenwald, & Robey, 1964). Included in this last category is violence perpetrated against unborn children during the woman's pregnancy. Gelles (1975) reported that 25 percent of the women were beaten during pregnancy.

Previous Criminal History/Activity

Men who batter may have a history of other types of criminal activity, such as sale and/or possession of drugs, property crimes, violent crimes, and the like (Falk, 1977). Although this information may not be readily available to counselors, it can shed light on how effective treatment is. This information can be obtained in several ways. If a client is referred by the court, probation officers can give you a copy of the individual's criminal rap sheet or at least a verbal report over the telephone. The client himself may be willing to discuss his past and current activities; however, his partner may be a more reliable source of this information.

Criminal history includes arrests and/or convictions. Criminal activity includes those activities for which the client has not yet been apprehended or of which he has not yet been accused. The degree to which a person is involved in antisocial behaviors is extremely valuable, as it may shed light on the potential for future such behaviors at home or outside the home. Be aware, however, that with respect to the issue of what the reporting responsibilities are of counselors learning this type of information, there is variation from state to state, and profession to profession. Anyone involved in this type of counseling should learn what those responsibilities are in their area.

Violence Outside the Home

Although many of the men with whom we have worked have re-
stricted their violence to the home, there are men who act violently
outside the home as well. Those particular cases which come to mind
are men who are involved in other criminal activity, such as the sale
and procurement of controlled substances (illicit drugs), and alcoholic
men who get involved in bar-fight situations. Also included in this
category are those individuals in occupations which intrinsically involve violence, such as police officers, security guards, military personnel, or bar bouncers. The question of concern here is how much is
violence a part of the person's life inside and outside the home.

Isolation

Isolation, as discussed earlier, is a particular stress that may increase
the likelihood of violence (Searle, 1982). Isolation increases dependency and loss of perspective, which may lead to paranoid ideation,
depression, and anger from not getting all one's needs met (Straus
et al., 1980). Most important, it creates a rigid mental framework,
causing the individual to fail to consider alternatives to violence when
confronted with conflict, frustration, or anxiety. As will be discussed
later, a decrease of isolation can have a concurrently similar effect on
lethality.

Proximity of Victim and Offender

If a couple has less contact with each other, there will be less exposure
to violent situations. A woman in a shelter and/or a defendant incarcerated is probably the safest possible situation. Couples continuing to
live together may be of highest risk depending on the history and
extent of the violence. One of the disadvantages of shelters developing
a men's program is that this may create a physical proximity between
the victim and offender, which may not be desirable, with the counselors getting in between.

Where the woman is not in a shelter and the man is not in jail, a
factor to consider is how much time they spend together. In cases
where the couples are separated, the counselor must assess the need for
restraining orders and supervision of child visitation and/or child
exchange for visitation.

Attitudes toward Violence

How does the batterer *feel* about the violence? Does he consider it all right to use violence? Does he feel justified, and would he use violence again? Does he feel bad about his behavior, and does he want to change? For whom does he want to change his behavior? You? His wife? The Court? Himself? This factor alone could give you some indication as to motivation for treatment and prognosis for success and the possibility of reoffenses.

Life Stresses

Stresses, particularly of a financial and/or unemployment nature, can create considerable tension in a relationship (Rosenbaum et al., 1981; Straus, 1980). These, and other stresses listed on the first page of the intake form, should not be underestimated nor should they be ignored in terms of formulating a treatment plan or utilizing a particular intervention for a client.

General Mental Functioning

When referring to this factor, professionally trained clinicians may want to make a formal diagnosis. If you are a paraprofessional, you are essentially asking yourself whether the individual appears to be of sound mind. It does not take a trained professional to identify an actively psychotic person or one with a paranoid personality disorder. If the person seems frightening to you, overly suspicious, incomprehensible, or out of touch with reality, he may have some psychological disorder. As a rule of thumb, though not always accurate, the more disturbed a person, the more unpredictable and, therefore, the more lethal a situation may be. The less formal training you have, the more I would recommend that you rely on trained individuals for consultation and backup.

Physical Health

This is not to replace a formal medical work-up, but we routinely ask clients whether they suffer any chronic illnesses, are currently on medication, have suffered past illnesses, have been on medication in the past, or have had major accidents or work-related injuries. The purpose of this questioning is to determine whether the violence can be attributed in part to medical disorders, brain damage from illness or accident, and/or medication or combinations of medications and/or other drugs or alcohol (Elliot, 1976; Lion, 1977). When in doubt, always consult a physician. Included in this category are developmental and/or neurological disabilities which may cause loss of muscle coordination or spasms. It is also important to assess when the violence in these situations is a function of the disability or a function of the stress one may experience from the disability.

In working with high-risk cases, it is highly advisable for counselors to seek consultation with colleagues. A co-therapist or fellow staff member from your agency frequently can offer valuable feedback and insight from a different perspective. We will often discuss our thoughts and feelings as to dangerousness with our client, his partner, other family members at risk, probation officers, attorneys, colleagues, or any person or persons who can offer us assistance in deciding on an appropriate course of action.

What follows is an outline of the 14 lethality factors previously discussed and a summary of the information elicited from the client during the assessment process. In the Appendix of this book there is the assessment form that the client completes himself. This form contains most of the content areas that follow in the outline below.

In a later chapter we will discuss legal and ethical obligations in treatment, with a specific emphasis on responding to threats of violence and the appropriate response to an assessment of high lethality or danger.

Lethality Factors: Domestic Violence Intake/Assessment

    I.   Homicide risk
        A.   weapons in the home
        B.   use of weapons
        C.   threats with weapons
        D.   threats to kill
        E.   most severe violence
   II. Suicide risk
        A.   family history of suicide
        B.   contemplation of suicide
        C.   attempted suicide
        D.   threats of suicide

III.   Frequency/cycle of violence
    A.   history of violence (when it started)
    B.   last violent episode
    C.   first violent episode
    D.   most severe violent episode
    E.   typical violent episode
    F.   inventory of physical violence
    G.   inventory of sexual violence
    H.   inventory of property violence
    I.   inventory of psychological violence
    J.   frequency of violence early in relationship
    K.   frequency of violence in last year of relationship
    L.   cycle of violence evident/current stage
IV.   History of violence
    A.   physical abuse as a child
    B.   sexual abuse as a child
    C.   offender's parent violent toward spouse
    D.   victim's parent violent toward spouse
    E.   offender violent in previous relationship
    F.   victim in previous battering relationship
V.   Substance use/abuse
    A.   offender's type, frequency, and amount of alcohol use
    B.   victim's type, frequency, and amount of alcohol use
    C.   offender's type, frequency, and amount of other drug use
    D.   victim's type, frequency, and amount of other drug use
    E.   offender's and victim's history of alcohol/other drug use
    F.   offender's and victim's family of origin alcohol and
       other drug use
VI.   Assaults on other family members
    A.   child abuse
    B.   child sexual abuse
    C.   elderly abuse
    D.   violence between children
    E.   violence of child toward parent
    F.   exposure of children to violence between adults
VII.   Previous criminal history/activity
    A.   history of crimes against persons (violence)
    B.   history of crimes against property (theft, burglary, etc.)
    C.   crimes involving drugs
    D.   police called; arrests and/or convictions

    E.   probation/diversion history
VIII.   Violence outside the home
    A.   violence with friends
    B.   violence against strangers
    C.   violence involving drugs
    D.   occupational violence
  IX.   Isolation
    A.   relationship to other family members
    B.   close friends and/or co-workers
    C.   other professionals involved with family
    D.   significant persons involved with family
   X.   Proximity of victim and offender
    A.   separate or same residence
    B.   separate or same places of employment
    C.   temporary restraining orders or other court orders
    D.   child custody/visitation
    E.   need for shelter or other housing
  XI.   Attitudes toward violence
    A.   not permissible at any time
    B.   permissible in some situations
    C.   permissible in most situations
    D.   attitudes toward members of the opposite sex
 XII.   Life stresses
    A.   Holmes and Rahe Social Readjustment Rating Scale
    B.   client's perception of stressful areas of his/her life
XIII.   General mental functioning
    A.   *DSM-III* diagnosis
    B.   history of psychological disorders
    C.   history of treatment
    D.   other therapists currently seeing client
    E.   prior hospitalizations for mental health reasons
    F.   medications, current and past
XIV.   Physical health
    A.   current condition
    B.   history of chronic disease
    C.   medications, current and past
    D.   family history of disease
    E.   major accidents in past
    F.   hospitalizations
 XV.   Therapist's evaluation

     A.   personal evaluation

     B.   group consultation

     C.   co-therapist consultation

     D.   consultation with other therapists, probation, offender, victim, etc.

     E.   client cooperation with treatment plan

     F.   number of reoffenses in treatment

     G.   client's ability to assure therapist that he will not act violently

     H.   client's participation in treatment

     I.   attendance

Assessment of Motivation

The second goal of the assessment, once it is determined that violence is part of a client's life, is to assess for motivation for change. In working with batterers, as with any client population, you will find men with varying degrees of motivation. There will be men who will come into your office and, with a little guidance and support from you, make the necessary changes in their lives. There will also be men who come to you, not because they want to be there, but because someone else wants them to be there, that is, either their partners or the courts. These men will clearly state that they have no problem with violence. The majority of men, however, probably will fall somewhere between these two extremes with a tendency toward being less motivated.

Motivation to change behavior is a complicated process and can be measured in many ways. Motivation, as with change, is not always obvious. Therefore, the counselor must listen and observe very carefully to determine to what degree someone is interested in changing his behavior. Change may be a difficult and frightening process, at the very least, for many people. One way of gauging motivation is by determining whether the motivation for change is coming from internal and/or external pressures and to what degree for each. We have found that the majority of men who seek counseling will be doing so initially because of the court or their partners, that is, external pressures. One of the goals of counseling is to make these men self-motivated.

The men who state from the outset that they are there because they want to change their behavior are obviously the men who are most motivated, but not necessarily the ones who will complete the program or even benefit from it. However, during assessment it is important to take a reading of the client's personal desire to change his behavior. Words do not always express this desire. We have seen men who have not wanted to come to counseling, but who have attended regularly and who have learned to control their anger. They were very clear that they were there because they had to be, not because they wanted to be, but would utilize the opportunity in spite of that fact.

We ask ourselves the following questions when determining a client's degree of motivation.

1. Does he acknowledge having a problem with violence?
2. Does he acknowledge having a problem with anger?
3. Does he acknowledge having any problems or difficulties?
4. Does he keep appointments?
5. Does he arrive on time?
6. Is he willing to discuss the violence?
7. Has he tried to stop the violence in the past? If so, what did he do?
8. Has he ever been to counseling before? If so, for what, when, and how long?
9. To what degree does he minimize and deny the violence?
10. Does he appear remorseful?
11. Does he feel his violence is justified? If so, would he do it again?
12. Does he acknowledge that he could benefit from counseling? If so, how?
13. Does he have any insight into why he uses violence? If so, what?
14. Does he see the violence as functional in the relationship? How or how not?
15. Does he state that he would like to be nonviolent in his relationship?
16. Is he willing to cooperate with program requirements?
17. To what degree does he externalize?

Different counselors have different criteria for motivation. Some say that as long as the client comes to the sessions, he is accepted into the program. Others say that the client must acknowledge having a problem with violence before he is accepted. Others fall in between. It is important for you to make your requirements clear throughout the counseling process. What may be acceptable motivation at the first session may be unacceptable six months later. The basic question is, To what degree does this person take responsibility for his behavior and want to change that behavior? This should probably be the ultimate goal for any counseling program for the male batterer.

Treatment Plan

Once a client has been identified as having this problem and is either motivated to do something about it himself or with the assistance of external pressure, it is essential to determine a treatment plan for this person and his family. From our experience, most men who experience this problem could probably benefit from an initial period of time in a group on anger management. We believe that the violence needs to be addressed before any other problem, and this seems to be addressed most quickly in group or individual counseling. Therefore, our treatment plan for each person includes a period of time in which they work mainly on managing their anger and lessening the possibility of recurrences of violence. This philosophy seems to be a common thread running through many programs working with male batterers (Ganley, 1982; Walker, 1979).

In choosing between group and individual counseling (assuming both are available in your area), we usually take into consideration several factors:

1. Can this person function well in a group? That is, will the group experience be so intimidating to him that it might be more beneficial to work on his anger on a one-to-one basis? In such a case, individual counseling may be more appropriate. Men who are the most psychologically disturbed may feel too different from others, feel even more isolated, or be too disruptive to the group. Cultural and language barriers can sometimes be a problem for some men in groups.
2. Does this person need a great deal of attention? If so, individual work could be helpful, either by itself or as an adjunct to group. A person who needs too much time at some point becomes a detriment to the group. One must balance the individual's needs against the group's needs.
3. Will he fit into the group or create an imbalance in some

way? Anyone who has run groups for any period of time will think of group composition as a means to keep good balance. We find it most important to keep a balance between court referrals and self-referrals and between races and socioeconomic backgrounds, as well as ages. Another balance which it is important to maintain in the group is between men with varying degrees of motivation.

4. What does the client want? Some men come into counseling wanting individual or group because of previous experiences with one or the other. It is just another obstacle for someone to be in a treatment modality which they do not want. Ultimately, it must be his choice, for this is what we are teaching in counseling, to make informed choices.

In some communities the local men's groups are often full, so the choice of individual versus group becomes a pragmatic one: "There is no room in the group right now. How about an individual counselor?"

For those men assessed to have an alcohol or other drug problem, we have found it necessary, like other programs (Ganley, 1981; Roberts, 1982; Walker, 1979), to make participation in our program dependent on their receiving concurrent alcohol and/or drug treatment. In addition to substance-abuse treatment, we have found rare cases in which residential treatment or hospitalization was necessary either because of alcohol and/or drug abuse or because the clients were more severely disturbed and in need of a more structured environment than once or twice weekly outpatient treatment. This is also true for clients who need medication.

A typical treatment plan for a man will be 6 to 12 months of group or individual counseling, with alcohol and/or drug treatment if necessary. If the man and his partner want to stay together, at some time when the man knows that he is managing his anger, we will recommend couples or family counseling. We will also recommend individual or group counseling for his partner as support for herself. We give her the very clear message that the counseling for her in no way carries a message that she is partly responsible for the violence. She may be partly responsible for the conflict, but the violence is the batterer's choice as a response to the conflict. We let her know that a referral for counseling is to give her support and to build up her self-esteem and personal strength.

In some situations you may discover that the victim has also been violent toward the batterer. It is important to speak with the woman to get a clear understanding as to the dynamics of her violence. Frequently her violence is in self-defense or in her anticipation of his violence. It may be that she is so angry at his violence that she now has also become violent as a way of expressing her rage. When the tension level becomes so high that it may be unbearable to the woman, she may attempt to take control by determining the time and place of his inevitable explosion.

We have found that most women will cease their violence once the batterer is in treatment and has stopped his violent behavior. Some women need to be encouraged into counseling so that they can effectively cope with their understandable anger. If a woman has an extensive history of violence, we will encourage her to participate in some form of treatment that focuses on anger management.

We have found it helpful to discuss a plan of action with the men in steps, to ensure that they clearly understand what is expected of them. It also gives them a time frame within which to achieve their goals. By engaging their partners, if they want to be part of the process, we hope to give the message that their partners and/or families are behind them in making the changes necessary to stop the violence, and that their partners are willing to work on their own problems so as to make problem solving/communication in the family easier.

Although treatment actually begins with the first phone call to the counselor, we find it helpful to separate assessment and treatment for the reasons previously described. In our program these two processes are clearly distinguishable because assessment is one to one, whereas treatment is almost always in a group. For a person working individually, this separation may not always be so clearly demarcated. It may also be said that even while a person is in group, the evaluation process continues and that counselors should not be afraid to change their opinion or plan for someone several weeks or months after their initial formal evaluation. However, at some point the focus turns from primarily information gathering to that of changing internal psychological processes and external behavior patterns.

Formal Testing and Assessment

As programs across the country have been developed to meet the needs in their respective communities, an interest has been rapidly growing in the area of clinical assessment. These various programs use different tools in documenting the presence or absence of certain psychological characteristics in their particular client population. Because so little research has been conducted on the male batterer, it is uncertain which assessment tools are the most effective in describing the male batterer.

As part of our initial assessment process, we utilize a number of assessment tools so that an effective treatment plan can be developed for each unique client. In addition to the interview process described earlier, each client is required to complete an alcohol and co-alcohol screening test (Sonkin & Durphy, 1982), a hostility toward women scale (Check & Malamuth, 1983), a stress inventory (Holmes & Rahe, 1967), and the anger and violence inventories described in the Appendix of this book. Recently we have begun to utilize the Minnesota Multiphasic Personality Inventory (Hathaway & Meehl, 1951) to determine serious psychological impairment as well as articulate general personality traits. Other clinicians and researchers have utilized other personality inventories (Carrillo, 1983), self-esteem measures (Walker, 1984), and measures of attitudes toward women (Carrillo, 1983; Walker, 1984).

In addition to the formal testing, each client is given a differential diagnosis as described by the *Diagnostic and Statistical Manual of Mental Disorders* or *DSM-III* (American Psychiatric Association, 1981). This diagnostic procedure is necessary to separate the more severely impaired from the more highly functioning clientele. Once-a-week, outpatient group psychotherapy may not be sufficient support and/or assistance for someone who is in crisis and/or is more psychologically impaired. The five-axis system for the *DSM-III* assists the clinician in determining an appropriate treatment plan as well as predicting and measuring success.

To date there is no formal clinical syndrome that adequately describes the male batterer. Unlike the battered woman syndrome, which is included under Post Traumatic Stress Disorder (Walker, 1984), the batterer's condition is yet to be formally recognized by the American Psychiatric Association. The American Psychological Association has recognized the existence of battered woman's syndrome (Kinports, Bersoff, & Ennis, 1983, 1984) and therefore recognizes the male batterer as being the cause of such a syndrome in women and children.

The *DSM-III* five-axis system allows the clinician to separate clinical syndromes, personality and developmental disorders, and physical disorders and conditions on three different axes. On axis one we would expect to find a syndrome that describes the condition that is the focus of attention or treatment. With a male batterer, this would be his violent behavior. An impulse disorder, such as intermittent explosive disorder, may serve to partially describe the batterer's behavioral problem. This axis may also include substance-abuse syndromes, Post Traumatic Stress Disorder for combat veterans, as well as psychotic and/or affective disorders that are concurrent to the violence. Axis two would describe any personality and/or developmental disorders such as schizoid, antisocial, passive-aggressive, or borderline disorders. The current thought among many therapists is that the batterer is characteristic of the borderline client; however, no research has substantiated this claim at the time of this writing. Until such research is completed, we are left with assessing each client individually in both diagnostic and behavioral terms. Axis three describes physical disorders that may or may not be related to one's violent behavior. A thorough physical examination conducted by a physician could provide valuable treatment information for the therapist, especially in cases where a client may be suffering from a chronic condition such as epilepsy, hypoglycemia, cardiovascular disease, and/or neurological disorders.

Axes four and five measure the severity of psychosocial stressors and level of adaptive functioning, respectively, in the past year. These measures can help the clinician measure success in treatment by examining a client's degree of stress and adaptation to that stress during his time in treatment. Axis five is a general measure of adaptive functioning in social, occupational and leisure situations. It is expected that a client will change his life in other areas in order to adapt from violence to nonviolence in his interpersonal relationships.

The differential diagnosis may change as you get to know the client better over time. Therefore, it is important for the clinician to be flexible and be able to recognize when a change in treatment plan is necessary in order to adapt to a new or different diagnosis. Although this discussion of diagnosis has been primarily aimed at the professionally trained clinician, we believe that the peer or paraprofessional counselor should be aware of these issues and routinely consult with trained individuals so as to improve on their treatment planning as well as protect the clients, the battered women and children, as well as the counselor from assault and/or legal liability should a client seriously assault or murder his partner.

4

Treatment of the Male Batterer

A primary prerequisite to providing effective counseling to male batterers is to have clear goals in mind as well as a way to measure the attainment of those goals. The primary goal of our program is to stop violent behavior, that is, physical, sexual, property, and psychological violence. Our primary method of reaching this goal is to help clients develop anger-management skills. By giving this goal top priority, we have found that there is a lowered risk for serious injury or death and consequently other individual and/or family therapy goals are more easily attainable. However, along with the anger-management process come secondary goals which, if achieved, are more likely to assure long-term change. These goals include:

1. *Decrease isolation and develop interpersonal support systems.* As described earlier, both men and women in domestic violence situations are socially isolated. This isolation creates more dependency on the relationship and ultimately more stress on each individual. The group provides an environment in which the man can learn to depend on other people at times of increased stress, as well as learn simply to talk about the problems he is encountering. The group becomes a release valve for the anxiety and tension the man experiences in his life and relationship. Each of the men in the group has the phone numbers of the other group members and is encouraged to call the others at times of increased stress, anger, and so on. A common pattern for men who batter is to withdraw at the times of crisis, which

ultimately exacerbates the crisis and resultant feelings. The group provides an opportunity to change that pattern of relating, encouraging men to utilize available potential support systems.

2.   *Increase feelings of personal control and power.* A typical description we have heard from men is that they are feeling out of control of their situation at home and that the violence is an attempt to take control of themselves and others. This is followed by feelings of remorse and guilt and ultimately of having relinquished control to their partner. It is our hope that through counseling men can see that their use of violence in an attempt to control the situation means that they are really *less* in control and feeling personally helpless and weak. Through controlling and communicating their anger in direct, nonintimidating ways, they can feel a sense of personal power which feels good and does not infringe on the rights of others. When anger is communicated in this way, there is no reason to feel guilt and shame and consequently no reason to relinquish the sense of personal power. As an individual begins to know himself, he also begins to feel more personal power.

3.   *Increase feelings of self-esteem.* Many of the men who batter have low self-esteem from abusive childhoods and/or the shame and guilt of being violent themselves. We want men to feel more accepting of themselves, including the fact that they have been violent. But acceptance does not mean they cannot change that part which they do not like. An individual first must accept in himself that which he must change or wants to change. Typically the men punish themselves with guilt, which neither increases self-esteem nor changes the behavior.

4.   *Increase his responsibility for behavior.* This responsibility includes his violent behavior as well as other behaviors. As mentioned earlier, most men who batter externalize their behavior by attributing their responses to external forces. The focus of treatment is to help men take responsibility for what happens in their lives and see how they may set themselves up for negative, as well as positive, events.

5.   *Increase awareness of the dangerousness of violent behavior.* This awareness is increased dramatically through the use of groups, when men talk to other men in the group who were either arrested for violence or seriously injured their partners. Also, the men often hear about cases in which we are involved and in which a homicide has occurred. For some men this serves as a reminder of the lethality of violence. We feel that this awareness is a necessary component to a counseling program.

6. *Increase acceptance of consequences of violent behavior.* Many of the men who are court referred to counseling need to accept the fact that the court acted because they broke the law, not because their partners are trying to get even with them. They need to come to accept the consequences of their unlawful behavior. Many of the men whose wives have left them continue to feel angry and to blame their wives for "giving up on them." However, we believe that if the men are able to accept the consequences of their behavior, they are more likely to take responsibility for either changing or not changing that behavior.

7. *Increased awareness of violence in society in general.* Although not a necessary ingredient of change, we have found it helpful for men to become aware of all kinds of violence, not just that against women. We discuss violence against children, other crimes against property and persons, international violence, and so on. This heightened awareness removes domestic violence from the personal-problem sphere and brings it into the societal-problem arena.

8. *Develop communication skills.* Although many men may have means to express themselves articulately in other areas of their lives, they have difficulty doing so in their personal relationships. Communication of anger and other feelings is a necessary goal of treatment. It is the development of these communication skills which gives the men an alternative reaction to the type of stress and conflict which led to violence in the past.

9. *Develop assertiveness skills.* These skills are easily taught by the counselor; however, they are the most difficult for the men to incorporate into their repertoire of behaviors. The men have difficulty in their relationships learning to ask for what they want directly and to say "no" without intimidation. The group becomes a laboratory in which the men can experiment with developing these skills. To say no becomes a way for them to separate from their partners, which can be very threatening to someone who is dependent. To ask directly for what they want may mean being rejected, which can be equally threatening. Overcoming these anxieties takes practice.

10. *Develop stress-reduction skills.* Through the use of visual imagery, self-hypnosis, progressive relaxation, and other stress-reduction techniques, men learn to control anger, anxiety, stress, and the like. We encourage the men to use their creativity in finding out what works for them. Learning this skill heightens awareness of the interrelationship between stress, anger, and violence.

11. *Develop the ability to empathize with their partners.* Through role-playing and group discussion the men develop an ability to empathize with their partners. This is most critical for them with regard to increasing awareness of when they may be intimidating their partners. This empathy can create the frame of mind which may focus their attention on the issue of managing their anger, rather than feeling victimized or attacked by their partners.

12. *Increase understanding of the relationship between violence and sex-role behavior.* In discussing this issue, men must become aware of how the socialization process they go through as children has set the stage for violence in their lives. This includes messages which limit their expression of themselves, as well as those which affect their attitudes toward women. This learning process provides the intellectual framework for the behavioral changes that the group process reinforces.

13. *Develop control over alcohol and/or drug use.* As discussed earlier, our policy is to refer individuals with alcohol and/or drug problems for concurrent substance-abuse treatment. It is also a function of the group to monitor and support the changes in substance use. Close coordination between programs develops a system of mutual support for violence control and substance abstinence.

14. *Achieve/support other individual, couples, or family therapy goals.* It is a function of the group to support the therapy goals of other professionals involved with an individual or couple.

Once a client is in treatment for a period of time, a group leader develops an understanding of that particular client and, therefore, works with him on other issues, either in addition to or related to violence. An example of this would be a person who has a problem accepting help from others and ultimately cannot accept what his partner has to offer.

The counseling approach we utilize is psychoeducational, that is, a combination of lecture/discussion and group processes. Our techniques are described in the book *Learning to Live Without Violence: A Handbook for Men* (Sonkin & Durphy, 1982). The focus of the educational material is the development of anger-management skills. The men are taught to increase their sensitivity to their anger. Both physical and behavioral anger cues are identified, and a time-out technique is utilized to provide a cooling-off period for the man to avoid escalation and possible violence. As described above, assertiveness skills, stress-reduction skills, and other communication skills are emphasized as alternatives to a violent response to anger.

As part of the intake interview, we explain to the men what the requirements are for participation in the program. These requirements are described in part A of the Appendix.

It is of the utmost importance that the client clearly understand what is expected of him if he is to participate in the program. In this way he clearly agrees to the conditions of counseling and acknowledges that he is expected to act and take responsibility for his actions. Since this is an important goal of treatment, how the men follow the rules and respond to the consequences of breaking them is a barometer of how the men are benefiting from counseling. In addition to the group rules, each client is asked to read and sign a confidentiality policy. This policy statement can be found in part B of the Appendix.

As with group rules, it is important for clients to read and understand each section of the confidentiality policy. Again, the purpose of having such a policy is to set clear limits and facilitate the process of the men becoming more responsible for their actions.

The Group Structure

The groups are ongoing, so each person enters the group on his own 12-week cycle. In this way the men who have been in the program longer can provide guidance and assistance to the men just entering. The groups are also a mix of court- and self-referrals. The self-referred men provide a positive role model for the court-referred men by being somewhat more motivated to change their behavior. Also, the court-referred men show those who are self-referred that the criminal justice system is responding to this problem by taking action. This model provides many men with additional incentive to change.

The groups are also mixed in terms of races and socioeconomic backgrounds. The bringing together of men from other cultural backgrounds shows men that this problem is universal. These differences allow men to explore their own racial prejudices and how classes of people, both men and women, can be oppressed by men and women with economic power. Homogeneous groups with regard to culture can be beneficial or necessary; for example, developing a group for Latino men whose primary language is Spanish; or a group with programmatic restrictions, such as a criminal justice group or a self-referred group, in areas where there are no criminal justice programs.

As described by the group rules and confidentiality policy, follow-up is a critical aspect of our treatment approach. The telephone follow-up is primarily a check to see whether there are further incidents of violence and whether the techniques discussed in the group are being utilized by the client at home with his partner. We rely heavily on the partner's perception of change to corroborate our observations in the group. The couples follow-up provides us with a firsthand opportunity to see how the men and women relate to each other. This session also provides the couple with a safe environment in which to discuss issues that may be difficult to talk about at home. The couples follow-up often becomes a safe forum in which the woman can express her fear and distrust of her partner, as well as to express her anger about past incidents of violence. We believe that this is a necessary step for the woman to take, particularly if she chooses to stay with her partner. If it is not expressed directly, this anger can come out indirectly and possibly become a catalyst for conflict and disagreement. Just as the woman needs to express her anger, the man must learn to hear it and to understand the reason why she feels that way.

The group meeting, like the program structure, is developed to reach specific program goals. The group is structured in three sections: (1) the check-in process; (2) the work/educational process; and (3) the closing process.

The check-in process consists of each group member responding to five questions to determine the priority of work which needs to be addressed during the rest of the meeting. These are

1. Was there any physical, sexual, property, or psychological violence this week?
2. How many time-outs did you take this week?
3. How many practice time-outs did you take this week?
4. How many times did you get angry this week when you might have taken a time-out but did not?
5. What would you like to talk about tonight in group?

Any group member who had an incident of violence during the week is required to talk first during the work/education process. Second priority goes to men experiencing other crisis situations. If neither violence nor other types of crises are occurring, the main focus of the group is on mastering the anger-management material. We look at how the men are identifying their anger; how they are utilizing or not utilizing the time-outs; and how they are working in their work-books and utilizing the other anger-management techniques. The process of responding to these issues usually brings to the surface other issues the men want to discuss relating to anger, other feelings, and the dynamics of their relationships. During this process feelings among group members and/or between members and the facilitator will also surface, which can be used to address the appropriate aspects of the anger-management material. Frequently, we will role-play difficult situations with anger the men have encountered or conduct group exercises to bring home a point described in the workbook (Sonkin & Durphy, 1982).

After each man's work in the group, other group members are given the opportunity to respond and offer feedback. This feedback is structured in such a way that the men are asked to focus on their feelings rather than making judgments or giving advice. This process can be an important means for men to understand their anger and develop skills in communication.

In addition to the anger-management material, the men work on a variety of other issues in the group. This work may include issues with respect to problems with fathers and mothers; developing friend-ships with other men; developing new relationships with women; and separation and divorce. Within the context of each of these issues, the discussion includes its relationship to anger and violence. For example, men dealing with a separation or divorce are informed that during this time they are likely to feel anger and frustration, which consequently makes them at a high risk for violence. Men who are experiencing stress on the job or who are angry at someone with whom they work are assisted with those problems, but are also made aware of how that stress or anger is brought home and projected on their partners. Specific coping strategies are developed to avoid future violence in their relationships.

The closing process of the group is an opportunity for the members to communicate any last minute feelings, angry or otherwise, and to avoid taking those feelings with them, possibly channeling them at home in a way which may contribute to a conflict situation.

When working with batterers, a counselor frequently encounters situations in which the men reoffend while in counseling. We believe that this situation needs to be dealt with consistently in order to lessen the risk of future violence. Reoffenses can be uncovered in one of two ways: either through our telephone follow-up or couples follow-up, or by self-revelation by the client during the check-in process at the beginning of each group session.

In each case of reoffense, whether the person is court referred or self-referred, we have five procedures the person must go through.

1.   The reoffender must be the first person to talk in the group. He will be asked to discuss what happened between him and his partner, how he was violent, and why he chose to be violent.
2.   He must develop and take home with him a specific strategy to avoid future violence which will impose some consequence for violent behavior.
3.   We make immediate telephone contact with the man's partner to assess her future safety, as well as to advise her of her options.
4.   We see the man and his partner in a couples follow-up session soon after the incident in order to make them aware both of the dangerousness of the situation and of other ways to avoid future violence.
5.   If a client is referred by the courts, he will be required to report any reoffense to his probation officer. Whether the client is self-referred or court referred, his partner will be urged to utilize the criminal justice options.

Initially our reoffense policy did not include criminal justice consequences for men self-referred into counseling. In fact, this issue became a concern of the men in the groups. They felt that it was unfair that a self-referred man did not have to report reoffenses to anyone. Although we made an argument that the court-referred men needed that consequence to motivate them to change, this distinction in policy represented an inconsistency in group rules and ultimately created tension within the groups. Consequently, we developed this reoffense policy for the noncriminal justice client.

As described in the confidentiality policy, when a self-referred client reoffends, it is our policy to strongly urge his partner to involve the criminal justice system. In the case of a more serious offense, we will utilize the privilege exceptions and report to the police a client who is a danger to himself or his partner.

The issue of reporting reoffenses is critical to successful treatment. Men need to know that their counselor will not collude with them in not changing their violent behavior. The message is that violence is both dangerous and against the law.

The Group Leaders

Like any form of group counseling, domestic violence men's group leaders play an important role in developing group process and group cohesion and in facilitating change in the men. The group leaders are both facilitators of the process and models for the participants. Although a discussion on groups and group dynamics could take up a complete book in itself (Yalom, 1975), the following discussion addresses issues which are relevant to working in domestic violence men's groups.

1. *Number of persons leading the group.* We have found having two leaders in each group to be the most effective means to counseling male batterers for the following reasons. First, two leaders can model together the types of behaviors they want the men to learn. Second, interactions between a leader and a group member may be facilitated by the other group leader. The co-leader can provide his or her colleague with valuable feedback regarding his/her interaction with the group member. Third, two group leaders can provide each other with feedback about how their own particular issues are affecting their work in the group. When these issues are discussed openly, they can enhance a group leader's effectiveness with the group members. Last, we have found having two leaders extremely helpful when making important decisions regarding lethality and the duty to warn a particular victim. The stress of leading such a group, and the decisions that leaders need to make regarding a client's potential for dangerousness, are better handled by two persons rather than one.

2. *Group leaders as models.* The positive role modeling of anger between group leaders as well as between group leaders and clients is a necessary ingredient for success with men who batter. Because of their position, the group leaders can be powerful positive role models for clients. In addition to anger, group leaders can model effective commu-

nication skills and demonstrate openness, vulnerability, a willingness to admit mistakes, and assertive behavior. Often many of the men have difficulty with authority figures, viewing the group leaders as police or father figures. By actively engaging yourself in positive role-model behavior, you are teaching the clients to develop similar patterns of relating and ultimately lessening the dichotomy between facilitator and client.

3. *Group leaders as facilitators of interactions between group members.* As described earlier, many of the men who batter are isolated and have difficulty developing meaningful relationships with other men. When in groups, these men have the tendency to interact with one or both of the leaders. This is especially true if they see the group leaders as having influence over their sentence or court disposition. Because of this we find it helpful for group leaders to make a concerted effort to encourage interaction between group members.

We do this through the use of role-playing; by encouraging the expression of anger and other feelings between group members; through the feedback process after someone has spent some time discussing an issue; and by the use of a buddy list which is comprised of each man's name and phone number for contact between group meetings. On occasion, men are given specific instructions to maintain contact with those men in crisis. In this way the men support each other in the changes necessary to prevent violence.

4. *Group leaders as guides for group process.* Frequently men will discuss issues which are not relevant to anger and violence. It is the role of the facilitators to bring this focus into their discussions to make them consistent with the group goals. This is less critical for those men who have been in the group for a period of time and have already demonstrated anger-management skills. It is more important for men who are new to the group and who are essentially still at risk for violence. Although these issues may be interesting to the other group members and even to the facilitator, it is important to keep sight of the priorities for a particular client.

An example of this type of situation is a client who reported at group an incident of psychological violence with his wife. She also happened to be leaving him at the time, and it was in his interest to discuss his feelings about his impending divorce. The divorce was of interest to all of the members of the group, including one of the group leaders. However, this person was new to the group and was still at considerable risk. Thus, the focus of attention was turned to the psychological violence first, with an emphasis placed on coping strategies to avoid future episodes of violence. This, of course, related closely to the stress and emotional turmoil of separation and divorce, but the focus was on coping strategies and not on the divorce itself.

5. *Counselors and self-disclosure.* Preferences regarding counselor self-disclosure vary from counselor to counselor. Some attribute their differences to style, others to opinions about the appropriateness of counselor role. Our style is one of self-disclosure. We have found it helpful in developing a working relationship with a man, in particular those men who are less motivated. This self-disclosure also somewhat reduces the tension between the client and the counselor, especially with those clients who are sensitive to authority and power differentials.

6. *Counselors as separate from group.* Although we encourage self-disclosure, we also encourage counselors to appreciate the difference in their role in the group from that of the clients. We feel that it is important for clients to know that they can depend on you for support and help if needed. In some ways, counseling men who batter is like reparenting, that is, providing men with the guidance and support which may have been lacking in their upbringing. One client described us as being the benevolent father figures in his life.

7. *Encouraging interpersonal support.* As described earlier, the role of the group leader is to encourage the participants of the group to support each other. We encourage them to call each other during crises and to relate to each other on a friendship/noncrisis basis also. This support lessens isolation and decreases stress. This mutual support prevents the counselors from being perceived as the only sources of support and helps to distribute power more equally between the counselors and the group members.

8. *Creating a safe place for men to explore their emotional side.* As with any psychotherapy group, physical and psychological safety is a necessary prerequisite to afford members the opportunity to explore their more vulnerable side. The leaders create this atmosphere by providing structure, consistency, limits, and encouragement for this personal exploration.

9. *Relationship between group leaders.* As described earlier, the group leaders can facilitate change in the group members by positive role modeling. The demonstration of two men solving problems together, sharing a role, respecting each other, communicating clearly, and being cooperative and noncompetitive can serve as a powerful male model for the group.

In order for this to occur, group leaders must spend time outside of group sessions analyzing how their relationship is influenced by the group. Time must be spent developing the type of communicative relationship which will be contagiously transferred to members of the group and their families. What feeling do you experience working with your co-counselor? Do you ever feel angry, competitive, sad, hurt, and so on? How easily can and do you discuss these feelings with your co-counselor?

Frequently issues from within you will surface during a particular group session. Are you able to talk about these with your co-counselor? If you are working with male batterers, being receptive to these thoughts and feelings can provide you with a powerful opportunity to experience growth yourself.

10.   *Connecting with individual members.* Through the assessment process, each group leader has an opportunity to form a personal relationship with each group member. This personal relationship allows the client to feel safe coming into a potentially threatening environment. If possible, we have found it most helpful for both group leaders to meet with a client for the intake process. This sets the stage for consistency between leaders as well as establishing in the client's perception who is the leader of the group.

11.   *Sex of group leaders.* Men and women can lead groups for male batterers. Sex is not as important as who the person is and how well he/she has examined his/her own issues regarding sexuality, sex roles, and attitudes toward members of the opposite and same sex. Programs across the country have found both male co-led men's groups and male–female co-led men's groups to be equally effective. Either alternative has its own particular advantages and disadvantages. A male–female team can model positive behaviors just as two men can model positive behaviors. Decisions regarding who leads the group often come down to who is available. We often recommend, if possible, that you try both, to see what model is comfortable to you, your program, and your clients.

The First Session, the Last Session

At his first session a new group member will be asked to introduce himself at the beginning of the session and to tell other members how he came to be in the group. Other typical questions may include:

1. What was the last incident of violence?
2. What was the worst incident of violence?
3. Why is he coming to the group now?
4. What would he like to get from the group?

Other group members are encouraged to ask the new member questions and to share any information they wish. When discussing the anger-management techniques with new members, we have found it very effective for the other group members to explain the various techniques they utilize and the rationale for these techniques. In this way the men can verify the effectiveness of these techniques, which will encourage new members to use them. In addition, this procedure helps develop group process and encourages interpersonal support between the participants.

As new members come into the group others will leave. Termination from the group can either disrupt or facilitate the group goals. Unfortunately, many men leave the group in less than desirable ways, such as failing to appear. However, we encourage men to attend one last group meeting before terminating. At this session we discuss why he is leaving the group, and each group member gives feedback on how he sees that person's progress. Each man is encouraged to have a plan of action to follow up his participation in the program. Frequently, men want to know when they are ready to leave the group. This is a difficult question to answer because it depends on the individual and his situation. We look primarily at how much the individual utilizes the anger-management material.

Clients who come to group week after week, discussing how they managed their anger that week, in our opinion are less likely to reoffend subsequent to group. The more the men talk about their anger on a weekly basis, the more confident the leaders and the other group members feel. This time period within which to learn the anger-management material varies from person to person. We have found that an average of 6 to 12 months is sufficient for a person to develop these skills. However, some men may take longer. It is our policy that the development of anger-management skills, however, is only a beginning step. Working on issues of self-esteem, power in relationships, parent–child interaction, and gaining a better understanding of one's self can take a longer time period than a commitment of 6 months in an anger-management group.

From our experience it appears that if the man and woman choose to stay together, couples counseling may need to be incorporated into the treatment plan. This has proven to be most helpful once there appears to be a clear commitment from the man to stop his violent behavior. Couples counseling often focuses on the system of interaction and may give the message, explicitly or implicitly, to both the man and his partner that the violence is somehow a function of this interaction. To repeat a point made several times earlier, the conflict and/or the anger is a function of this interaction. However, the violence is solely his choice of how to deal with that conflict and/or interaction and consequently is in his control. Realization of this fact will empower the man in such a way that he does not have to depend on his partner to change for him to control his anger and stop his violent behavior. Although there may be deep psychological causes to his feelings of helplessness, depression, anger, or whatever, behavior change is possible without completely working through these issues. In fact, the man may see stopping violent behavior as a necessary first step toward bringing these issues to the surface and thereafter resolving them.

Problem Areas

One of the problems most frequently encountered in working with the male batterer is that of continual reoffending. These reoffenses can vary in degree of seriousness, and one may see a reoffense of lesser violence as progress rather than a problem. However, in an informal study of two groups of batterers, we found that the self-referred men reoffended more frequently than the court-referred men. The message is clear that when you stand to lose something, you are more likely to change your behavior quite rapidly (Gelles, 1982). Although there are numerous reasons why a person may have trouble changing his behavior, we encourage the counselor to look at several factors.

Client Resistance

There are many theories on the issue of resistance. Some believe that there is no such thing as a resistant client, only therapists who have difficulty connecting with clients. Erickson and Rossi (1979) point out that clients make the best choice they can in a situation and that resistance is essentially the habitual framework in which clients view their lives. Other more traditional views of psychotherapy frame resistance as a self-protective process in which clients may view change as destabilizing or as threatening in some way. Regardless of the orientation, change is a difficult process for both counselor and client. It is important for the counselor to come to some personal understanding of how and why people change. We recommend seeking advice from colleagues whenever there seems to be a problem with a particular client who consistently reoffends. Many times we have found it to be a function of developing a closer, more meaningful connection with that client, and at other times, it simply is a function of his still believing that violence is acceptable in his life.

Not Treatable

How does one work with a client who believes his violent behavior is not a problem and feels completely justified in using it? Our belief is that every client, even one such as this, feels bad or has some remorse for using violence. On some level he knows that it is not totally functional in his relationship. At the other end of the continuum is the client who has had only one episode of violence in his life and is convinced that it will never happen again. He does not have any "problem." What the client says is usually not as important as what he does. If either one of these clients were attending group regularly, we would be less concerned than with clients who do not attend regularly and/or do not utilize the anger-management material. However, these are the clients who are more likely to have attendance problems. At what point do you determine that this person is not a good candidate for your program? If this person has the same problem in other programs, at what point do you determine that this person has not yet reached a time in his life when he can benefit from counseling? This is perhaps the most difficult question with which a counselor may have to come to grips. Can we help this person? Can our profession help this person? It is important to ask and answer these questions routinely. As a matter of practice, if a client is terminated from our program for attendance reasons, we will consider his trying another program.

Counselor–client Problem

Just as a counseling style could inhibit change, so can a particular counselor–client relationship be problematic to the point of inhibiting change. Although something may be gained from a problematic relationship, time is of the essence in many of these cases. If such a situation should develop, we would consider making a second referral to another counselor who can develop a more meaningful relationship with the client. It is important to keep in mind that the woman is still at risk during the first several months of counseling or until the client makes a firm commitment to stop the violent behavior.

Co-therapist Problem

One of the roles of the counselors in a group is to model appropriate expressions of anger and other feelings. The counselors can demonstrate that one can feel powerful without dominating others or infringing on their rights. However, the demonstration of these principles takes a commitment between the counselors to work on their own interaction. Their relationship needs constant attention to be functional in the group. The group will affect this relationship. Each therapist's individual personality will affect this relationship. The system within which these people all work together necessarily will affect this relationship. It is our belief that the more cooperative and functional the interrelationship between the therapists, the more likely it is that the group will respond favorably to the process. As with parents, group members often will try to divide the counselors by labeling one the good parent and the other the bad. There are times when differences between the counselors is a healthy model for the group, and there are times when mutual reinforcement is of primary importance.

Frequently problems within an agency will be reflected in the group. One agency wanted to provide a batterers' group with only enough money to pay one counselor to do all the follow-up contact with the women, intakes with the men, coordination with probation, as well as performing the administrative responsibilities for the group. The other counselor was paid only to be in the group and for one hour of consultation a week. As a result of this agency policy, a discrepancy in power between the counselors was evident to the group. One counselor was perceived as the leader of the group, for it was he who chose the members of the group, had all the information about the victims, and handled all the reoffenses and problems and contacts with probation. This power differential took its toll on the counselors' relationship. This problem between the counselors came to a head after six weeks of reoffenses by members of the group. It was the crisis period which helped the counselors look at their relationship and how it had been affected by the system within which they were working. This awareness and making the necessary systemic changes ultimately brought about an end to the crisis in the group and thereafter a more solidified group.

Lack of Consequences for Violent Behavior

As mentioned earlier, men are more likely to change their behavior rapidly if they get consistent messages about what the consequences of that behavior will be (Gelles, 1982). Although we do not want to become the overcritical fathers or parents, we feel strongly that there should be some consequences to a single reoffense or a continuing reoffense pattern. For court-mandated clients this can be anywhere from a stern warning from their probation officers to the reinstitution of criminal charges. For self-referred clients it can be anywhere from specific homework, to encouraging the victim to report the incident to the police, to our making the report.

Reoffenses, even less violent ones, need to be taken seriously. They must be viewed as a warning that the client needs more attention or help. Although the counselor is not responsible for the violent behavior perpetrated by the client, he/she is responsible for responding to that situation in a timely fashion. We are trying to empower our clients emotionally so that they do not have to resort to violence as a means of feeling powerful. However, we may begin to feel somewhat responsible for their behavior. We must remind ourselves that there is only so much we can do; the rest is up to the client. However, failures in the form of reoffending often include physical and psychological injuries to the victims. At some point, and it varies from client to client, our focus shifts from helping him change his behavior to helping her remove herself from a dangerous situation.

A similar kind of change in focus occurs with men who have attendance problems. Again, at some point we will abandon our concern for his attendance in the group and focus our concern solely on the victim's safety.

Individual, Couple, and Family Counseling

Frequently when a man has been in an anger-management group for 6 to 12 months, there comes a time when the need for specialized attention becomes evident. This need for attention may be for personal psychological issues and/or issues relating to communication or dynamics within the couple and/or family. Often violence is only one of many problems plaguing these families. Once the batterer has begun to address the violence problem, these other issues begin to surface and call for attention. Many times we will make a referral for individual counseling concurrent with group counseling for the high-risk cases, men needing more attention, and those interested in pursuing deeper work.

Couples who seem to be constantly in conflict or having difficulty making critical life decisions will frequently benefit from couples work while the man attends the group. Families with children who are acting out problems between the parents could benefit from family therapy. Often a second referral such as this is optional for a participant in the group. On the other hand, referrals for alcohol and/or drug treatment are often a requirement for participation in our program. Financial considerations are frequently an issue in dual referrals.

When making the decision to utilize adjunctive individual, couples, and/or family counseling as a part of the counseling program, we will not see that person, couple, or family ourselves. We will utilize other resources in the community. As with alcohol and drug referrals, we will turn to colleagues with whose work we are familiar and who we know understand the dynamics of domestic violence clients. This cooperation between service providers is necessary for success with clients. In each Bay Area county, therapists and other service providers involved in work with domestic violence clients meet periodically for support, continuing education, and political networking. In this way we become aware of the variety of services available, the persons offering those services, and their policies and procedures. Frequently small case conference groups and the involvement of service providers on a political level of activity in the community are outgrowths of these meetings.

Client Process—Counselor Process

The degree to which personal issues or emotions surface with group members will depend on how a group is structured. Groups which are more educational in nature, comprised mostly of didactic and some experiential material, will focus more on intellectual processes and less on emotional issues. At the other end of the spectrum, a group focusing on process will bring emotional issues within an individual and between individuals readily to the surface. Obviously the structure will be a reflection of the counselors' own attitudes, and it therefore is a model for members in the group.

We have found that the degree to which clients are willing to confront their own issues is reflected by the degree to which the group leaders are willing to confront theirs—both issues between counselors and within individuals. As co-leaders, we are constantly confronting issues of competitiveness, communication of anger, control, expression of vulnerability, and feeling taken care of or supported by a co-leader. As co-leaders we are in a close relationship. This relationship exists whether the counselors are aware of it or not. When they are not aware of it, it may undermine the process in the group, and ultimately it may undermine or impede the success of the group members. When they are aware of it and work with it, their relationship becomes another tool for helping the men change. It becomes a working model, a force that affects both the counselors and the members of the group.

An obvious way to make this relationship work for you is to confront these issues with your co-leader. We encourage co-leaders to meet before and after group sessions and at other times during the week, if possible. We have found it useful for us to be aware of issues occurring in each other's personal lives, for these problems may affect our work in the group. When a group leader is aware of what his co-leader is experiencing in a particular interaction with a member or in listening to a group member discuss his problem, it allows his support to be felt more strongly. This may be in the form of taking over for his partner, or it may be sensitivity in the form of a touch, a look, or verbal support.

Frequently when group members work on issues of alienation, loss, anger, sadness, and the like, the intensity of the process will affect other group members and the leaders as well. The more the group leader is able to welcome and allow these feelings in himself, the more likely the group members will be able to do the same. To see a leader be affected in a profound way is a powerful model for everyone present. This is not to say that the group leader uses the group to work out his own issues; however, the group leader *cannot* be unaffected by the experience of the group.

The issue of domestic violence reflects issues which are universal and therefore affect everyone. That is, how men and women relate to each other; how men relate to the male and female within each of them; how people communicate with and feel connected to or under-stood by other people; how we face our own alienation and aloneness in the world; how we love others and how we love ourselves. These are issues which all people at some time in their lives confront and attempt to resolve. When this process begins varies from person to person and from time to time, depending on the circumstances. A group for men who batter women can be a place where these issues must be recognized and dealt with.

5
Special Issues in Treatment

When counseling men who batter women, whether the modality is group, individual, couples, and/or family, issues will arise which at one time or another surface for all men. The following is a discussion of 17 of these issues which seem to surface with regularity. We will discuss how each fits within our philosophical framework and how each is addressed clinically.

1. *"She is constantly bringing up the past. She doesn't appreciate all I'm doing to change."*

High levels of anger in battered women have been well documented from both clinical observation and research (Martin, 1981; Rosewater, 1982a, b; Walker, 1979). Much of this anger is exacerbated by being continually abused physically, sexually, and/or psychologically. Although typically women retroflect their anger, that is, turn it inward, causing psychophysiological complaints, depression, and severe distress, the anger is frequently directed toward their partners who are perpetrating the violence. When women become aware of this anger and its causes, the expression of those emotions is sometimes overwhelming for the woman and her partner. Often this anger is expressed indirectly in the context of the relationship because the direct expression of such anger can lead to further victimization. The withholding of anger becomes functional in the context of the relationship in the short term even though it may have long-term self-destructive consequences.

110

When men enter our program, we discuss this issue with them. They may be expecting a gold star for their efforts, but instead they get a barrage of anger, following an initial short honeymoon-type period when they begin counseling. We view her beginning to express her anger as healthy for her and for her partner as well, and also as a sign of progress. The direct expression of her anger is healthy for her because it may be a sign that she is not taking on the total responsibility for the violence, as women often do when men blame them, and this may also be an indicator of her feeling better about herself. This is also a positive model of expression of anger when it is done in a direct way. We believe the men need to hear this anger because it forces them to take responsibility for their violent behavior.

The expression of anger may also be an indication that the woman is feeling safer to express feelings she once withheld or communicated in indirect ways. Typically male batterers have a great deal of difficulty identifying and communicating their own anger and even more difficulty hearing the anger of others. For some men this can be a sensitive issue. We use the group and couples follow-up sessions to help men learn to hear anger without getting defensive, blaming, or angry in return. We will frequently ask men to just listen, to let it sink in, and then to repeat back to the person what they have heard. In this way the focus is on understanding and communicating, and not on their typical defensive response pattern.

2.   *"She says she doesn't trust me. I don't get it, she knows I won't hurt her."*

As well as being angry, many battered women are afraid of their partners long after the violence ends (Rosewater, 1982a, b). This fear is genuine and very real and needs to be validated by the counselor and by her partner. Often battered women exhibit symptoms of Post Traumatic Stress Disorder (Walker, 1984), including anxiety reactions which result from ideational or environmental stimuli, such as his walking into the room, talking in a particular way, moving toward her in a particular way, or even looking at her in a particular manner. Like anger, this fear needs to be discussed, and the man needs to understand it.

Men who were abused as children or were afraid of one of their parents can understand this type of fear, the fear of someone bigger and stronger than you, who has hurt you before. As with the anger listening exercise, we will instruct the man to just listen and to repeat what he hears. What are the feelings that come up for him when he hears this? Most typically men feel sad and hurt, which is sometimes masked by their angry defensiveness. Frequently when men hear their partners tell them that they are afraid of them, the men think they need to do something to make that feeling change. We find it helpful to reassure the men that often there is nothing they can do about it, but they can listen and validate what their partners are saying to them.

3. "I feel so depressed sometimes I feel like ending it all."

Men typically feel at their lowest point after an arrest, especially when their partner has left them. Statements such as this may be only a plea for forgiveness and/or her return home; however, I would caution any counselor to take all such suicide threats seriously until you have information which leads you to believe otherwise.

We take such statements seriously and will directly confront a client on his suicidal thoughts. Has he thought of suicide? How so? How would he do it? Has he contemplated suicide before? Has he attempted suicide? Does he know anyone who has attempted to commit or committed suicide?

In cases where suicide is a concern, the group approach can be very helpful. In most cases a high-suicide-risk person will be instructed to attend an individual session with one of the therapists as well as contact someone in the group each day between group sessions. Specific days and times will be arranged before he leaves group that day. He will also be asked to agree to make a contract with the group not to take his life without making contact with one of the therapists first. If a client cannot make this agreement, we will initiate a 72-hour hold with the police department and notify his family as well. Although there may be instances where suicide threats are used to control another person, it does not necessarily mean that an actual act of suicide is not possible. For this reason, our assumption is that suicide is a risk no matter what the motive for such a threat.

When a man discusses suicide in the group, the following week he may begin to feel embarrassed after such a discussion and may want to miss the session. To avoid the turmoil that kind of reaction foments for both the man and the group, we may predict those feelings of embarrassment and consequent desire to miss the next session in order to let him know that those feelings are normal and that we would like him to return with those feelings and talk about them.

4. *"She left me."*

A common consequence in domestic violence relationships is divorce and/or separation (Levinger, 1966; Walker, 1984). Like other types of problem relationships, domestic violence relationships have their ups and downs. Often following an initial period of separation, there is a reconciliation. It is estimated that over one-third of the women who seek refuge at a battered women's shelter return to their relationships (Carsenat, 1975). However, battering marriages do not last any longer than the general population of marriages (Walker, 1984). The typical question asked is, "Why do women stay in an unhappy relationship?" We prefer to ask the question, "Why does the man stay if the woman is such an awful wife or partner?" The specific answer to this question may vary from man to man, but there are some general or commonsense reasons reported by the men, which are very similar to the reasons why the women stay. These include love, dependence, fear of being alone, uncertainty about whether or not he can do better or whether someone else will love him, family pressures, financial pressures, children, and the list goes on and on. However, when someone leaves, it is most often the woman who does so. Once separated, women tend to function better, given similar support systems, than the men. Many men tend to have a great deal of difficulty living on their own.

After separation the initial impulse for most men is to put on the hard sell: "I will do anything if you come back." Our recommendation is to leave her alone. "If she wants to talk with you, she will contact you. Forcing yourself on her in a loving way can be as intrusive and abusive as forcing yourself on her in a violent way." Separation may be viewed as a necessary step to reconciliation. Explaining the separation in terms of analogies can be helpful to some men.

I once interviewed a man who was referred to me by his wife. She had left him and was staying at a shelter. Neither he nor I knew where she was, and he was calling everywhere trying to find out her location. I tried to explain to him that what his wife wanted was not to have to talk with him and not to have him impose himself on her as he would do when he battered her. He could not hear what I was saying. All he could do was try to find her to get her to come home. He wanted to assure her he would not batter her again. He needed a repository for his guilt and an object for his dependency. This man had been raised on a ranch, and one of the animals they raised was sheep. After giving up on getting through to him directly, I told him a story about myself:

When I was a boy my family used to visit some friends who had a farm, and they had sheep also and a wonderful sheepdog. Because I liked that sheepdog so much, I own one today. Anyway, that dog was always busy finding the sheep which had wandered from their area into the cattle area.

At that point the client said to me, very nonchalantly, "They probably kept escaping because they may have been overcrowded in their area." I said to him, "I guess that's where the expression 'If you want to keep your sheep, you need to give them a bigger pasture,' came from. Sometimes the correct and necessary thing to do is just the opposite of what comes naturally." The client gave me a big smile and nodded his head up and down as he left the office.

We tell men right from the outset of treatment that there is no guarantee that their partners will come back, and that her return is not the focus of treatment. However, if they do want their partners to return, there is a better chance of that occurring if they begin to acknowledge their problem with violence and start to work actively on changing those patterns in their lives.

A common response is, "I need her to make those changes." We disagree; they do not need their partners to begin to look at their past history of violence, develop anger-management skills, and change their attitudes toward themselves, their partners, and the relationship. At some point in the future, if and when they reunite, he may want to work on his anger-management and communication skills with her, but she is not a necessary ingredient for developing those skills.

Men will sometimes say, "If she's no longer with me, then I no longer have a problem." It is difficult to convince a man otherwise if he has never been violent in prior relationships. Other men in the group can speak about their experiences, and the counselors can speak about their observations, knowledge, and experience; however, some men will drop out of treatment if they discover that there is no chance of reconciliation.

5. *"Should I tell her? I don't want to scare her away."*

With the high probability of divorce in domestic violence relationships (Levinger, 1966), the men will inevitably begin to date other women. The question then comes up, "Do I tell her, and if so, how and when?" From our perspective as therapists, we want to have contact with any woman with whom our client is involved, for several reasons. First, to assess how he is dealing with his anger in his new relationship. Second, to determine how she is dealing with the knowledge of his past history of violence. Third, to provide us with the information about how to contact her and/or her family in the event that we have to issue a warning of dangerousness.

Two questions remain, "When does a date become a significant relationship?", and "When does therapy begin to intrude into the other aspects of the client's personal life?"

The answer to the first question, obviously, varies from person to person and relationship to relationship. Typically, we will ask the client, "Are you in a significant relationship with this woman?" Most men know when they are just friends with someone and when they have serious intentions. Depending on the client and his history and patterns of violence, we will require that we have contact with significant others whom he may be dating. This becomes a problem mainly when the men do not want to tell the women they are dating about their violent histories and their involvement in the program.

For most men, revealing this information is a matter of time and language. At what point do you tell a prospective partner of your history and current involvements? An argument could be made that informing every person that there exists a risk of becoming a victim of violence is the ethical and reasonable thing to do. An argument to the contrary can also be made that it is necessary to tell only someone with whom he is seriously interested in getting involved. For many men the violence started months or even years into the relationship. For others, it started on the second or third date. Most unhealthy patterns of relating, poor communication skills, and unresolved personal issues begin with the first word. This is a very controversial issue to address in counseling.

Our basic policy is that if the man goes out with a woman three times or more in a month or is sexually involved with her, we need to have contact with her, and, therefore, he has to tell her. We encourage the men to use the group sessions to brainstorm how and when they do this, and how to be prepared for her reaction. Having such a policy puts the responsibility on the man to confront the problem in his life. Not acknowledging this problem to the potential partner can be a way of not acknowledging this problem to himself.

The problem of violence is not like other emotional problems one may have in that it is the type of issue which has a direct impact on the health and safety of another person. This may parallel the informing of potential sexual partners as to the risk of their developing a particular type of venereal disease. Although doing so can be very uncomfortable, and there may be a risk of losing the relationship, the long-term consequences of failing to inform the other person may be as bad as or worse than telling them at the start.

As to whether or not this type of policy is intrusive into a person's private life really depends on your belief and their beliefs. Many men have had no problem informing the new women in their lives about the past and the counseling program. When men feel it is intrusive, they have two obvious options: to be in a program that does not require them to tell their partners, or to talk about it with the men in the group to get their support and to hear their suggestions and perspectives. We prefer the latter, but the former is always an option.

6.   *"I'm afraid of myself."*

To reach this conclusion and to realize it is, in our opinion, reasonable and healthy. It is reasonable because of the past. It is healthy because it is an indication that he is beginning to view himself from his partner's perspective, which is a sign of empathy, and because making that statement is another way of saying, "I'm a batterer; I have been violent, and I have the capacity for violence." It is an expression of feeling—a feeling of fear. Having a man make this statement, feel it, and mean it, embodies some of the major long-term goals of counseling. Those goals are taking responsibility for his behavior; acknowledging his feelings; and acknowledging his past behavior.

When men start new relationships, especially when expressing excitement about that relationship, and when men discuss their partners' fear or distrust of them, we seize that opportunity to explore their own feelings of fear and mistrust. Within the context of an exercise utilizing "I statements" or expressing feelings, asking a client to say he is afraid of his violence and/or anger can be an effective means to start a group discussion of each man's fear of himself.

7. "I'm afraid of letting go."

For many men the fear of showing their feelings can equal or exceed their fear of their violence. Men who have been violent when experiencing extreme emotional eruptions frequently begin to associate intense feelings with violence. When asking men what they have done to try to control the violence, we most frequently hear, "I try not to get angry" or "I try to keep my feelings in." We explain that intense feelings do not cause violence. Violence comes from an inability to deal with those intense feelings, and those intense feelings come from lack of expression of less intense feelings on a daily basis. The group becomes a laboratory for the experimentation of experiencing those feelings and communicating them in positive and productive ways.

8. "My father didn't have much of an impact on my life."

Although historically men's relationships with their mothers have filled the psychological literature (Chodorow, 1974; Dinnerstein, 1976), little has been written or known about men's relationships with their fathers. Men often state that they did not have a relationship with their fathers; therefore, the assumption is that the fathers had no effect on their lives. When given the opportunity to talk about or even with their fathers (in role playing) in the context of the group, emotional temperatures rise and vivid memories, long forgotten, resurface. Devoting a group just to the discussion of fathers can be an unforgettable event.

Although many of the men were right that their fathers were peripheral to the family activities, their presence was certainly felt. Men growing up with alcoholic, explosive, and/or violent fathers, who experienced the most trauma as children, have the most difficult time discussing their fathers. It is a frightening realization for men growing up saying that they are not going to be like "that" to discover that they *are* like that. Men are reassured that their fathers probably did not have the advantage of, nor would they have taken the opportunity to utilize, a program such as this. Coming to terms with their anger and their love for their fathers can be an emotional event for those talking, as well as for all those listening.

9.   *"Why me? Why did I get arrested? Others don't!"*

This is certainly a valid question. At the time of this writing great variances exist from jurisdiction to jurisdiction (and within jurisdictions from officer to officer and from court to court) on the enforcement of domestic violence laws. To some degree this is true for many laws. However, the question would be more accurately stated as, "Why *not* him?" That question may be easier to answer. Most probably it was not him because of the evidence, the attitudes of the responding officer, his response to the officer, and so on, but *he* also broke the law. It was him because he broke the law, and there was evidence to prove he had done so. It was him for one or more of a myriad of possible reasons.

We believe people are where they are by choice, either consciously or unconsciously. It may be argued that a man finds himself arrested because on some level he knows that that is what he needs to solve his problems. A man who comes to the group on his own obviously does not necessarily need the system on his back to be there. For the man who is arrested, perhaps if he did not need the system, he would have been in counseling long ago.

10.   *"She's no angel; she should be in counseling too."*

An implicit statement contained within this comment is, "Somehow she plays into the violence, so she needs help too." The way we diffuse this issue is by separating conflict and anger from violence. The long asked question is, "Do women provoke violence?" From our point of view, the answer is no, for the most part. However, women can and do provoke anger and conflict, just like men. What men (and women) do with that anger and/or conflict is within their own control. We agree that it would be helpful for the women to get counseling as well as the men, but such counseling will not stop a man's violent behavior. He is in counseling to manage his anger so an argument can occur between him and his partner without him or her having to fear violence. A second way in which we channel this discussion is when we discuss the possibility of couples counseling at some point in the future.

Frequently the "she's no angel" syndrome is a function of her living in a violent relationship for some time. She may be depressed, defensive, anxious, and angry; and counseling, in the form of group or individual sessions, could greatly decrease the tension between the two people during the transition phase of going from a violent to a nonviolent relationship.

Another aspect of this statement is deciding what, if any, action justifies violence. Our personal philosophy regarding this issue is that there is no justification for the use of violence outside of self-defense, and even in self-defense, one can often choose to escape from the attacker rather than retaliate with the use of force. Unlike battered women who kill their batterers, men who batter usually have the means to escape, and if the men do use violence, it is commonly used as a means to express anger and frustration and/or to get even rather than actual self-defense.

11. *"I didn't get angry this week."*

As described in the preceding chapter, our groups begin with a check-in process which includes the discussion of incidents of anger during the previous week. The above statement is perhaps one of the most common responses a group leader will hear. Take a moment to think about how you would respond to this statement.

Men who batter (like many men) are generally insensitive to their anger. They are also frequently unable to identify a particular anxiety response or bodily response as being anger. They also may not feel the need to communicate or to deal with any emotional response they can successfully repress. Many men (and women) do not value this expression of emotions, and therefore they lack the skills to deal in such currency. The expression of such emotions has not been a skill men have needed to succeed in business or pleasure.

We approach this problem in a number of ways. First we discuss the various degrees or levels of anger. For the most part, men associate only rage, and the feelings they experience when they are violent, with anger. When learning to focus on bodily and behavioral clues to anxiety and/or anger, men learn to become sensitive to lower levels of anger not often associated with arguments and/or conflict. It is explained to them that these low-level angers are usually disregarded on a daily basis, but that they can add up to explosions which may be initiated by a seemingly unimportant issue or conflict.

Another way we approach this issue is to explain that some people associate the word *anger* with a particular level of anger or anxiety. For example, given a range of anger on a scale from 1 to 10 (1 being low and 10 being high), men will refer only to levels five through eight as "being angry." Other words are used to describe lower or higher levels. An exercise we do in the group which brings out this issue is to put three columns on a blackboard. The first column is headed with the numbers 1, 2 and 3; the second, with 4, 5, and 6; and the third, with 7, 8, 9, and 10. We explain to the group that each of these numbers represents an increasing level of anger, and we ask the men, "What words do you use to describe the anger in each of these columns?" This exercise (described in *Learning to Live Without Violence: A Handbook for Men*) helps the men discover their various levels of anger and helps the therapist learn the language each particular client uses to describe the various levels of anger. When using the words they use to describe low-level anger, such as irritation or annoyance, we learn that everyone experienced these low levels of anger almost every day.

12.   *"I guess I was psychologically violent this week."*

Men often do not grasp the difference between direct expression of anger and psychological violence. Perhaps for some men the direct expression of anger itself (in a nonintimidating manner) is perceived as violence. When discussing with the man what happened, you may discover that in fact the manner in which he expressed his anger was direct and clear, without infringing on the rights of others. It is important to clarify the difference between psychological violence and direct expression of anger. Likewise, it is important to discuss all episodes of anger between a man and his partner to pick up cues of psychological violence which are unreported or unnoticed by the man. The couples follow-up sessions and the telephone follow-up are helpful to determine the woman's perspective based on her fear of him during the arguments or conflicts.

Outside of obvious arguments or conflicts, men may give subtle cues which may be a form of intimidation as perceived by his partner. A thorough assessment with his partner can give counselors an idea of how nonverbal threats or intimidating messages are conveyed in the relationship.

13.   *"Why doesn't she make up her mind?"*

Frequently women who leave battering relationships do not altogether cut off contact with their partners. There is uncertainty as to the future of the relationship. For men in general this is perhaps one of the most difficult aspects of their situation. The uncertainty and the resultant anxiety can be overwhelming. Many men have great difficulty living with ambiguity. From their viewpoint, they are either together as a couple or not. The counselor is often just as uncertain as to the direction of the relationship; however, we believe that it is important for these men to come to grips with this uncertainty. Their tendency is to see things as black and white. Someone has won or lost; someone is right or wrong. The gray areas are not very tolerable. This rigidity is part of the reason why some men find themselves with no other option but to be violent. They are handicapped by the inability to look beyond their understanding of the possible alternatives in a particular situation. To have to choose only between right or wrong, win or lose, really narrows the possible viable alternatives in a conflict situation.

We work with men to help them learn to live with the uncertainty and the feelings of fear and insecurity which may result from such a situation. We help them to understand their partner's ambivalence as being a natural response to the situation and that by working on their own problems, they are paving the way for a better relationship, should they reconcile, or should they move on to other relationships. We help them see that there may be other areas in their lives where such uncertainty is not only normal, but accepted by them, and that they can derive strength from how they deal with those situations as well.

14. *"I didn't need a time-out."*

Frequently, men come to group with several incidents of conflict with their partners during the previous week in which they handled themselves appropriately, but were unable to utilize the time-out. However, if they are new to the group (under six months), our response is that they need to use those situations when they are still in control of themselves to practice using the time-out. It has been our experience that they will be less likely to utilize the time-out when they really need it if they cannot use it when they do not need it.

The practice time-out was developed for the purpose of giving the men practice in simply saying the words of the time-out ("I'm feeling angry and I'm going to take a time-out") and then walking away from their partner. They use the practice time-out when they want practice at going through the motions but are not feeling angry. The real time-out is used any time they feel angry, whether at a low, medium, or high level. During the first six months of group, the main priority is for the men to develop the skill of identifying their anger and using the time-out procedure as a means to deescalate the situation.

In some cases men will return to the group stating that their partner "will not allow me to take a time-out." This usually happens when men do not explain the time-out procedure before using it and/or they use the time-out as a way of punishing or getting even with their partners. An example of the latter is when the man leaves for his time-out and does not return until hours later, or uses the time-out as a chance to be with friends and/or go out drinking. Frequently men use the time-out to get away from their partners even though there is no anger at the time.

In explaining the time-out procedure to the men, we find that it is very important that it be used only in the way we prescribe in order to avoid possible negative repercussions from the use of the technique. For example, some men will just walk away without telling their partner anything. This leaves her uncertain as to whether or not he is taking a time-out. Some men stay away longer than the prescribed hour and/or do not check in upon returning. Some men use the time-out as a chance to be with friends, which could cause friction between a couple upon his return, whereas we prescribe it as a chance to be alone. We encourage the men to discuss with their partners at the end of the time-out what they got angry about in the first place. Many couples have a hard time with this aspect of the technique, so they will simply avoid it altogether.

Much of the time in the group is spent on helping the men learn to use the time-out and other techniques in the identification and communication of their anger. Although this process can be tedious in the short run, the long-term benefits of preventing violent behavior far outweigh the drawbacks.

15.   *"In my culture it is okay to hit a woman."*

All cultures give implicit (if not explicit) permission to hit a woman to one degree or another. Frequently, a statement such as this represents a man's minimizing and denial of his violence problem and his tendency to externalize responsibility rather than a desire to engage in a philosophical discussion about societal messages regarding violence toward women and children. Differences in the societal responses and messages do exist between cultures; however, several points remain the same:

1. In American society woman battering is against the law.
2. Psychological and physical injuries do result from violence.
3. Violence has a detrimental effect on relationships, marriages, and families.
4. Children will repeat patterns of violence as adults.
5. Violence has negative psychological consequences on the offender as well as the victim.

When clients bring this issue to attention, we also may discuss the fact that although the society tolerates other types of unhealthy behavior (e.g., cigarette smoking, use of alcohol and drugs), whether to engage in that behavior is a matter of personal choice.

Beyond the issue of violence, significant differences do exist between cultures, to which counselors need to be sensitive, such as:

1. The importance of the nuclear or extended family.
2. Hierarchy within families.
3. Attitudes toward discussing problems with people outside the family.

Additionally, employment issues, language barriers, and citizenship status must be considered in working with individuals from different cultures.

16. *Recognizing the feminine: "Who is this woman inside of me?"*

Much of what we focus on in our program is how men come to face their emotional side. That side is neither supported in men nor seen as a valuable tool for men to have to succeed in life. Men have a difficult time understanding these feelings, and most importantly, what to do with them. The group is a laboratory in which the men can experiment and explore their emotional side and how it can be functional in their day-to-day existence.

Communicating emotions is a high priority in the group. The communication is encouraged and facilitated between group members, between group leaders, and between members of the group and a group leader.

The opportunity to explore feelings is presented in every meeting. When members leave the group, reoffend, break the rules, or come into the group, each group member and leader will have his/her own unique response to the situation. This response is encouraged. Men can and do discover that the bond between men can be emotional as well as based on a project or other activity.

Over time, as group members begin to appreciate their own emotional side, they can appreciate their partner's expression of feelings. In this way, men are able to respond to more of what their partner is communicating rather than to react simply to the intensity of the feelings being communicated. As they begin to accept their own feelings, it becomes easier for them to accept their partners' feelings.

17. *Appreciating the masculine: "I need to be a man."*

Accepting the feminine does not necessarily mean rejecting the masculine. It means increasing options for responding to a situation. The most evident masculine characteristic which comes out in a group (and it could be said that sitting in a group discussing feelings is far from the male stereotype) is the team spirit that develops when men have been together for a while. It is as though each man is cheering on his teammate to succeed. What makes the group different from normal male team activities is that the process is as important as the outcome or product.

Another aspect of the group which seems to be typically male is the incredible amount of advice which is given to members by members. As facilitators, we encourage members to incorporate their feelings and observations into their more typically advice-oriented feedback. Frequently, there develops a competitive aspect to telling success stories and giving the most enlightened feedback to one of the group members. Facilitators need to give equal time to success and failures alike to avoid the men's competing in failure to get group attention.

One man came to group one night, after a lengthy discussion the previous week on the masculine and feminine sides of ourselves, happily stating that he finally understood this week what we were talking about. He related the following story.

> As you all know my company, which is based in San Francisco, has a small office in Santa Cruz. Well, to avoid any rush hour traffic coming back to San Francisco from Santa Cruz, I always drive up the Coast Highway. Well, at the end of the day, I always look forward to getting

home, relaxing and eating dinner. But this week my wife and kids were visiting her parents, and so I wasn't in a hurry. I took it very slowly. In fact, I realized what a beautiful ride it was up the coast. I saw things this time I never noticed before. I'm usually in such a hurry that all I can think about is getting home. Well, this experience made me think about what we were talking about last week in that men are product oriented and women are more process oriented. This week I really saw what I was missing by being so focused on the finish. It was as if I had never driven that way before. It made me think of how much I might have missed in the past.

Predicting Success

When discussing the treatment of male batterers, it becomes easy to focus on the problem areas from a negative perspective. For example, how can one predict risk for future violence? What should be the consequences for a reoffense while in treatment? However, prediction of success can be just as valuable an assessment as prediction of future violence. In this section we pose the question: How can one predict success in treatment? This question is addressed by examining various aspects of treatment in conjunction with characteristics of male batterers.

1. *Length of time in counseling.* It can be argued that the longer an individual is in counseling, the more likely he is to be affected by that process. The implicit assumption of this factor is that the client is actively participating in the process and utilizing the suggestions given by the counselor. Although many of the programs for male batterers last three to six months (Roberts, 1982), our experience tells us that most men need to be involved in some form of counseling for a minimum of one year, and in many of the cases, more than a year. The changes the men need to make are much more substantive than simply learning new anger-management skills.

2. *Probation/diversion mandated treatment.* Through mandated treatment the counselor is given the time necessary for the men not only to develop anger-management skills, but also to make the necessary long-term psychological changes to assure nonviolence in the future. It is our routine recommendation that men participate in some form of counseling during the entire period of their probation or diversion. This time can be anywhere from one to five years, depending on the seriousness of the offense.

There are two implicit assumptions made here. First, that the counselor is actively engaging the client in the counseling process, and, second, that the probation officer will institute court sanctions on those who do not cooperate with the conditions of counseling and/or supervision (whether probation or diversion).

3. *Time with partner.* Success is easier to predict when the man has had time with his partner and has demonstrated that he can control his anger and not be violent. We do not tell the women that they are needed to assure his change; however, for men and women who are still together or at least having some form of contact, how the man deals with his anger with her can be a barometer for change and ultimately for success.

4. *Use of time-outs, practice time-outs, and other anger-management material.* Obviously the more a client comes to counseling and discusses his success with utilizing the anger-management techniques, the more likely it is that he will continue to use such techniques subsequent to counseling. The men who use the techniques the least are more likely to reoffend during the course of counseling.

5. *Generalizing of issues from counseling to outside life.* When a man transfers insights or ideas originally discussed in group to outside situations, this is indicative that by his generalization he is now able to apply skills learned in counseling to day-to-day situations. This generalizing indicates that he does not see the group session as separate from the rest of his life. What he talks about in counseling is thought about during the intervening week.

6. *Wanting to change.* The degree to which a man takes responsibility for his violent behavior is probably one of the best predictors of success. The man who comes into counseling wanting to be nonviolent will frequently work the hardest to change that pattern in his life. Some men will come to counseling and say that they want to change, but they do not really hold that conviction. Those people are likely to be physically present, but they do not utilize the anger-management material and the other treatment techniques.

7. *Not being involved in criminal activities.* People who want to stop battering but do not want to give up other antisocial behaviors, especially the use and sale of drugs, property crimes, and so on, are less likely to give up their violence. Even if they do give up the violence, they do so only while they are in counseling. When conducting your assessment, success can be predicted by how willing an individual is to

change other areas in his life in order to assure that the violence will stop.

8. *Alcohol and drug free.* Those people who continue to use low to moderate amounts of alcohol and/or drugs will continue to be at risk for future violence. The clients who have seriously limited their use of alcohol and other drugs have been the ones who are more likely to succeed in counseling. This is not necessarily an iron-clad rule, particularly when dealing with a former alcoholic or addict who may still be on a dry drunk or high. Former substance abusers may employ psychological coping patterns similar to those used when still using/abusing. These may include depression, avoidance, and possibly violence.

9. *Length of battering history.* Those men who have had the least history of violence and who have stayed in counseling have the best success rate. The one notable exception to this rule is the man who has only battered once. These men frequently will drop out of counseling earlier because they believe that they do not have any "problem" and that it will not happen again.

10. *Frequency and severity of violence.* As with the preceding factor, those men with the least frequent and least severe violence are more likely to succeed in counseling. Occasionally men who perpetrate the least severe violence may not view their behavior as violent, as compared to the more serious offenders. Those men with the most serious history of violence may want to change their patterns but have difficulty in doing so.

Success will vary from client to client. For some men it may mean the cessation of violent behavior. For others it may also include the attainment of other personal goals. Some of these goals may be a change in attitudes toward women, more effective communication skills, and/or a deeper understanding of themselves in relation to the world. In any case, an important aspect of any program for batterers is the realistic assessment of the degree to which you can help a particular client.

We routinely apprise each client of the factors which will contribute to the outcome of his treatment. This gives the client a firm and realistic assessment of treatment expectations. We also inform our referral sources of this assessment. Most importantly, we discuss these issues with the victim of the violence, with a clear statement that although these factors can affect success, we cannot ultimately guarantee success with her partner. We reiterate that she cannot stop his violent behavior; only he can do so. For this reason the woman understands that as long as she continues to have contact with the batterer, she puts herself in jeopardy of further victimization. This discussion will also include a statement of her options for dealing with the situation, for example, separation, divorce, criminal justice intervention, use of shelters, or temporary restraining orders.

The special issues discussed in this chapter were viewed from the perspective of facilitating therapeutic change. However, a second category of special issues relates specifically to violent behavior and a counselor's duty to respond to both the potential victim(s) and/or the offender. The following chapter will discuss the legal, professional, and ethical issues confronting the counselor who works with men who batter.

6
Legal, Professional, and Personal Ethics in Counseling Men Who Batter

As with any specific clinical population, domestic violence clients present their own legal and ethical issues which must be addressed in order to effectively provide counseling services. Distinctions among legal, professional, and personal ethical issues are necessary so that a service provider can be clear when certain actions are mandated by law, are highly advised by their professional standards and/or the courts, or are matters of personal choice in acting in a professional and ethical manner.

Laws vary from state to state; therefore, parts of this chapter may or may not be relevant, legally speaking, to your location. However, all of this chapter is relevant ethically to your work. I would like to begin by defining the difference between legal, professional ethical, and personal ethical issues.

Legal issues refer to aspects of our work by which we are bound, by the laws of our individual states, to perform in a certain manner. For example, child abuse laws require certain professionals to report such cases. If one is negligent in reporting, the individual is breaking the law and as a result can be found guilty of a crime.

Professional ethics refer to rules or standards of conduct by which a person is bound to act in a particular way. A law has not been enacted, but a ruling has been made by a court or professional licensing board saying that a professional must act in a particular way when confronted by a certain type of situation or suffer the consequence of a lawsuit and/or loss of professional licensure.

Personal ethics are neither law nor court rulings, but are instead a personal choice to act in a certain way because of personal beliefs. The possibility of a lawsuit is always present, but no precedents have been set so far for this particular choice. The usual result of this type of choice is either loss of a client, because of a difference in philosophy, or impeding progress in treatment. No current laws or professional ethics are transgressed.

Because of the high risk of injury and/or death in domestic violence cases, and the fact that it is also criminal behavior, working with this client population has unique legal and ethical issues which must be addressed by the counselor. Although laws differ from state to state, and within a state from professional license to professional license, all persons working with batterers must address these issues, if not for their own legal or professional safety, for the safety of the women and children in these families who are at risk.

The primary issues that we will be discussing in this chapter will be those of confidentiality and privilege. Confidentiality refers to a client's right to have information which he has communicated in confidence not revealed to a third party. Privilege refers to a service provider's right to resist having to reveal confidential client disclosures in a court of law. The client is the holder of the privilege, and it prevents others from discussing this information without his permission. The related concepts of privilege and confidentiality grew out of every person's right of privacy.

When a batterer comes to you for counseling, everything he says is confidential, and he is the holder of the privilege. You may not discuss his communications without his permission. However, given the dangerousness of violent behavior, service providers are faced with the dilemma of having to break a confidential relationship under various circumstances. A discussion of several of these instances will follow.

Legal Issues

Child Abuse

In the State of California, as in most other states, laws require any child-care custodian, medical practitioner, nonmedical practitioner, or an employee of a child protective agency who has knowledge of or who, in his or her professional capacity or within the scope of his or her employment, observes a child whom he or she reasonably suspects has been the victim of child abuse, to report such suspected instance of child abuse to a child protective agency immediately or as soon as practically possible by telephone and to prepare and send a written report within 36 hours of receiving such information concerning the incident.

The law states that the person needs only a reasonable suspicion, and it is the child protective service which makes the final determination as to whether or not abuse is occurring. The child abuse law includes cases of neglect as well as physical and sexual abuse. The consequences for failing to report in California are that the individual may be found guilty of a misdemeanor, which is punishable by a jail term of no longer than six months and/or a fine not to exceed $500.

As stated in the child abuse statute, California Penal Code §1172(b), this law is not intended to deny parents the right to raise and control their children by imposing reasonable discipline but is to ensure the protection and safety of the child. Unfortunately, no clear guidelines have been developed to delineate the point at which reasonable discipline ends and abuse begins. This is a gray area, and in the final analysis it may come down to a personal choice for the clinician.

Frequency of child abuse, like spousal abuse, is difficult to pinpoint in exact numbers. Davidl Gil (1970) estimates that between six and ten thousand cases are officially reported each year. Estimates based on surveys indicate over three million cases occur each year. Again, these findings vary depending on the definitions of abuse. In Walker's study of battered women's syndrome (1984), it was found that 53 percent of the women reported that the batterer was abusing their children. Straus et al. (1980) found that 28 percent of the sample families agreed that some violence is acceptable. J. J. Gayford's survey (1975a) of 100 battered women found that 37 percent of the women admitted taking out their frustrations on the children, and 54 percent claimed that their husbands committed acts of violence against the children. Although there is much controversy as to what constitutes (unlawful) abuse versus (lawful) corporal punishment, the fact remains they are both acts of violence. This distinction will be discussed in the final chapter of this book.

Child Sexual Abuse

As mentioned above, child sexual abuse legally speaking falls under the heading of child abuse. As with child physical abuse, there are varying degrees of sexual abuse. Difficulties arise in assessment and ultimately in bringing legal action against the offender in the least blatant degrees of child sexual abuse. Although no statistical correlations have been found between men who abuse their spouses and sexually abuse their children, overlap is most probable. Many programs treating men for child sexual abuse behavior have reported spousal abuse as well (C.S.A.T.P., personal communication). Again, as with child physical abuse, if a counselor "suspects" child sexual abuse, he or she must report in the fashion mentioned above. A failure to report can lead to criminal charges being lodged against the counselor.

Physicians' Report of Victims or Offenders of Violent Crime

By law in California physicians must report any victims or offenders whom they treat whose injuries have resulted from being a victim of a criminal act or were acquired while in the commission of a criminal act (California Penal Code Section 11160, *Deerings* 1983). Specifically, Sections 11160 and 11161 state:

> §11160. [*Reporting injuries inflicted by violence.*] Every person, firm or corporation conducting any hospital or pharmacy in the state, or the managing agent thereof, or the person managing or in charge of such hospital or pharmacy, or in charge of any ward or part of such hospital to which any person suffering from any wound or other injury inflicted by his own act or by the act of another by means of a knife, gun, pistol or other deadly weapon, or in cases where injuries have been inflicted upon any person in violation of any penal law of this state shall come or be brought, shall report the same immediately, both by telephone and in writing, to the chief of police, city marshal, town marshal or other head of the police department of any city, city and county, town or municipal corporation of this State, or to the sheriff, if such hospital or pharmacy is located outside the incorporated limits of a city, town or other municipal corporation. The report shall state the name of the injured person, if known, his whereabouts and the character and extent of his injuries. . . .
>
> §11161. [*Same: Report by physician or surgeon.*] Every physician or surgeon who has under his charge or care any person suffering from any wound or injury inflicted in the manner specified in Section 11160

shall make a report of the kind specified in this article to the appropriate officers named in Section 11160.

Although this law is infrequently enforced in woman battering cases, it is a law which could leave a physician vulnerable to criminal charges, lawsuit, and/or loss of licensure.

Professional Ethical Issues

These legal responsibilities have thus far created a professional dilemma for the clinician. Should a person know that a report will be made if he discusses certain aspects of his problems, it may discourage the person from seeking help. In addition, many counselors feel concern about being cast in the role of police officer or judge.

The concept of a person's duty to respond or inform is not a new one in the legal profession. Cases have been documented throughout legal history where private citizens and professionals have been accused of irresponsibility by persons who have suffered personal injury or other harm in some manner and have felt that the other party should have intervened on their behalf. Courts have for the most part ruled that people do not have a duty to warn or intervene, particularly in cases involving family violence (McNeill, 1984). These decisions reflect the attitudes of society: what happens in the privacy of one's home is one's own business. The attitudes of the healing professions, such as physicians and mental health professionals, and the clergy have likewise reflected this societal attitude in that confidentiality is the cornerstone of these professions. In the past 10 years, this attitude or belief has been changing, and the change is beginning to be reflected in the courts.

The laws described above also are indicative of these changes. The following court rulings in California are further evidence of this change in philosophy, in that we are our brothers' and sisters' keepers.

Tarasoff v. The Regents of the University of California, 17 Cal.3d 425 (1976).

In *Tarasoff*, the court stated that a psychotherapist has a special relationship to a person whose conduct may need to be controlled. The therapist has a duty to determine, within his area of expertise, whether or not a patient poses a serious danger to others, and if so, to exercise "reasonable care" to protect the potential victim. The *Tarasoff* decision was based on a situation in which a specific threat to kill had been made. The therapist warned the police but did not warn the intended victim. A violation of this duty, which constitutes a proximate cause of injury to such victim, creates a liability in tort against the psychotherapist (Jefferson, 1982, p. 1402).

The standard in California which psychotherapists use for "poses a serious danger of violence to others" is a direct or indirect threat of violence made in the presence of the therapist. *Jablonski v. Loma Linda Veterans Administration*, although a separate case, clarifies, expands, and reinforces *Tarasoff*.

Jablonski v. Loma Linda Veterans Administration, 712 F.2d 391 (9th Cir. 1983).

This June 1983 decision takes *Tarasoff* one step further. In this case a man was being seen by a psychiatrist at a V.A. Hospital. The patient made no specific threat; however, it was known that this patient had a history of physical and sexual violence toward a former wife and a current woman friend. Although the woman attempted to solicit help from the man's psychiatrist, no specific warning was issued. The patient ultimately murdered her. The psychiatrist was held liable. The court stated that "Jablonski's [the patient] previous history indicated that he would likely direct his violence against Kimball [his woman friend]. He had raped and committed other acts of violence against his previous wife. His psychological problem indicated that his violence was likely to be directed against women very close to him." The court held that the psychiatrist had to "exercise reasonable care to protect the foreseeable victim of danger."

Hedlund v. Superior Court of Orange County, 34 Cal.3d 695 (1983).

The rationale of this case was further expanded by *Hedlund v. Superior Court of Orange County*. In this case, two psychotherapists were seeing a couple in treatment. At one point during the course of treatment the man reported having told his partner of his intent to cause her great bodily injury. Thereafter, the man used a shotgun to inflict such injury.

The act occurred while the woman was in her car with her child. In an attempt to protect her child, she covered him with her body. Although the child did not suffer physical injury, he did suffer extreme psychological trauma.

The court ruled, as it had in *Tarasoff*, that the therapists, being informed as to the threat, had a duty to exercise "reasonable care" to warn the foreseeable victim. In addition, it ruled that the therapists also had a duty to inform the foreseeable victim of the risk of harm to bystanders, in particular to those in a close relationship to the intended victim.

This decision does not mean that therapists have to warn every one, known or unknown, but it does mean that under the facts of this case it was reasonable to believe that if the woman was to be victimized, it was highly likely that her child would be nearby. Therefore, the therapists' duty extends to that child. Although not clearly spelled out by the court, a warning to the mother of danger to her and to her child, clearly documented, would have sufficiently carried out their duty to warn.

The primary controversy about these three decisions concerns the dilemma for a psychotherapist, who risks being sued for violation of confidentiality if his or her assessment was inaccurate and the client decides to file suit. Another dilemma which counselors experience is how one can expect a client to be honest with the therapist if a report must be made to the police or if confidentiality is otherwise violated. A further concern expressed by counselors is that they are being placed in the position of acting as an arm of the law.

Interestingly enough, these three cases all involved domestic violence. In all three the offender previously had been or currently was in an intimate relationship with the victim at the time of the incident or shortly before. In *Jablonski*, the offender also had a history of physical and sexual violence toward his previous wife and in *Jablonski* and *Hedlund* toward their current women friends. In *Tarasoff* a specific threat had been made in the therapist's presence.

Our knowledge of domestic violence suggests that the likelihood of continued violent behavior is high unless some form of treatment is sought (Walker, 1979). Therefore, in order to comply with *Tarasoff*, *Jablonski*, and *Hedlund*, in California at least, we must make an unequivocal statement at the outset of treatment to both the offender and the victim that continued violence may end in serious injury or death. In addition, at times when risk of violence appears to be significantly increased or imminent, we must formally warn the potential victim(s), our clients, and the authorities. In this way we are protecting ourselves from contributing to the possibility of the injury or death of another, as well as informing our clients as to the realistic danger he and she are in by his continuing to use violence and her continuing to choose to stay in the relationship.

In California a psychotherapist must keep all statements made by a client in the presence of the therapist confidential and is required to claim the privilege of confidentiality if asked by third parties. This privilege is inapplicable in several circumstances:

1. If in the psychotherapist's assessment that person is a danger either to himself or to others. Examples would be a client who is suicidal, threatening violence toward others, or abusing or neglecting children.
2. If assertion of the privilege aids or enables the commission of a crime. Examples would be the sale or purchase of illegal drugs, violence toward another, violation of temporary restraining orders.
3. If assertion of the privilege aids or enables an individual to escape detection or apprehension for criminal behavior. An example would be a batterer who has a warrant out for his arrest or is being pursued for questioning or arrest, or has violated a temporary restraining order.
4. If the evaluations are done for the court or the probation department. Examples are a report to the court for termination or revocation of diversion or probation; evaluation for the court as to the appropriateness for treatment.

Essentially, the exceptions to the psychotherapist–patient privilege protect the counselor from lawsuits or other actions if any of the circumstances mentioned above arise in a counseling relationship. In fact, a failure to act in these situations could result in legal culpability under *Tarasoff*, *Jablonski*, and/or *Hedlund*.

As mentioned earlier, these decisions allow the therapist to see his or her responsibilities more clearly and determine what actions are within the limits of the law. Although much latitude is given by these rulings, many counselors choose not to utilize them.

Below are a number of situations which we have encountered in counseling. How would you proceed?

Example 1. A client on probation comes to counseling and tells you that he went by his girlfriend's house today and knocked on the door. You are aware of a court order that he is to stay away from his girlfriend.

Example 2. A client comes to group agitated over the fact that he was just served with divorce papers, and his wife is seeking custody of the children. He is very angry at her and refuses to deal with his feelings in the counseling session. He leaves more angry than when he arrived because of the confrontation he got in counseling.

Example 3. A client comes in and tells you that he and his brother stole some auto parts from their neighbor because the neighbor sold him some defective parts in the past.

Example 4. Your client boasts in group about how much money he makes dealing cocaine.

Example 5. Your client admits that he smokes marijuana and that he keeps himself supplied with it regularly.

Example 6. Your client describes a situation in which he was out drinking with his wife, he was very intoxicated, and he drove off by himself after an argument with her, almost hitting her with the car.

Example 7. Your client's driver's license has been suspended for driving under the influence of drugs. He tells you that he drove his car to counseling that night.

Example 8. Your client tells you that last week while with his girlfriend he threatened to cut her throat.

Example 9. You are referred a client for an assessment by the probation department. He is on probation for wife battery. You suspect child abuse.

Example 10. Your client tells you that he is going over to his wife's house after your session. You know that there is a restraining order in effect.

Example 11. Your client tells you that his wife left him. He is depressed and says he has considered suicide. He refuses to agree not to take his life during the next week or to call you should he decide to do so.

Example 12. A self-referred client is assessed by you. You determine that lethality is quite high. You feel great concern when he leaves your office, even though you have another appointment with him in a week.

These examples are very common. There are laws and court rulings which can guide your actions in each of these situations; however, some of these actions are more discretionary than others, thereby forcing you to make personal decisions.

Aside from the legal and ethical factors related to these exceptions to the psychotherapist–patient privilege, there are clinical issues at stake here as well. To confront a client as to your concern about his violent behavior may be clinically indicated. It may be in his best interest to be aware that you have notified his partner about your concern for violence. This intervention may preclude or intervene in an escalating situation between them. When conflict increases and the concern for safety concurrently increases, decreasing isolation and opening lines of communication can decrease the stress, and ultimately lessen the risk. We will routinely ask to meet with the man and his partner to discuss our concerns. Probation officers, and other therapists involved with the family, are also informed about our concerns. Increased stress, conflict, and/or violence indicators are interpreted as a plea for help. Our response is one of concern and assistance, not the intention to intrude into the private lives of our client and his family, nor to impose limits on his freedom.

In the following section it will become evident to the reader how we make provisions for these types of interventions from the onset of treatment.

Personal Ethical Issues

Reporting of Reoffenses

There are no laws or rulings which mandate or encourage counselors to report reoffenses of men referred by the criminal justice system, although courts can and do sometimes make it a condition of probation that such reports be made. In the absence of a specific court order, policy on this issue varies from probation department to probation department. Some probation officers want the therapist to report reoffenses and make that a condition of the referral of clients. Other probation officers expect to hear it from the defendant or the victim. Still others simply check the computer for subsequent arrests. If there are none, then they assume that there has been no further violence. This decision, in the past, has been a personal choice requiring policy that must be made by the individual therapist. Because there is such variance in policy among probation departments, and within departments among probation officers, we have developed a policy which requires our reporting and the client's reporting of further acts of violence. Should you have any doubts as to whether or not you are violating confidentiality, the previous sections specifically state that the psychotherapist–patient privilege cannot be claimed when the client has committed a crime or is trying to escape detection. In addition, a reoffense may be indicative that the client is a danger to others, specifically his partner.

Other concerns that counselors have expressed are that reporting puts them in the position of being an arm of law enforcement. In part this is true. Another way of viewing the reporting issue is that you simply have your client's and his partner's best interests at heart. A reoffense may very well be a signal that the person needs more stringent limits. The initial reaction of many therapists to our reporting of reoffenses is, How do you expect your clients to be honest if you are just going to turn them in? The response is that our clients are honest for just that reason. They know we will set limits and be consistent in enforcing them. We believe that paradoxically this may help develop a more trusting relationship between client and counselor.

Reporting of Poor Participation

As with reporting of reoffenses, policies vary between probation departments and between probation officers. Some probation officers call the counselors periodically for reports of attendance and participation, others wait until they hear from the counselor. Others are interested only in additional acts of violence, so even if the clients never attend counseling but stop the violence, or there are no reports of violence, the probation officers will rate them as having successfully completed probation or diversion. As with reporting of reoffenses, policies vary from therapist to therapist on the issue of reporting poor or nonparticipation. Each counselor needs to determine how many sessions a client has to miss before he receives a poor participation or attendance rating. Our policy is that each client needs to make a 12-week commitment every 12 weeks. During each 12-week period, he is allowed to miss two sessions for emergencies. If more than two sessions are missed, the client is terminated from the program and referred back to his probation officer, if he is on probation or diversion.

As with the reporting of violence, clients usually want and need limits. They understand from the outset of treatment what is expected of them. Clear and consistent expectations as to participation in treatment are necessary to help these men take seriously their problems with violence and the consequent urgent need to address those problems.

Reporting of Likelihood of Further Violence

As we discussed, with *Tarasoff, Jablonski*, and *Hedlund*, counselors are very reluctant to predict future behavior. In addition, probation officers and the courts rarely require or request this information. This action is a personal choice. For several reasons, we typically make this choice when dealing with cases of high lethality and when reoffenses occur while the man is in treatment. First, this is an attempt to educate the probation officer and the victim as to the reality of the situation. There is no guarantee that the offender will stop his violence just because he is in treatment. Second, this serves as an attempt to create concern on everyone's part: the victim, the offender, and the probation officer. Third, this is a means of lessening our liability in case of serious injury or death. Included in the Appendix are two forms we use for progress and termination reports. These reports include our assessment as to risk of further violence. This rating is based on the factors described in the previous chapter and the relationship of any or all of those factors to a client's particular situation with his partner. Examples of how these issues are addressed follow.

Coordination with Other Therapists

Although this would seem to be a commonsense approach when dealing with any kind of client, we have been surprised by how many counselors seeing our clients have not considered this policy. As with any client who has been acting out problems, the most important therapeutic intervention is having clear, consistent limits. When multiple therapists give different messages to a particular client, they essentially undermine each other's efforts and invite further acting-out behaviors. Our policy always is to have contact with other counselors involved with the family to assure consistency and mutual support.

Follow-up with Victim

In our opinion the most critical aspect of our work is that on a bimonthly basis we have telephone contact with the victim to determine whether there have been any reoffenses and whether the client is utilizing the material we are prescribing in the program. This follow-up is a condition of treatment, and it is explained as such from the initial session. It is the knowledge that we are going to have this contact with their partners which in part assures honesty in self-reporting of reoffenses. Although admission of a reoffense may be seen as an admission of failure by the client, it becomes an incentive to be honest with themselves and others, when the alternative is to be confronted by the group leader and subsequently to be viewed by the group as lying or withholding information.

Our policy has been viewed by some of our colleagues as contraindicated. One reason for this attitude is that it potentially puts us "in the middle" of communications between the man and his partner. It has also been criticized because it clouds therapeutic allegiance, which can result in mistrust between the client and the counselor.

In response to these criticisms, we believe that if one is clear and consistent as to the purpose of the contact with the partner, the information sought, how that information will be used, and that if our relationship with each person is clear to both, we find little difficulty with issues of indirect communications between the couple and trust issues with the man.

In addition to the telephone follow-up, we meet with the man and his partner once every six to eight weeks to help them address any issues between them which they have difficulty addressing on their own. For ongoing couples counseling, we refer to our colleagues. This policy also may be criticized in that it can lead to some confusion as to therapeutic allegiance. Some people criticize this practice because conjoint sessions may be seen by the woman as ones in which she is outnumbered by the men or in which she may be held responsible for the violence. Our experience is that if the woman's discomfort is evident, we can respond flexibly by including her counselor if she has one, or by only one of us meeting with her and her partner. Often, however, letting her talk about the violence will ease her discomfort. With regard to responsibility for the violence, we consistently give every woman the clear message that she is not responsible for it, and that there is nothing that she says or does which justifies his battering her.

Although there are potential problems with these practices, the helpful information which these contacts yield far outweigh any drawbacks.

Encouragement of Use of Criminal Justice System

Whenever there is a reoffense by any member of our program, we encourage the victim to either contact the probation officer, if the offender is on diversion or probation, or to call the police and pursue the case through the criminal justice system, if her batterer is self-referred. This action is an outgrowth of several of the issues discussed in the professional ethics section of this chapter. When a reoffense has occurred, there is no privilege, so that concealment of such an offense could put the clinician in jeopardy. However, unlike the laws with regard to child abuse, in California there is no procedure whereby a counselor who knows of a criminal offense such as assault can initiate an investigation. Unless the victim reports the offense, nothing will be done legally, which is why we encourage her to pursue the case through the criminal justice system.

We have been criticized by some counselors for "turning our backs on our clients" or for "getting them into more trouble." Our clients see it as a reasonable response, given the dangerousness of the situation. We see it as perhaps the additional limits a client needs to control his anger and utilize the anger-management material.

Treatment of Choice

As therapists, we often get locked into one particular counseling philosophy or modality. As we are referred clients, we attempt to fit them into our mold. It is important, no matter what our personal approach and modality are, to try to assess accurately our client's needs.

You are about to start a group for batterers. You want to start with four members; you have three. You get a referral of a man who probably could benefit more from individual work. He can only afford one or the other, not both. Could you avoid the temptation to choose the group? Would you recognize his needs or yours as affecting your decision?

A client is referred to you. You would like to see him individually. He has no friends or support systems outside of his relationship with the victim. He could afford individual work, but it would be a struggle. You are trying to build your private practice, and you are anxious to work with a domestic violence client. Could you recognize his need for a group?

These are difficult choices for counselors. We always like to think that we can help everyone who walks in the door. But can we? Are there others who can do more? Is there some way we can develop a treatment plan with a client which may include several modalities of counseling over a period of time?

Client Treatability versus
Client–Therapist Relationship

When treating domestic violence clients, we frequently find that some clients will continue to reoffend and others will continually miss sessions. One conclusion you may draw from either of these situations is that a client lacks the appropriate motivation to attend counseling or to acquire and utilize the skills necessary to manage his anger appropriately. As discussed in a previous chapter, a common characteristic of male batterers is that they externalize their behavior so that they are likely to feel less responsible for it and consequently less motivated for change.

However, I do not want to underemphasize the importance of the counselor–client relationship as a critical factor in facilitating change. Therefore, it is important to examine or consider the lack of a meaningful relationship with a particular client as a possible factor in the reoffenses and/or attendance problems. This is not to say that the client is not responsible for his behavior. There should be some consequences for his acting out. In some cases, however, it may be appropriate to make another referral to a different therapist with the same or different modality and/or style. We have seen a number of cases in which a referral to another therapist proved to be the key to success with that particular client.

This issue needs to be addressed with individual cases of problem attendance, participation, and reoffense, with an openness on the part of the therapist to distinguish between untreatability and client–therapist relationship problems.

Treatment Goals and Philosophy

This may seem like a treatment issue rather than one of personal ethics, but we feel it should be included in this category because it is usually a personal choice based on one's own beliefs about how and why people behave as they do and what should be the goal of counseling. We believe that because domestic violence cases are generally of high lethality (Browne, 1983; Walker, 1979), it should be the priority of counselors working in the area to focus on lowering this risk before attending to other individual, couple, and/or family issues. It has been our experience that unless this risk is attended to, other therapeutic goals are, at the very least, difficult to achieve and, at the worst, impossible. Just as with a suicidal client the risk for suicide is dealt with immediately before tackling other issues, the goal with domestic violence clients should be to lessen the risk of homicide or serious injury before addressing the in-depth issues of individual, couple, and/or family dynamics.

　　Some of our colleagues see this as a contradiction. How can you minimize the risk of lethality without dealing with these in-depth issues? While working on the underlying issues, we have found a series of behavioral interventions to be very successful in lessening this risk. Many of the people working with domestic violence clients have been trained in traditional psychodynamic and/or systems theory. It has taken a great deal of flexibility to develop and utilize interventions inconsistent with our training in order to achieve this goal, so that we might ultimately use our training to produce long-term change in our clients.

Responsibility for Violence

One final ethical issue I would like to address is that of responsibility. Coming to grips with this issue personally is a necessary prerequisite for working with domestic violence clients. It is our belief that violence is not a function of an interaction with a particular person, nor is it caused by women who want to be abused. There is nothing special about the victim or the nature of the relationship with this particular victim which creates a violent interaction. Instead, the violence is a function of the offender's lack of alternative resources for dealing with anger, stress, and conflict, and it is not something which the relationship or the victim brings out in him. This idea is corroborated by other clinicians working in the field (Ganley, 1982; Walker, 1981). If a clinician adheres to this value, then a particular treatment approach will necessarily follow. If, however, a clinician believes that the violence is a function of the relationship and that both are responsible, then another approach to treatment will necessarily follow.

It is very important for a counselor to come to terms with this issue prior to or soon after beginning to work with domestic violence clientele. It is our belief that both persons may be responsible for conflict, stress, and problems in a relationship, but how each person deals with each of those pressures is an individual responsibility. It would be misleading to try to convince a client that a change in his partner's behavior will necessarily change his behavior, specifically the violent behavior.

This approach has been criticized by some counselors as a blaming one. It is not meant to be blaming, but empowering. We want men who batter to begin to feel in control of their lives and their behavior. If the woman is seen as somehow partly responsible for the violence, then he could never be totally in control of himself. The issue here is not blame; it is responsibility for one's own actions, and ultimately, responsibility for acting in a way which can build trust, intimacy, and a sense of personal power that is not achieved at the expense of someone else's powerlessness.

As can be seen, the issues facing counselors working with men who batter are many and complex. When making legal and ethical choices, we suggest that you not do so in a vacuum. Consult with colleagues as much as possible. Develop an attitude that no choice is a failure, that there is something to learn from each choice you make. Many times there are no perfect or clearly right choices. You can only do what *feels* right.

The following case examples illustrate how we have dealt with the above issues.

Case 1

Upon intake a woman describes violence in her marriage of three years. She also describes what appears to be abusive behavior by her husband toward their two-year-old child. Wife states husband is not interested in counseling.

Action
Report of child abuse to protective services and police.
Assessment of woman battering.
Husband/defendant pleads guilty.
We evaluate defendant for treatment and recommend:

  1. Child abuse treatment/education.
  2. Anger management for woman battering.

Current Status
No reoffenses.
Currently in treatment.

Relevant Issues
Child abuse reporting.
Warning to wife regarding her and child's safety.
Jablonski and *Hedlund* warnings.
Treatment of choice.

Case 2

Client referred by probation, having pled guilty to several misdemeanor charges of assault and battery. Client reoffends twice in one-week period after six weeks of counseling. Wife moves out into friend's house and secures a temporary restraining order. Client leaves group and gets drunk, goes over to wife's house and pounds on door, then leaves. Client comes to group the following week and reports his actions.

Action
Client required to notify probation within 24 hours.
We contact probation; warning issued.
We call wife to corroborate information; warning issued.
Reevaluation for alcohol treatment.
Client warned by probation; one more incident, return to court.

Current Status
No reoffenses.
Anger-management group and alcohol treatment.

Relevant Issues
Privilege exception: aid or enable the escape of detection or
    apprehension; danger to self or others.
Jablonski warning to victim.
Reporting reoffenses to probation.
Reporting likelihood of further violence.
Follow-up with victim.

Case 3

Client referred for treatment by couples therapist. Last incident of
violence occurred three nights previous. Client was arrested and released the following morning. Client wants to be in counseling on his
own without criminal justice system forcing him. After evaluation of
man, woman is seen for individual evaluation. She wants to drop
charges if he agrees to come to counseling. We discuss with her our
typical experience with domestic violence cases, in that if she does not
follow through with the complaint, he may eventually drop out of
counseling prematurely and then she will have no leverage. We offer to
send an evaluation to his attorney recommending treatment in lieu of
prosecution and/or incarceration.

Action
Release of Information procured from man and woman.
Evaluation sent to Public Defender.
Evaluation for alcohol abuse.

Current Status
Domestic Violence Diversion.
No reoffenses after five months of counseling.
Alcohol counseling not required.

Relevant Issues
Follow-up with victim.
Release of Information for written evaluation.
Coordination with other therapist.

Encouragement of use of criminal justice system.
Evaluation stating need for violence treatment.

Case 4

Couple wants to be seen together. Upon initial interview, domestic violence is assessed to be occurring regularly. Last incident occurred six months before; incident before that, six months prior. We explain that we are very concerned about the violence, and that couples counseling would be difficult if the man did not agree to attend concurrently an anger-management group or program. Both agree to that condition of treatment. We refer him to a domestic violence men's program and secure a Release of Information to contact that program. It is explained that one way of predicting violence in a relationship is to look at the frequency of its occurrence. We warn that violence seems to occur for them every six months or so, and we express our concern for future violence to both. We also warn that their two-year-old child could also be injured during a violent episode.

Action
Referral made to men's program.
Release of Information procured.
Woman informed about police protection and shelters.
Evaluation for alcohol for man and woman.
Woman informed of women's group in community.
Child abuse assessment.

Current Status
Couples counseling terminated after two months upon suggestion
    of both man and woman.
Woman in individual counseling.
Man in men's group.
One incident of physical violence after one month of couples
    counseling.
Woman also attends Alcoholics Anonymous.

Relevant Issues
Treatment of choice.
Release of Information to coordinate with other therapist.
Priority of treatment.

Warning for potential violence (*Jablonski* and *Hedlund*).
Encouragement of use of criminal justice system.

In each of the above cases, the therapist was confronted with any one or a combination of legal, professional, and/or ethical issues. In most instances a colleague was consulted to determine the implications of the various options when alternatives were a possibility.

Although many of the actions involved the notification of the police or other criminal justice personnel, which in some instances may have had serious consequences for the client, we feel that setting clearly defined limits can facilitate the change process. Some clients become very angry at such actions by the therapist and may drop out of treatment. However, such anger could be utilized creatively by the counselor to help men learn new ways of working through such strong emotions without withdrawing or becoming violent. No matter whether the client stays and works out his anger or leaves, the counselor must face the issue of responding to the potential for danger to others in a responsible manner.

7
What Counselors Should Know about the Battered Woman

Lenore E. Auerbach Walker

The voice on the other end of the telephone sounded soft and frightened. "I'm scared my husband is going to kill us all one of these days," Janet whispered, confirming my own perception of her fear. "But what can I do? Nothing seems to work for long. He might stop his slapping us around for awhile but then he just hollers and makes us all so nervous. I want him to stop his violence but I don't want to leave him." Her voice got stronger and more confident. "I love him. He is really a good man, you know!"

Janet is typical of the battered women who reach out to counselors and therapists all over our country. She recognizes that her husband has a problem with his violence and she is frightened of his potential to physically and psychologically harm her and their children. Sometimes that fear is openly expressed; more often it gets buried underneath a myriad of psychological responses. If she had her way, her most fervent wish would come true: her husband's violent behavior would disappear and the kind loving person she fell in love with would be there all of the time. Perhaps by the time Janet and other battered women like her finally call for help, in their hearts they know that the batterer has a serious problem which wishing will not make go away. And if her husband (or lover) gets into a treatment program, she usually believes that he can change in order to stop his abuse. Most battered women are willing to do anything to help his treatment process, even to their own detriment. Many want to believe that it will help them regain the kind, gentle, nurturing man they fell in love with. Others feel less guilty and safer leaving the relationship when they know the man has someone to help him through the emotional hurdles ahead. Some believe that his acceptance of his need for treatment validates their own mental health. Given their personal investment, battered women need a support system to look out for their own interests while the batterer is in his own treatment.

Historical Perspective

The attitudes toward battered women have been unkind to their image. Either they have been portrayed as meek, passive, helpless victims or provocative, scheming, manipulative masochists. It was said that battered women like to be abused, it met their psychological needs and thus, they set up or encouraged the man's violent behavior. Therapists may adopt this attitude because of their own frustration in helping the battered woman keep herself safe. Indeed, there are many battered women who may appear to "provoke" a man's anger by their behavior. Battered women specialists, however, are clear that even if her behavior is outrageous, it is his responsibility not to react to his angry feelings with abusive behavior. *There is no justification for violence, except in self-defense or defense of others.* Thus, nothing she does causes her to deserve to be hit.

Early psychiatric literature which discussed battering relationships supported the notion that the woman was mentally ill. Dependent personality, hysteria, and schizophrenia were the most popular diagnostic categories, and therapists believed that strengthening a woman's characer would prevent further beatings. Today's message to battered women is not always all that different: "Be strong," women are urged. "Don't rely or depend upon men who might harm you!"

The political message when violence is "clinicalized" or given a psychopathological explanation supports the belief that a man has the right to judge a woman's behavior if she "misbehaves." This originated from the days when husbands were legally responsible for their wives' behavior, a concept no longer recognized in our common law. But the patriarchal message that women belong to the men they marry continues to reinforce men's dominant behavior over women. The analysis of sexism as well as violence in society is of major importance in avoiding an individual mental illness model. Nevertheless, living in violence does create psychological effects on battered women and children which must be understood by those who counsel the men.

A feminist analysis assumes that battered women, like all women, should be entitled to social, political, and economic equality with men. Presently, there is inequality between women and men in our society. This inequality causes mental health problems in women and men, making it imperative that societal change be part of any therapeutic effort. All mental health problems, then, must be scrutinized to differentiate between those which come from within the person and those which come from living in a sexist society. Everything, including violence issues, gets such scrutiny.

Psychological Injuries to Battered Women

Perception of loss of control, which is inherent in battering relationships, is one of the critical factors causing psychological injury to the battered woman. Most of us understand that we never have total control over our lives, but we do not expect to lose involuntarily the ability to protect ourselves. This perception causes women to focus on the reality of men's greater physical strength and increases the level of fear. It forces women to come to an understanding of the limits of their own strength. The process by which such an understanding is reached is unsettling as it disturbs the psychological equilibrium and creates a feeling of non-well-being. The process of living with someone who could unpredictably cause her harm keeps the battered woman off balance. Her behavior is often designed to help her feel more balanced in an unsettling environment. She often perceives that she is in less danger if she is close to the batterer and hides her true feelings. This perception is supported by reality. The most dangerous time in a battering relationship is at a point of separation; more serious injuries and deaths occur at that time.

Feeling betrayed and recognizing the violation of love and trust needed to keep an intimate relationship growing are other major causes of psychological injury to battered women. We are socialized to believe that someone who loves you cannot hurt you. Love and violence are seen as unable to coexist. Yet in battering relationships, they do.

The constant worry that the loving period will be replaced by the painful abuse causes the battered woman to be constantly vigilant, trying to avoid another incident. Yet feelings of betrayal occur, especially from the humiliation and psychological harassment. Even when he stops the physical abuse, most battered women continue to hold the man responsible for violating their marriage commitment. Although many try to forgive him if he gets into counseling and starts to change, it is the inability to trust her own perception that he won't cause her harm which will not let her forget the past. This sense of betrayal and violation of trust usually stands in the way of successful reconciliation or ability to co-parent children.

Mythology about the sex-role standards expected for women is another cause of psychological injury to battered women. The expectation that a woman will marry a good provider still exists despite the increasing numbers of women who work. Being judged a good wife and mother is important to most women and this includes cooking, cleaning, entertaining, and making a home in which she, her husband, and others can take pride. Most battered women have high expectations of their ability to conform to the "Sally Homemaker" standards and are vulnerable to their husbands' criticisms when they perform less than perfectly. This is also true for their expectations for being a mother. A battered woman tends to want a family and will go to great lengths to protect her children from the break-up of a home, even when to outsiders it appears that she would do better as a single-parent family rather than remain in a violent situation.

In my own research based on observations of their behavior, I hypothesized that battered women would rate their own sex-role attitudes toward women as very traditional. Instead, their responses were more liberal than 80 percent of the college women on whom the *Attitude Toward Women Scale* (*AWS*) was normed (Walker, 1984). Their perceptions of the batterer's attitudes toward women indicated he was very traditional. Their fathers also were perceived as having very traditional attitudes toward women, while they saw their mothers as about average. We included questions about relationships with nonviolent men, which about half (200) the women had experienced. They perceived that these men were closer to the norm in their attitudes toward women's role, indicating that the battered women we interviewed had different perceptions of abusive and nonabusive men. Rosewater found similar results in her investigation of 100 battered women, using the MMPI (Rosewater, 1982b; 1985). Although her sample said they often behaved in a passive way, they did not accept their passive role.

These empirical data support the anecdotal stories battered women tell. Their fear of another beating often forces them into behavior which they would not voluntarily choose otherwise. It is possible that many batterers do not realize the extent to which the women feel coerced by the ever-present threat of violence. My own clinical experience includes contact with many abusive men who cannot understand why women are afraid of them when they are not being directly abusive. They do not see how the potential for an explosion forces women's behavior into the rigid sex-role-stereotyped patterns which are perceived as safer than the nonconforming way they would prefer to act.

Weighing costs and benefits of a relationship continuously permeates an unstable marriage. Most battered women are psychologically harmed by the confusion which results from the lack of justice they perceive for themselves. If the man gets angry over little things, he's permitted to express his anger. But she cannot get angry with him when he does the same things for which he previously complained about her. If she demonstrates anger, the battered woman risks psychological or physical punishment.

While compromises are always part of a relationship, battered women feel that they are called upon to make the most sacrifices. Nevertheless, most stay with an abuser until the costs get too high. Sometimes, a large disposable income and other material benefits are part of the compromise battered women temporarily make. Economic advantages such as good schools for the children, opportunity for their own education, or basics such as food, shelter, and medical care are part of the bargain. Women know the economic realities of trying to make ends meet, and the forecasters tell us about the feminization of poverty: women still earn only 59¢ for every $1.00 a man earns.

There are other dangers of being single which figure into this cost-benefit ratio. The loneliness experienced by many who have been in a primary relationship can be unbearable. Battered women learn to identify intimacy with the batterer's intrusive, overpossessive style. A less intense relationship can be misperceived as not as loving. Some find other men boring after years of living on a rollercoaster. And the reality for single women is that the pool of eligible men diminishes as we get older, given the earlier mortality rate of men as well as their trend toward remarrying younger women. There are also those women who have lived with violent men who choose to relate only to women once they leave their relationship. However, this may not be an alternative given the negative societal values against lesbian relationships. When women choose this type of lifestyle they may live in fear that they will lose custody of their children should their sexual preference become public knowledge. Understandably, they may be less than forthright about their lifestyle.

Another factor which figures into the costs and benefits of a relationship is the provision for continued parenting of children. Battering often continues, following dissolution of marriages when child visitation and joint custody arrangements have been ordered. Women fear that men will make good their threats to take away their children, either literally or figuratively through psychological manipulation. It is probably unrealistic to expect a batterer to be able to co-parent a child fairly and without intimidation toward the woman he has beaten. Women believe that the bitter custody fights are simply one more technique with which the batterer causes them pain with his need for power and control.

Coping Skills for Psychological Survival

In order to minimize psychological injury, battered women may adopt a set of behaviors which can protect them and cause others frustration. The five most common skills observed are manipulation, indirect expression of anger, splitting of mind and body (dissociation), denial, and compliance or a willingness to please.

Manipulation is usually used by the women as an attempt to regain control over their unstable world. They frequently are quite successful at keeping the batterer from acting out by smoothing the external environment for him. Most men reward the women for doing just what they tell them to do. To keep the house clean, the kids quiet, the neighbors away, the family in line and protect their men from the external pressures of the world is quite a feat. Many battered women are able to do it all, even if it is only for a very short period of time. They are always anticipating potential violence cues and are trying to keep the peace until the tension finally gets out of hand. Because they are so successful during the early part of the tension-building period, it is not easy to persuade battered women to give up their manipulative techniques. Therapists and counselors need to gently confront the women with concrete evidence of such manipulation should it get in the way of the batterer's treatment. However, the exhaustion women feel after such continuous hypervigilence can be necessary to success-fully arrive at a natural intervention point.

Indirect expression of anger is usually the only way a battered woman can express her angry feelings without being subjected to more abuse. Many battered women become frightened of any angry, con-frontative stance, even when it is unrealistic to expect more harm. They have become conditioned to expect anger to generalize into a painfully dangerous situation and, thus, avoid it or push it into a "safe" place to get beyond the inevitable explosion. The inability to tolerate anyone's expression of anger, and fear of potential harm if they express their own anger, often pushes women into indirect ways of expressing their feelings. Sometimes it is called passive-aggressive behavior. They say yes, but really sabotage whatever plans are availa-ble. Confrontation is too dangerous in a battering relationship but essential if the women are to build honest relationships. Thus, direct expression of anger as well as assertive behavior and requesting that their rights be respected are important skills for former battered women to develop. Care must be taken not to unleash a torrent of rage which could be stored up from long-term abuse. A slow, moderate approach tends to be most beneficial, reaffirming the woman's right to own her own anger. This anger may be expressed verbally or in the form of action, that is, in leaving a violent relationship.

Splitting of mind and body is part of a dissociative state which protects battered women from feeling the full impact of physical and psychological pain. Mild hypnotic-like trances are described which serve to anesthetize the abuse victim from pain. The ability to expe-rience altered states of consciousness sometimes scares the woman, who fears going crazy, but more likely, she becomes able to withstand much greater levels of pain and survives more beatings.

In children for whom there is severe physical, sexual, and psycho-logical abuse, the splitting may be complete and cause a multiple personality. More frequently, there is incomplete splitting of the ego, which fragments a basically integrated personality. Guided imagery techniques can be used to heal the split and to teach the battered woman control over her "trances."

Dissociative states become more common and last for longer periods of time as the abuse becomes more severe. If life threats are perceived, there may be memory loss (partial or complex psychogenic amnesia) and a telescoping of events out of the normal time sequence. Many battered women who are terrified exhibit this behavior, as do those who have seriously harmed or killed their batterer. Women who have an out-of-body experience become very scared that the batterer's threats to drive them crazy may indeed be coming true. Body therapy and awareness constitute one way to help battered women reintegrate the mind–body split (Moss, 1985).

Denial and minimization of the violence to themselves, their children, their families, their lawyers, and anyone else who will listen is one of the most common traits of battered women. Most of us have been trained to believe that if there is a discrepancy between two people's stories about a single event, the truth must be somewhere in the middle. Not so for battered women and their batterer's descriptions of the violence. Both tend to minimize and deny the abuse so that the truth is almost always worse than either person's account. Denial and minimization are considered psychological defense mechanisms which are adopted as a way to lessen the anxiety caused by perceived psychological threats. Once a battered woman feels safe, her anxiety drops so that she can perceive the danger she has been in. However, if she gets scared again, she will revert back to minimizing and denying the potential danger, using denial as an anxiety-reduction technique. Obviously, her knowledge of the true danger is most likely to be revealed when a battered woman is in a shelter. Even then, however, if she is contemplating returning to the relationship or is involved in threatening legal proceedings, the chances are that she will be unable to reveal her true feelings.

Compliance or a willingness to please is another survival skill developed from living in violence. This behavior is widely reported in the literature of other survivors of trauma, such as concentration camp victims/survivors and prisoners of war (Browne, in press). Learning to recognize nonverbal cues of how to please one's captors can result in special favors in an otherwise bleak existence. Women, who are socialized as girls to be nurturing, will try to calm a batterer's anger by such behavior. A fear of getting anyone else who is in an authority position angry with them causes battered women to be overly pleasing when feeling threatened. In one homicide trial at which I testified on behalf of a battered woman who had killed in self-defense, this behavior was found so unusual that it was commented on by the press. They observed the battered woman revert from her genuine sad mood and become lively, chatty, and even laugh as she responded to the prosecutor's cross-examination. This was her way of minimizing the potential threat; she tried to smile, be agreeable, and not express her true feelings.

Battered women have been known to repress their feelings so that they appear to have no affect at all. Sometimes this masks a depression, but more often it simply allows them to protect against possible abuse for expressing themselves. Another example of the unfairness perceived in battering relationships is that the man can express any emotion he chooses, and usually expresses a wide range of feelings in a short period of time. She, however, is expected to antici-pate and respond to his feelings without any expression of her own. One woman explained it to me this way: "If I let Ed know what made me unhappy he'd use it against me when he was angry. If I let him know what made me happy, like going to see my granddaughter, he'd use that to make me do for him. So, it just got easier not to show any feelings so he couldn't use them to make me hurt more."

Theory of Learned Helplessness

The inability of a battered woman to predict whether or not her behavior will successfully protect her from further abuse creates a perception of no voluntary control over her life. This lack of con-tingency between response and outcome has been labeled "learned helplessness" by social scientists. It is not that women think they are helpless all of the time, but rather it is the inability to predict when they will succeed and when they will fail which constitutes learned helplessness. Psychologists have been able to create the learned help-lessness condition experimentally in the laboratory and have demon-strated the distortions in perception, feelings, thinking, and behavior in those animals and people who receive "helplessness training" (Se-ligman, 1975). In my work, I have tried to correlate degree of vulnera-bility to developing learned helplessness with childhood and relation-ship factors found when there is family violence (Walker, 1977, 1979, 1984).

If a battered woman has learned not to trust her ability to choose responses which will keep her safe, she tends to use only those few methods which have been the most successful previously. Her reper-toire of responsive behaviors becomes smaller, as she discards from consideration any alternatives for which she has no proof of effective-ness. This lack of faith in the predictability of new or different options is seen in her lack of trust that others might be able to help her and in her need to keep control of the environment. It also causes her to view the world in a myopic, personalized way. Much of her distortion in perception is intertwined with the batterer's constant verbal messages, usually a function of his own distorted logic and fears.

The battered woman begins to develop a stereotyped routine which meshes with the batterer's stereotyped routine, and this response set tends to function as tightly as narrow, closed systems generally do. The response set protects the system from outside harm, which is often defined as separation or termination of the relationship. It is fueled by the coping responses each makes to keep the abuse from escalating out of control. She may be more active and have more control during the beginning of the tension-building period while he has more control and is more active during its latter stages and during the phase two explosion. The third phase of loving kindness or at least an absence of tension is an attempt to restore the system balance. The cycle theory of the three phases of violence is more fully explained elsewhere (Walker, 1979, 1980, 1981, 1984). It is important for therapists and counselors to note that intervention techniques which might be successful at one phase are inadequate during another.

The learned helplessness model is based upon the lack of perception of successful response/outcome prediction. Random and variable abusive attacks interspersed with rewards and lack of abuse keep the system perpetuated. Thus, teaching the man and woman to measure their own violence cycle—plotting out tension-building incidents, the acute battering incident, and postexplosion and loving contrition phases—helps eliminate the perception that the violence is unpredictable. Therapists and counselors who teach the batterer to use a time-out technique, for example, when he feels his anger and notes where he is on the violence cycle must be assured that the battered woman also understands that time-out is to deescalate the anger, not ignore the issue under consideration. A woman who does not understand this may respond by trying to keep the man within her presence so as to get him to talk things out or finish the argument, unaware that she is sabotaging therapy efforts.

The battered woman's perception that she must control this man's behavior on her own comes from a lack of belief that anyone else will perceive just how dangerous he can be. His Dr. Jekyll-Mr. Hyde personality, which allows him to act charming sometimes and mean at other times, makes her fear that other people, including professionals, will not believe her accounts of his violence. This is especially true when he denies or minimizes his violence. Sometimes the men have forewarned the women that they will make everyone think the women are crazy and thereby invalidate the women's stories. Battered women scrutinize professionals' behavior to try to determine whether they believe her or the batterer. She will interpret any attempts at neutrality or impartiality to mean the person is on his side. Thus, she cannot trust that she will be safe with any counselor or therapist who tries to be "fair." You believe her or you don't; and if you don't, then you believe him.

This is one of the major reasons why a family therapy approach is so dangerous with couples in a battering relationship. To be effective, a family therapist must be neutral, objective, and out of the dysfunctional system. Violent relationships have such a powerful system, necessary to guarantee life survival, that therapists tend to get enmeshed even against their conscious awareness. Individual and group therapy approaches to reverse the effects of learned helplessness are necessary before any family systems approach is tried. Occasionally, the only way to get a couple into treatment is to begin with marital therapy. In those rare cases, two therapists are preferred, each one taking primary responsibility for one person. This allows both the batterer and the battered woman to perceive that each has an advocate and creates a parallel system which can become an alternative model to their original destructive one. In my practice, we use a male and female co-therapy team when such a treatment approach is indicated. Occasionally, children within these families are in therapy, also with their own therapist. Flexibility of our staff permits various combinations of the family to be seen with their respective therapists whenever appropriately indicated. This type of modified family counseling is more effective and less dangerous than a more traditional approach.

Assessment of Impact of Abuse on the Victim

Most batterers do not understand the full impact their behavior has had on the women they love. Her attempts to minimize its effects reinforce his belief that it really was not so bad. The physical bruises often heal quickly, particularly if there was soft tissue swelling and discoloration. But the psychological injury remains and forms a constellation of symptoms named Battered Woman Syndrome, which is a subcategory of the Post Traumatic Stress Disorder diagnostic category in the *Diagnostic and Statistical Manual of Mental Disorders* (*DSM-III*, 1981, p. 236). Those using the *DSM-III* multi-axial diagnostic system usually give an acute (308.30) or chronic (309.81) Post Traumatic Stress Disorder diagnosis on Axis I; defer diagnosis on Axis II until some of the Battered Woman Syndrome symptoms are reduced, to see what—if any—long-term disorder remains; rate health problems, physical or sexual injuries on Axis III; choose a psychosocial stressor rating for Axis IV, usually between 5 and 6 (*DSM-III*, 1981, p. 36); and rate the previous year's level of functioning on Axis V. Many clinicians confuse the symptoms adopted as a survival strategy in a violent relationship with those expected in a long-standing personality disorder or even a psychotic episode. A period of safety is needed to see what caused the confusion, paranoid-like thinking, and difficulties with reality. Rosewater (1985) discusses some of the common diagnostic errors made by clinicians in greater detail.

There are a number of common emotional, cognitive behavioral signs of Battered Woman Syndrome. These include anxiety, fear, depression, shock, anger, compassion, guilt, humiliation, confused thinking, intrusive memories, uncontrolled reexperiencing of traumatic events, rigidity, lack of trust, suspiciousness, hypervigilence, and increased startle response to cues of possible violence. Certainly, not all are seen in all battered women. Battered women often show some disturbance in their interpersonal relationships because of living with violence. The areas where these disturbances may be observed include degree of physical and emotional isolation from others, the quality of friendships with men and women, family support system, parenting skills (battered women tend to be both harsh and lenient in their discipline, depending on the batterer's mood), mood swings, degree of toughness, and ability for emotional intimacy. Some women are ready to work on all of their own issues quite rapidly. Others, particularly if there has been a history of chemical abuse, need to deal with them one at a time. The woman's typical coping style needs to be determined— how does she survive and cope with the impact of the violence? The length of time in the relationship, the severity and frequency of the abuse, the damage to their children, and the battered woman's prior abuse and emotional history all need to be assessed before there can be a full understanding of the effects of the battering on any particular individual woman.

One of the most popular questions asked of the woman is to defend why she stayed with the batterer. Those counseling the woman prefer to rephrase the question and instead ask why the batterer will not let her go. Typically, battered women will rescue the men: they bail them out of jail, go to their side if ill, suffer through financial adversity together, and continuously build up the man's ego at the expense of their own. However, it is usually the man who keeps coming back to them, calling, pleading, cajoling, and threatening the women so that fear, loneliness, and need for companionship enter into the women's decisions. Counselors and therapists working with the man need to help him become less dependent on the woman and encourage him to let the woman go when she wants to leave. On the other side, counselors and therapists working with the woman should be helping her become more independent, reviewing job skills, educational needs, financial management skills, and her other resources. The specific treatment approaches for women are detailed elsewhere (Walker, 1984; 1985). An individual and/or group counseling approach from a feminist perspective is the most successful in reversing the effects of learned helplessness as well as the other effects from the violence.

Can This Relationship Be Saved?

Initial counseling sessions usually spend a lot of energy focusing on whether or not this relationship has a future. It is usually best for the battered woman to put aside that question, unanswered, for some time. She needs to find who she is again, separate from her identity with her abusive partner. Often women are relieved not to have to make decisions, and enjoy the opportunity to pay attention to their own needs in the therapeutic relationship. Relieving external stress and pressure is important to create a therapeutic climate where the woman can learn to listen to herself. Once she begins to feel safe, she will get in touch with her anger at having been abused. Teaching her to judge where it is safe to express the angry feelings, in the therapist's office or more carefully at home, is crucial to avoid an acute battering incident. Contact between the man's and woman's therapists can help prepare them to protect their clients from a particular therapy stage, if it could be dangerous.

The battered woman is usually much slower and more reluctant to want to work on any reconciliation plans once she is engaged in therapy. Her focus rightfully should be on her own personal growth, and she often becomes resentful of the need to spend time compromising or submerging her needs to his needs any longer. Those working with batterers usually request joint sessions as the men have less ability to live with the anxiety created by such unresolved issues. The woman is more focused on rebuilding her strength; the man wants to rebuild the relationship. Sometimes, he cannot tolerate her timing and precipitates a crisis. Either one could push for resolution that results in a divorce.

Therapists or counselors working with those involved in family violence may also have to help their clients deal with the impending divorce, if that is their decision. The goal should be to keep it nonviolent, settle the property fairly, and decide upon child-raising responsibilities in a mature, reasonable fashion. Easier said than done in any divorce, with battering couples it becomes a potentially lethal situation. It is imperative for professionals to monitor their own myths, beliefs, and subtle or overt messages given to these clients. Assisting attorneys to understand the level of dangerousness is always helpful. While mediation is seen as useful in resolving differences amicably, the same admonitions about marital or family therapy can sabotage mediation efforts. It is useful for the individuals' therapists to play a more active role in keeping conflicts from escalating through prevention and rapid intervention efforts. A realistic perspective is needed by the clients as well as the judicial system.

The area most fraught with violence potential concerns child custody and visitation decisions. Most battered women resent the batterer who becomes a "born-again" parent. She feels she has done the major child raising, sometimes even fought against him to have the baby when he did not want it, and that she has the psychological bond with the child(ren). She believes he is requesting sole custody, joint custody, or unlimited visitation for reasons that are not in the children's or her best interest. Financial manipulation, power control issues, and a way to continue to hurt her are her assumptions as to why the batterer demands rights to his children. Although she responds to the continued psychological (if not physical) abuse in typical battered woman ways, the man often pulls himself together as he gears up for the fight. It is hoped that those therapists and counselors working with the men at this time will recognize the danger to the children and long-term destructiveness to the man, and attempt to confront these issues in therapy.

Confidentiality and Ethical Issues

Counseling in the field of family violence raises numerous confidentiality and ethical issues which must be addressed. This is one of the few areas when confidentiality may have to be broken, to warn of impending abuse, and to deal with past abuse, especially if it involves children. The mandatory child abuse laws in most states demand the reporting of any case of suspected or known child abuse to appropriate social services or law enforcement authorities. Willful nonreporting is punished by fines and jail sentences: it is a crime. In most spouse abuse cases there is a greater risk of child abuse, especially from the men (55% in our research study; Walker, 1984). Women's potential to abuse their children is eight times higher when living with an abusive mate. Yet it takes time to get a good grasp of all the actual violence in any abusive family. Caution in sorting through the details and good personal liaison with the child protection workers often smooth this potentially difficult process. Regular communication with the woman or her therapist is another way to reduce the damage to the therapeutic relationship but still get information back and forth on the regular channels.

   Carefully kept, accurate records, reflecting that which can be documented and not personal opinions, are also important should records be subpoenaed in a legal proceeding. Always respond to a subpoena but do not turn over raw data or records without a court order following a hearing on the attorney's motion to produce records. Psychologists can fall back upon the APA ethics code, incorporated in most states' licensing laws, to refuse to turn raw data (notes, test protocols, correspondence, and other nonreports) over to anyone who is not a trained licensed psychologist specialized in spouse (or child) abuse. To do so, without the judge's order, is in violation of the license to practice. Usually, I place the material in a sealed envelope and offer it to the judge, stating my objections to turning it over to a person untrained in psychology. This takes the ethical issue away from me and puts it on the court.

Revitalization for Counselors and Therapists

Many of the counselors and therapists working with these difficult family violence cases on a daily basis begin to get overwhelmed by the staggering amount of violence they are exposed to. If it results in their becoming less effective, or in experiencing burnout (the need to expend more energy to get less accomplished), then frequent vacations, retreats, and conferences are critical to becoming revitalized. Sometimes it is important to think of the work we do with women victims and batterers as just a period in our lives; we will move on because we all grow. Each of us probably needs to put some volunteer time into making the system more responsive to battered women and their families. Then, this time is not a burnout, but just time to finish passing through.

8

Developing Counseling Programs for Male Batterers

Ten years ago treatment programs for male batterers were essentially nonexistent. Shelters for battered women were confined primarily to urban areas, and woman battering was not viewed by either the general public or service providers as being a serious or prevalent problem.

As shelters began to flourish and domestic violence advocacy programs were developed to have impact on public policy, the question was asked, "What is being done for the male batterer?" It became evident with the increased awareness of the problem, new criminal justice policy and procedures, and the greater availability of counseling for victims, that counseling services for men had to be developed to meet the needs of future criminal justice clients, and self-motivated clients seeking help. In addition, over time it became obvious to shelters that they could not meet the needs of their entire community and that many of the women who did seek shelter services ultimately returned home to their abusers only to be further victimized.

During the mid-1970s a number of people interested in this issue in different parts of the country began to counsel male batterers. As interest in the batterer grew, so did the number of programs and people counseling men. Today, the networking between programs serving the offender has been greatly facilitated by conferences, written materials, and the various battered women's organizations. Since the early development of services for batterers, there has been a great deal of controversy over who should provide the services and how the services should be structured.

These questions and more need to be closely examined and answered as an agency or group becomes interested in developing services for male batterers. This chapter asks some important questions and suggests some possible answers to those questions as a necessary prerequisite to developing services in your community.

In developing a counseling program in your community, you must ask several questions in the planning stages:

1. Is there a need for this service in your community?
2. Who has the skills to offer the service?
3. Who will ultimately sponsor the service?
4. How will referrals be generated?
5. Who will pay for the services?

I would like to discuss each of these points in detail so as to help you and/or your agency come to some conclusions in developing a domestic violence offender counseling program.

Is There a Need in Your Community?

Domestic violence cuts across all socioeconomic backgrounds, races, religions, and cultural groups (Straus et al., 1980). In our travels across the country we have talked with many people from many different types of communities that experience this problem. We have spoken with people from both urban and rural communities, culturally specific communities, suburban communities, transient communities, and military communities all wanting services to meet the needs of their particular population. This question would most accurately be worded as: How can a domestic violence counseling program meet the need in your community? Questions such as the following must be answered:

For military programs, should the program be on or off base? Which type of program would servicemen be more likely to attend?

In large rural counties, where would a program be most utilized: in a central location or in the largest town?

For counties that have barriers to travel, such as a mountain range or a river or lake, how will those barriers affect someone who also has internal barriers to change?

In areas where there already are a number of domestic violence men's programs, will developing another program be a wasted expenditure of energy if the other programs are struggling to stay alive?

If a community has many domestic violence programs but few referrals from the courts, from shelters, or through advertisements, time and energy may be better spent in training police and the courts on more effective responses to this problem. Although offender programs are in vogue with foundations and other funding agencies, I would caution you about getting on the bandwagon unless your community is ready for such a program.

One way of assessing this need is to conduct a formal or informal needs assessment in your community. Talk with police, district attorneys, probation officers, public defenders, judges, mental health practitioners, shelter workers, crisis lines, military personnel, hospital emergency rooms, and members of the clergy to find out what their needs are. Is it training or is it services? Besides conducting a needs assessment, you are essentially beginning to do the networking prerequisite to running a sound program.

The Family Violence Project in San Francisco did just this in its early stages of development. Offer to observe an evening in the emergency room or a day in court, or go on a ride along with the local police or sheriff. Not only will you see how many cases can possibly be referred but you will also appreciate the difficult jobs these people have to do, and how they can better respond to this problem.

Once it is determined that there are cases available and a need for a service in a particular area, it is important to ask the next question.

Who Has the Skills to Offer the Service?

The best experts on domestic violence in your community are the shelter and/or hotline workers. These women have usually read a great deal about this issue and know about it from direct experience with battered women. They will be your most valuable resource in terms of training and expertise. Although few of the women will have experience in working with the batterer, their general knowledge of the issue and experience with the victims can lay the groundwork for your skills in counseling men.

There are a number of consultants who travel around the country offering workshops on this issue, which could be rather costly to a new program. There are now programs for batterers in nearly every large city in the country. It may be more cost efficient for you to travel to them rather than have them travel to you.

One way of bringing in experts is to do so in the form of a conference, if you have a relatively large number of people who would pay for such training. An expert can generate interest and enthusiasm; an expert can also drain pocketbooks. Much can be done on your own through reading the available materials on the topic and utilizing the experts in your own community.

Who Will Sponsor the Service?

A seemingly innocuous question can be the subject of much controversy. There are several options on which we will elaborate. They are:

1. Shelter program
2. Criminal justice program
3. Community mental health program
4. Social service agency program
5. Men's program
6. Private mental health practitioner
7. Treatment team approach.

Shelter Program

Shelters offering counseling services to batterers are a subject of much controversy. Those in favor say that it makes sense that a shelter treat men as well as women. They have the knowledge, experience, and skills to do so. Some shelter workers feel that if the shelter offers the service, the counselor working with the man will adhere to feminist principles and not collude with the man in blaming the victim, which historically has been done by mental health practitioners. Many shelter workers believe that it will strengthen their image in the community to offer counseling for men so as not to appear sexist or anti-men. Some shelters have simply developed programs for men because of a lack of interest on the part of anyone else in the community or because the funding sources which support them have told them to do so or lose funding. In the San Francisco Bay area two shelter programs, Battered Woman's Alternatives in Concord and Marin Abused Women's Services in San Rafael, have shown that a men's counseling program can be successfully incorporated into a shelter program for women.

Those against the idea say that shelters have enough trouble staying afloat without taking on another financial burden. Some workers say shelters exist for women, not to help men. Some women have told me, "Women have always taken care of men, especially in battering relationships. For a shelter to start a men's program is only propagating a pattern that breeds inequality and contempt."

Another possible disadvantage of a shelter offering services to batterers is that some women and men could use this connection as a way of getting information about each other. If men come to counseling knowing that their counselor can contact their partners while they cannot, it might cause some tension between the men and their counselors. Opponents also say that treatment for batterers needs to be institutionalized in the community mental health centers.

Criminal Justice Programs

The most advantageous aspect of this type of program is that its presence in the system can help determine the fate of cases which ordinarily might have been dropped or inappropriately referred. The Family Violence Project has been able to institutionalize the many policies it has because of its presence within the criminal justice system (San Francisco Family Violence Project, 1982). Counseling can be started soon after a defendant comes into contact with the system. Cases can be closely monitored because of a criminal justice program's close ties with probation and the courts. Information about the current offense as well as about prior offenses is more easily accessible to the counselor.

Two possible disadvantages of these programs are:

1. *Confidentiality.* What are the limits of confidentiality in counseling sessions? Is the counselor an arm of the law or an advocate of the system? This distinction would make a difference in how the men perceive the counselor.
2. *Homogeneous groups.* Many criminal justice programs work only with men referred by the courts. The absence of self-

referred men may change the dynamics of the group because of the lack of the positive effect it has on men to see that there are other men who are internally motivated to solve their problems on their own.

There are a number of criminal justice programs in the country operating successfully. These programs, however, are usually dependent on governmental funding whose priorities may vary from year to year. Another issue of concern is, if the criminal justice system is getting into the business of counseling, which department of the system would host such a program where there would not be any conflicts of interest? This issue is currently being addressed in several programs.

Community Mental Health Programs

Historically, city/county community mental health programs have not worked with criminal justice clients because of their lack of expertise on the issues, as well as some potential problems with confidentiality being an issue for city/county agencies. In addition, many psychotherapists have difficulty with the idea of reporting to probation and courts. Most mental health professional training programs do not familiarize students with the criminal justice system, so for most practitioners it is an unknown to be feared and probably mistrusted.

Offering a counseling group for batterers at community mental health centers has several advantages:

1. Trained mental health professionals are already on staff.
2. Student interns can be used as a way to save some staff time and money and train future mental health professionals.
3. Many community mental health centers have 24-hour crisis clinics for late-night referrals.
4. Staff support for consultation and emergency backup already exists.

Community mental health services can and do respond to this issue. West Oakland Mental Health in Oakland, California, started one batterers group several years ago and currently has three groups for men and one group for women.

Social Service Agency Programs

A private nonprofit social service agency in the community can be an excellent location for a batterers program. Family Service Agency of Marin County, California, has offered a batterers program in the past. As for other private nonprofit agencies, the problem of money is of great concern. Paying two therapists to run a group properly can be an expensive proposition on a tight budget. Often these agencies have access to counseling student interns which can defray a portion of the cost of running the group with client fees.

One major advantage to private nonprofit groups over community mental health and criminal justice programs is that instituting a counseling group for batterers may entail less red tape and bureaucracy with the former. In addition, many of these agencies have already made good contacts with the criminal justice system for other types of clients which they may already be seeing.

Another advantage of both social service agencies and community mental health is that they can make internal referrals of batterers being seen at the agencies for other reasons. Having a batterers group in such an agency can raise the consciousness of all of the staff as to the seriousness and prevalence of this problem.

Men's Programs

Many communities have men's centers active in issues of sexism, homophobia, gay rights, and so on (Adams and McCormick, 1982). These centers may be an ideal location for a batterers' program in that the issues of power, sexuality, and sex roles are those underlying domestic violence. Programs like EMERGE in Boston or Men Overcoming Violence in San Francisco, which grew out of the men's movement, were developed by men interested in changing how men and women, and men and men, relate. Many of these peer counselors have personally struggled with their own sexism issues and want to support other men in doing the same.

Private Practitioners

Many mental health professionals choose to work privately or in a small group rather than for a large agency. Some of these individuals could be persuaded to start, or may already be interested in starting, a batterers' group. Many people working in agencies for little or no money often look at private practitioners with suspicion: they are out there making a lot of money. However, any private practitioner who is running a group for batterers properly is not going to make a lot of money, which probably accounts for why you cannot find many volunteers in the first place.

At this point you have a major decision to make. Who will provide the service? If you are lucky, you will either have the money and/or the enthusiasm and expertise to do it yourself or someone else in your community may offer his or her services. If you are truly lucky, you will have a number of people from both agencies and private practitioners expressing interest in providing services to batterers. This is what we had when we started the Family Violence Project in San Francisco. From that we developed what is now known as the San Francisco Domestic Violence Treatment Team.

Treatment Team

A group of counselors from San Francisco was interested in providing services to male batterers and battered women. These counselors came from Community Mental Health, Catholic Social Services, private nonprofit clinics, and private practitioners. Each wanted to work with this population of clients. Some offered individual counseling, others offered group or family counseling.

Requirements to be on the team included attending a number of workshops on domestic violence and a willingness to meet once a month as a group to discuss cases and issues. The probation officers in charge of domestic violence cases would also periodically meet with the team. Clients referred to the Family Violence Project for assessment would then get referred to members of the treatment team for counseling. The treatment team concept worked well in a city where a number of persons were interested in working on this issue and the number of referrals or clients needing counseling was too much for any one program to accommodate. Ideally, this should be a goal of any program—to get too many referrals for one program to handle. If this happens, you will know that you are making progress.

How Will Referrals Be Generated?

This question has already been answered indirectly in the previous discussion. Below is a list of possible referral sources.

1. *Criminal justice system.* Each member of the system can make a referral as the wheels of justice slowly turn: police, district attorneys, public defenders, judges, and probation officers. Each can make a referral while cases are pending.
2. *Mental health workers.* Where properly trained on how to identify domestic violence cases, other practitioners in your agency or in the community who know about your service will find it invaluable and will want to refer clients to a domestic violence program.
3. *Hospital and medical personnel.* Although usually catering to the battered woman, medical personnel can inform women, and sometimes men, of the services in the community dealing with this problem. Many battered women utilize emergency room services.
4. *Shelters for battered women.* As discussed earlier, many men will go into counseling if they are threatened with loss of their relationship. Women in the shelter can inform their partners of the counseling services for men in the community and may go so far as making their participation in treatment a condition of their return home or to the relationship. In addition, many more women call the hotline or just need to talk than go to shelters. These women can also be informed, not only of their own criminal justice options, but also of services available for their partners.
5. *Other crisis hotlines.* Other crisis lines, such as for suicide prevention or child abuse, get many calls from battered women and batterers. These hotlines are in a position to make many referrals to community agencies.
6. *Clergy.* Many times battered women and batterers turn to their priest, minister, or rabbi for support and guidance. Members of the clergy are often unaware of new services in the community and would make referrals if they knew of your services.

Do not underestimate the power of advertisement and the media. Local newspaper coverage as well as television news coverage can help reach the men who just need to know you are out there. KPFA-FM in Berkeley, California, did a series of programs on domestic violence over a period of a year which generated many referrals for local counseling programs. Public service announcements on both radio and television are available at any time at no cost. An excellent book which discusses getting free media coverage is called *How to Get Free Press*, published by Harbor Press (Delacourt, Kinsey and Halas, 1981).

Public speaking in the schools as well as brief educational seminars for other agencies in your community may generate referrals, as well as serve to educate other professionals. Alcohol and drug counseling programs are especially fruitful for referrals. So are military programs in your area. The bottom line is that the clients are everywhere you look. Any service imaginable probably serves people who are experiencing this problem. All it takes is some imagination and energy to reach out into the community and make your presence known.

Who Will Pay for the Service?

A discussion of developing a counseling program for batterers cannot be complete without a discussion of money. I am not going to try to convince you that money is not important. In fact, the more money you have the better off you are. In the Bay Area a bare bones program could cost as much as $25,000 to $30,000.

The point of the preceding statement is to make you really look at what your current resources are. What already existing services in your community can be augmented to serve this population of people? Even if you have $30,000 at your disposal needing to be spent this year, I would caution you to think for a minute. What about next year? The $30,000 this year will need to be generated next year. Taking inflation into consideration, you will probably need $35,000 next year. If you think you can pull off the funding for three or four years easily, I would say go ahead and do it, and face the later fiscal crises when you get to them. The most stable programs tend to be those institutionalized within the system of an already existing agency.

I have seen many programs do quite well on collecting fees for services and surviving on donations. A colleague and I have been running a group for batterers that sustains itself solely on fees for services. The point I am making here is that we cannot always depend on foundations and government to help sustain programs for batterers. The men can and do pay for the services received. Those who can afford the higher fee, pay it, and that helps to defray the loss incurred through low-fee clients. Granted, this method would not pay for a full-time position or probably not even a half-time position. It does, however, pay for the group and a few additional hours, which is a start. One does not need a grant to start a *service* in the community (rather than a program) such as a batterers' group.

No matter which approach you ultimately decide to take, it is critical that you coordinate closely with the criminal justice system, local domestic violence programs (i.e., shelters), other service providers for men, and general services in your community. This coordination is critical for several reasons.

1. It is very easy to feel isolated in this work just as our clients do. This feeling of isolation creates additional stress on already very stressful work and ultimately makes us less effective in our work.

2. Many of these cases are high risk, that is, high in lethality. We encourage people not to make decisions in a vacuum; discuss your difficult cases with other people working in the field.

3. Just as making decisions about difficult cases can cause stress, so can not discussing your successes be stressful. Hearing about other people's successes can be inspiring for all persons working in the field.

4. Duplication of services can be a problem if there is not that particular need in your community. Keeping in close contact with other programs keeps you aware of those services currently being offered, as well as those being planned.

5. A relatively small number of people are working on this issue, and there is truth in the adage that there is power in numbers. Institutions respond more quickly to large gatherings rather than to small groups.

6. Domestic violence is not something most people want to think about because of the discomfort it elicits in us. For this reason it is important for programs to stay visible, through monthly coordination meetings, workshops, speaking at agency staff development meetings, and the like. When you are in the courthouse, stop by and visit your favorite probation officer, district attorney, or public defender. The more they see your face, the more likely they will be to think of you when a domestic violence case appears. Developing a program advisory board consisting of representatives of agencies that make referrals to the program can be an excellent way of

cutting down on isolation, staying visible in the community, networking, and coordinating with other service providers in the community.

Follow-up / Program Evaluation

As described earlier, a necessary aspect of a successful treatment approach is to have continual follow-up contact wth the victim(s) of violence, children, probation officers and other counselors involved in a particular case. The primary purpose of this contact is to assess for further violence; however, this contact is also helpful in determining the general success of treatment.

Success may be measured in any one or a combination of ways. You may want to measure the number of cases identified, the cessation of physical violence while the client is in the program, the cessation of all types of violence while the client is in the program, the length of time a client stays in treatment, the participation level of the client, and the cessation of any one or a combination of the four types of violence subsequent to treatment. In measuring posttreatment success, one needs to decide how long one will measure the batterers' behavior subsequent to treatment. This is a significant factor, in that some of the men may have either had a long cycle of violence prior to treatment, or as a result of treatment have been able to prolong the tension-building phase of the cycle of violence. Another issue in determining long-term effects of treatment is how the information is collected. Will you only depend on the client's report? Or will you talk with significant others? Many of the men will have broken off their relationship with the woman they initially battered and may or may not be in a new relationship. How will you measure success in this case?

Program evaluation, especially in treatment outcome, is a very difficult and complex endeavor, however in order to solidify our knowledge in the area of treatment for the male batterer we must now closely examine what works and what does not work in stopping violent behavior with this particular client population. The risk to human life is too great to ignore this element of program development.

We encourage persons wanting to work with male batterers to either receive education themselves on program evaluation, or consult with professionals in their community familiar with this aspect of program development. Many schools offer continuing education classes on program evaluation. In addition, a number of books may be found in any college library which have been written on this topic. When developing either a program or a service in your community we encourage you to ask yourself how you will determine the success of your treatment.

Preventing Burnout

In developing a domestic violence men's program, it is essential that staff be aware of how working on this issue affects them personally. Domestic violence is an issue which touches the heart of what it is to be a man and what it is to be a woman. In this way, it has an effect on everyone: the clients, the service providers, the administrators, neighboring agencies, and the community in general.

The concept of parallel process (Haley, 1976; Ritterman, 1983) helps a counselor understand how a particular victim of violence experiences her batterer. Men often will treat their counselors and/or their counseling groups in much the same fashion they treat their partners. Co-counselors in a men's group often will act out the dynamics between the men and their partners or between men in the group. The relationship between a counselor and his or her supervisor may be very similar to the relationship between a counselor and a client. Men and men, women and women, and men and women, all working on this issue could sometimes act toward each other much as battered women and their batterers interact. Agencies and individuals can isolate themselves, become overburdened or burned out, and lose perspective, a phenomenon similar to what happens in families which experience violence.

We believe that this parallel process is real, and understanding it can help us deal effectively with the problem of violence in the family on individual, community, institutional, and political levels. We encourage persons involved in direct service, administration, and/or sociopolitical activities to meet frequently, not only to talk about what they are doing, but also to talk about how they are working together. This process-oriented interaction can provide a healthy balance for the "let's get something done" ethic which can predominate any social movement.

In closing, we would like to remind the readers that the counseling of male batterers is a relatively new specialty. Although some programs claim to have a certain "success rate" or particular experiences with their clients, we encourage service providers to experiment with different techniques and approaches and to broadcast their own unique experiences to other service providers counseling men who batter, within and outside their community.

9

Confronting the Violence Within Us and Around Us

Several months ago I saw the movie "The Night of the Shooting Stars," an Italian film, highly recommended by friends and colleagues. The film is set in a small Italian village at the end of World War II. The town and surrounding area are occupied by the Fascists and Nazis, and the townspeople meet to discuss their fate. The Americans have landed, and a group of townspeople decides that they are going to leave at night to find the Americans to ensure their safety. Another group of townspeople decides to stay and face the consequences. The first group leaves at night and along their route in search of the Americans, they have adventures and meet other people, including a group of Fascists. In this group are a man and his teenage son. It is obvious to the viewer that the son has been molded by his father. He is violent, and it appears that he gets a sense of power from his group and a thrill out of killing the peasants. I found myself gradually growing to despise this boy and his father.

Later in the film we find the boy and his father literally up a tree without weapons or supporters. This time the Italians have the guns. The townspeople get them down from the tree and point a gun at each of them. The father begins to plead with them not to shoot his son. "Take me instead," he says. As I sat in the audience caught up in the horror, the anger, and the rage, I found I was saying to myself "blow them both away." As it turned out, the villagers shot the boy, and the father killed himself. As I walked out of the theater, I found myself thinking, here I am, someone who is supposed to be sensitive to this issue, and yet I was caught up in the story to such a degree that I wanted one of the characters in the film to act out my anger, in addition to his own. One of the people I was with said, "Of course you're going to feel that way. It has special meaning to you because you're Jewish." I thought to myself, "That's not a good enough explanation." It made me wonder, if I responded that way, how did other people respond to that movie? In the weeks that followed, I asked colleagues and friends who had seen the film what their reaction was. Most of the people told me they did not remember the scene, and those who did remember, did not have much more of a reaction than, "Of course they deserved what they got."

A few weeks later I saw the film "The Verdict" with Paul Newman. The first time I saw the film, I did not like it, which made me very unpopular in my circle of friends. How dare I not like a Paul Newman film! Unable to explain clearly why I did not like it, I went to see it again. From the second viewing it became clear to me why the film was distasteful. We have our hero, a hard-working attorney who is working with a woman on a case. The long and short of it is that the woman is also working for the other side in the case and betrays our hero. What does he do when he finds out? He punches her in the face, at which time the audience applauds.

Several months later I was conducting a training for the military in South Carolina. My hotel room had Home Box Office on the television. The movie I watched was "Absence of Malice," with Paul Newman and Sally Field. Again, our hero was betrayed by a woman, and again, his response was to be violent. In neither of these films did the hero reap any adverse consequences for his violence; in fact, all indications point to his behavior being justified.

This is nothing new; the movies and television are full of violence, specifically violence against women. However, what effect does this exposure to violence have on us? When surrounded by excessive stimuli of a particular kind, do we unconsciously develop a blindness or deafness to those stimuli? Do we become desensitized? Does the behavior become a part of our attitudinal repertoire?

In his early studies, Bandura demonstrated that children observing violent behavior by adults in person or in filmed models will imitate such observed acts of violence (1973). Children exposed to violence in the home have a much greater chance of demonstrating aggressive behavior later in life (Lefkowitz, Eron, Walder, & Huesman, 1975; McCord, McCord, & Howard, 1961). Although parental modeling has a major impact on a child's development, exposure to violence on television and in movies may add to the possibility that children will act aggressively later in life. For the past two decades television has become "one of the family" (Singer & Singer, 1975) such that a child grows up not only with his or her parental models, but also with powerful models and images conveyed through television and film (Williams, Zabrack, & Joy, 1982).

Many of the studies on the effects of television and/or movies have been conducted on children; however, recent experiments have shown that exposure to sexual violence in some forms of pornography has a similar effect on adult males (Malamuth & Check, 1983a; 1983b).

In addition to the modeling effects, it has been suggested that long-term exposure to violence on television may have a systematic desensitization effect, decreasing one's sensitivity to pain in others or diminishing one's awareness of violence (Cline, Croft, & Courrier, 1973). Investigators in the area of systematic desensitization (McGlynn, Mealiea, & Landau, 1981; Proctor, 1968; Wilson & Davidson, 1971; Wolpe & Lazarus, 1966) suggest that when one is exposed to a great deal of violence either directly or vicariously through the media, one develops a tendency to turn off his/her feelings about, responses to, or awareness of such violent stimuli.

This desensitization was evident during the Vietnam War. It was during this period that people at home, for the first time, through television witnessed the tragic effects of war. Although initially shocked, over the years most people developed an indifference toward the violence and death. Ten years after the war, public broadcasting presented a 10-part program on the Vietnam War. Viewers for the most part had a strong emotional reaction to this program, perhaps similar to that initial reaction years ago. (A similar phenomenon occurs with sex in the media. What was probably censored 20 years ago is now part of daily programming. Like violence, sex has become a part of our everyday lives; we expect it, and we notice when it is *not* there, but we accept it when it *is* there.)

People frequently need to be shocked into awareness. During the anti-Vietnam War days, you may remember the slogan, "Would you be against the war if it were fought on your front lawn?" When people are desensitized to violence, it takes an extreme form of violence to get their attention. Sometimes it takes violence touching their own lives in some way. People's feelings about crime change drastically when they become victims of violent crime. People's feelings about war are affected when they lose a relative or other loved one. One unfortunate response people have to violence and helplessness is to become frustrated and angry. Frequently they are not aware of this anger until something or someone touches it. It is like opening Pandora's Box. When this occurs, a "last straw" or "I've had it" response is forthcoming. A target for anger and rage is finally found, and violence is thought to be justified. Public reaction to the 1984 case of New York "subway vigilante" Bernhard Hugo Goetz is one recent instance. In 1983, the attack on the Marine installation in Lebanon, and the Soviet attack on the Korean jetliner were used as justifications for the further escalation of militarism. However, tragic events such as these can also be an opportunity to look at our own violence and to develop creatively a plan to avoid further violence.

People experiencing domestic violence in their relationships frequently undergo a similar desensitization process. Men will say, "I wasn't violent this time, I only pushed her." For many men physical violence has become such a way of life that the lesser forms of physical and psychological violence are not viewed as violence but are in fact seen as justifiable punishment (Bograd, 1983).

One of the goals of the battered women's movement has been to raise general public awareness of woman battering. However, what are the consequences for the individual whose awareness of this problem is heightened? One consequence for most people seems to be a greater general awareness of violence around them. For most people this can be an emotional experience. Feelings long forgotten from violent incidents in our own history rapidly surface and once again ask for recognition and resolution. For some people this means anger and sadness, for others it may mean fear.

For many women it means past incidents of victimization remembered or at the least, fear of vulnerability. For some men this may trigger guilt about their own violence in the past or their use of force and intimidation. No matter what the association, our emotional response can become overwhelming and leave us feeling impotent. For this reason many people do not want to hear or talk about violence. They often do not know what to do about the feelings which result. Think about how violence effects you. What is your emotional response? Now, think about what you do with those feelings. In order to confront effectively the violence around us, we must be able to deal effectively with our own responses.

When conducting workshops on domestic violence, the issue of child discipline always sparks heated debate. Those who have never had children usually say that hitting is not necessary at any time, whereas the parents in the group are usually less sympathetic to the opinions of their nonparent counterparts. The reality is that 81 percent of parents use corporal punishment on their children (Johnson, 1974) and that "6 out of 10" parents spank or beat their children an average of once a week; boys are typically subjected to up to three times as much spanking as girls (Pogrebin, 1980). Not all of these cases would be considered child abuse; however, corporal punishment *is* violence and therefore several messages are conveyed when a parent chooses to respond in this way.

When using corporal punishment on children, the first message which a parent hopes to convey, but which may be obscured by the process, is that whatever the child is doing, it is *not* all right with the parent. The parent is angry, unhappy, and disappointed and wants the child to stop. While this message hopefully is communicated, several more subtle messages are also coming across.

1. Being angry may justify the use of violence.
2. If someone loves you enough and they feel hurt or angry, they can hit you because of that love. This creates an association between love and violence.
3. When you disagree with someone and you believe in your cause, you should use violence.
4. Being hit is going to help build your character. You will be a better person because of it.
5. If I hit you, it is going to hurt me more than it hurts you.

Straus (1980) found that boys had a 61 percent greater risk than girls for physical injury. This fact may be attributed to many theories, which include boys are more difficult to raise than girls, boys need to be toughened up for the violence they may confront in the world, and boys can take it better than girls. No matter what the reasons, the violence boys experience may have negative effects on healthy sex-role development (Pogrebin, 1980).

This toughening process for boys may be one of the root causes of domestic violence. Early on in life children are taught that there are behaviors acceptable within the purview of being female and behaviors acceptable within the purview of being male, and never the twain shall meet. Males are treated like males from birth, and these behaviors are reinforced by almost all people and institutions imaginable. Boys are taught that being male is superior to being female; feminine character-istics are devalued in terms of power in society (Jung, 1961). The message is that feelings are not going to help you be successful at being male, so why have them?

In a recent book by Linda Leonard, *The Wounded Woman* (1983), she discusses this complementary conditioning of women in this so-ciety, noting that when men devalue all that is feminine in themselves, they will ultimately devalue the female figures in their lives, objectify them, and eventually relegate them to a status of limited utility, such as sex objects, violence objects, or servants.

Dr. Leonard is suggesting that men batter the woman inside themselves. They neither understand her nor relate to her. Men have not experienced the sense of power or wholeness that understanding and assimilating the feminine can bring about.

A man's sacrifice of the feminine nature within himself is in part an underlying cause of the troubles which individuals, couples, families and societies experience today. However, this sacrifice is not a recent phenomenon. It is evident in the art, literature, and history of our ancestors.

The relationship of men and women to the various aspects of their psychological selves can and does have an impact on their behavior. These relationships have been defined historically by soci-eties of people conforming to the standards put forth by powerful models.

Kings and queens, fathers and mothers, have all served as such powerful social models, defining the rules of behavior for men and women, past, present, and future. These values are learned by living in society and are reinforced by every conceivable institution in our society. Not to oversimplify a complex psychosocial problem, but a man who batters appears to devalue all that is feminine. This is evident in his traditional sex-role expectations, his lack of ability to express his emotions, his intolerance of his partner's emotions, and his ultimate battering of his partner into submission.

The battering of the feminine is common in all men, to a greater or lesser degree. Every day in order to get through the day, men need to keep that anger down, cover up that sadness, and keep a check on that fear. If we do not, we are left unbalanced, venturing into unfamiliar, unstructured territory. This territory is not easy to demarcate, like yard lines on a football field or the balance in a savings account. It is a place of indefinites, ambiguities, and uncertainties.

As men allow themselves to explore this feminine side of themselves, as they learn to trust their feelings as much as they trust their intellect, they will achieve a greater balance. As this internal balance becomes more pronounced, it will be manifested in their relationships with other people. The dream of an equal relationship with another person becomes a greater possibility.

A recent American Psychological Association convention had a workshop on whether men will ever understand women. Carolyn Peyton, a psychologist and former director of the Peace Corps, made the point that there is no advantage for men in understanding women. There is nothing to be gained from understanding that which you perceive as having less power than yourself. However, it is in women's best interest to understand men, to enable them to gain more power for themselves. Dr. Peyton made the parallel between blacks and whites. At this workshop the point was made that before a man can have an equal and understanding relationship with a woman, he must first understand and have a relationship with the female inside of himself. He must face the potentially terrifying territory of his emotions. He must come to terms with his issues of control. These are lifelong issues and are not discrete in time. It would be easier for most men if they would work on "it" and finish "it" in a prescribed amount of time. However, an appreciation of the indefinite, the sometimes undefinable, is a part of the essence of the feminine. This is the nature of internal violence: the abuse by our own choice of the feminine inside of all men.

This should be our personal journey in our work in domestic violence, asking such questions as, "What is it to be a man?" and "What is it to be a woman?" It is my belief that the process of answering these questions is really that of revolution. The changes will affect women, men, children, and, hopefully, the world. Because of the effects, changes will occur on every level: within and between the men and women working on this problem; within and between the men, women, and children experiencing this problem; within city, state, and national institutions, thereby affecting the policy on domestic violence and other violent crimes, and, hopefully, on an international level, thereby affecting peace among nations.

As an advocate of a systems approach to change, I caution people working with or wanting to work with men against viewing this problem as a product of individual pathology or even of interpersonal dysfunction. Such a narrow view creates limited options for the helpers and those in need of their services. When the problem of domestic violence is viewed in broader terms, the options available for solving it effectively open up and are limited only by one's own creative abilities.

Epilogue: One Man's Story

Nik

My name is Nik, and I have had a problem with anger and violence. This is my story. It isn't pretty, but it does have a positive outcome.

The memories of my childhood are not happy ones. There was no abuse of either the children or my mother that I can recall, however, there was violence. The rod was not spared, when we didn't perform as desired. The spankings were done in anger, and belts were used at times.

My parents' relationship can only be defined as unilateral. Dad was the head of the family and as such was above us all. The atmosphere was one of authority and absolute rule. My mother was passive, and the children had no input. There are memories of a great deal of yelling and what I will call psychological violence between them. I don't believe he ever hit her, but I wouldn't bet on it.

I had a recalcitrant relationship with my parents. My brother and I fought constantly. There was little real interaction with my sister. Although I was the first born, I cannot remember feeling any more than second rate and definitely not loved. My brother was deaf and every move the family made centered around him, and I hated him for that. We were at each other's throats, literally, constantly. There was never a family meeting or any opportunity for the family to communicate as a unit. This did nothing but prolong misunderstanding and create resentment. It did nothing to produce a cohesive family circle and provide any nurturing.

Learning about violence was a constant process. I was always the skinny kid the bullies liked to pick on and was forever getting hit by "the big kids." I swore that someday nobody would ever pick on me again. Today I'm six feet tall and weigh 220 pounds with only a small amount of fat. Therein lies some of the conflict I've experienced over the past several years.

My earliest memories of how I felt as a child can best be described as feeling sensitive, loving, and soft. The messages I received were always diametrically opposed to those feelings. You know the standard lines such as, "Big boys don't cry" and "You must learn to control your feelings." I had to be everything my Dad was and be able to do everything just like Dad. Every time I tried, I failed and the results were, "You'll never amount to anything." I was well on my way to proving he was right. I was not like him, although I kept trying to be for 26 years.

There were times that the rage was so intense that I wanted to beat the hell out of him, but I stuffed it deep. The opportunity to express those feelings was never there. If they were to surface, I was punished and told I should not feel that way about my father. I learned early to suppress those feelings and my feelings of softness and sensitivity.

There have been four significant relationships with women in my life. My violence erupted in its fullest during the last. Two of the others had a great deal of psychological abuse, and one was too good so I ran away from it. What that means is that I was accepted as I was, and was able to talk and express my feelings in ways I've never been able to do until now. Success was not in the plan of my life.

The last relationship bore the brunt of the majority of my violent behavior. We met and were living together within six months. That in itself wasn't a problem. The problem was too many outside influences, and we didn't even take real time to develop our friendship. We seldom discussed our differences, and I stifled all my little upsets with her. I was having trouble coping with my oldest daughter's needing psychiatric treatment and with my not feeling as though my partner could understand.

Looking back over those four years, I can only define our relationship as unhealthy love. She was jealous and possessive, and I was "macho" and demanding. She was just coming out of a relationship full of violence. I was her savior on a white horse who would protect her always. I'd never do that to her.

Within two years I had left her three times and just before the third time I battered her and fractured her rib. I left two weeks after that. But I didn't see that as a problem. I left because "she always pissed me off." She wouldn't listen to me or do as I said.

Four and a half months later we were back together and basically as happy as kids with new toys. There were problems, but we "were working on them." We never truly dealt with the real issues for either of us. I can't imagine our therapist's frustration with us. I never faced my anger. I could intellectualize it and say I had unresolved issues with my parents, and so on. Our therapy sessions were usually superficial in that we never did what we needed to do to pull ourselves together. Within a very short time the aggressive acts began again. We often walked out of the sessions facing a potential disaster.

In the late spring I overdosed with a muscle relaxant and alcohol. The drugs came from a back injury I had and the alcohol was the chaser. I dislike the taste of alcohol, which shows my desperation. I was released from the emergency room although I could have been detained under this state's laws.

Our therapist and I knew that I knew the system and I'd be out fast and madder than ever. The problem would not be dealt with properly. Our therapist is a neat lady, and I feel she was really caught in a very difficult position. For a short time afterwards things were good, but the violence returned more frequently and was more serious. I never was violent toward others while under the influence of alcohol or other drugs. It was in me, and in some ways I think it was even more dangerous.

I felt the violence was justified because "she pissed me off," "I lost control," or "she pushed the wrong buttons." But worst of all was "she asked for it" and "she liked it or she wouldn't make me so mad." Our relationship was intense but there was never room to grow, either together or in our individual lives. It was too threatening to either of us. Our own insecurities and lack of self-esteem poisoned any growth as friends or lovers.

Almost a year after getting back together I had a secret plan to kill her. In early December we had a fight which was probably the worst. The violence was hard and fast. We were attacking each other and getting in as many hits and emotional digs as possible. As I was choking her, I realized I was killing her and I wanted to do it. IT STOPPED THERE. I left. I found my own place because I knew I'd finish what I'd started if I stayed. I couldn't risk that. I still didn't recognize my problem.

A month later I heard a radio talk show about men who batter, and it hit me like a sledge hammer. I called for help.

I've been asked about my partner's response. I can only say that after each time she was abused, she felt it wouldn't happen again. When I left, she felt I was running. In a way I *was* running. Each time I was remorseful and she was forgiving. Now we have nothing between us but sadness and hurt.

That January call began a process that I will maintain for the rest of my life. The process itself will change as I grow and will always be something I cannot ignore. The potential will always be there, and I'd be a fool to think that 38 years of anger improperly dealt with will be erased in one year. But the beginning is terrific.

My first feelings of going to group were, "Now I'll get a handle on this in 12 weeks and all the trouble will be over." *Wrong!* After about six weeks I was frantic to change for her. I bought a copy of the workbook we use in group and went to her place to give it to her. "See, this is what I'm doing for you." The reception I got was a shock: as I rounded the corner of the house I was confronted with her and her boyfriend. There was plenty of anger but no physical violence. That experience said that she was more interested in other things, and it was the beginning of my true process of change.

Through this and other experiences with the group I began to *feel* the need to change for myself. I was not happy with me and those feelings began the actual change. Not until this time did I begin to put the program to work for me. There is a definite difference between intellectualizing a problem and feeling it. Now I was feeling and overcoming one of the two big obstacles to my changing.

The other obstacle was confronting a part of me that was 180 degrees out of phase with the image I had of myself. I was sensitive and caring and had a very soft side of me that was not consistent with violence. It took many weeks and much turmoil to accept both sides of myself. But as I began to recognize my anger and deal with it effectively, both sides became accepted.

My self-esteem grew each week that I was not physically aggressive during an angry moment. My self-confidence grew each time that I dealt with my different levels of anger. I was beginning to like me. Part of this process was giving up that euphoric feeling during violence and the fear of giving up my strength, that is, my masculinity.

What is truly amazing to me is how much more "masculine" I feel now. My strength is not in my fist. My strength lies in my self-confidence and the love I have for me as a unique person. It is in the awareness of my feelings and the knowledge that even though I'll experience down times, I have the power to come out of it alive and well. Suicide is a permanent solution to a temporary problem . . . but it isn't worth it. Violence is also not acceptable.

The process of change isn't an easy one. Dealing with an ugliness such as violence in each of us can be very painful, but the rewards are bountiful. We can learn as men that we can control our own lives and that our partners are our best source of support.

The feeling that I am OK is a love that grows endlessly and once felt for ourselves can be truly felt for others. It becomes a love that is healthy and unconditional and free. We begin to see women as partners in life, not as competitors for life. Our masculinity is not in our fists. *It is in our hearts* and in our ability to love, cry, and share our lives with another human being. That is happiness.

To those therapists reading this and to those interested in working in this difficult area, I can't emphasize this point enough. Be confrontational. We don't need Mr. and Ms. Niceperson helping us; you won't be effective. Don't stick to the traditional forms of therapy; they won't work. Do what must be done. If this means a 72-hour hold, do it. It seems we need that shock value. Don't take a chance with someone else's life. It isn't worth the loss. If you have any negative feelings about us, confront them, work them out. If you use any form of violence or abuse in your relationships, you won't do us any good.

We do need the support of other men and the realization that we aren't alone. Most of all we need a place to go and people willing to share new ways to deal with our anger, frustration, and relationships. The problem is not the women we batter; it is us the batterers. Unless we face the problem, all the shelters in the world aren't going to do a damn bit of good in the long run. Provide us with the opportunity to help ourselves.

For myself, I haven't erased the problem. I have learned to deal with it effectively. No one, especially me, will have to experience my violent side again. My own home county is beginning to face the problem, and I am active in developing the program. For the first time in 38 years I am happy with me. My present relationship is one of friendship first and acceptance of each other as individuals. I am happy and I hope others will find their happiness outside of violence.

Appendix

Included in the Appendix are a number of forms we have found helpful in our treatment program, Learning to Live Without Violence. Although these forms are the most recent versions at the time of this printing, we are continually revising them as we encounter new situations that require such revisions. What follows is an explanation of how each form is utilized in assessment and treatment.

A. Welcome to the Group

Each client is required to read, initial, and sign the group rules as a condition of treatment. The client gets a copy and one is included in his file.

B. Confidentiality/Release of Information

Like the group rules, each client is required to read, initial, and sign the confidentiality policy as a condition of treatment. After a preliminary interview, the client is then asked to sign a release of information so that we can contact other significant persons, such as other therapists, probation officers, attorneys, and so on.

C. Facts Women Should Know about Treatment for Male Batterers

This discussion was originally developed for women in shelters who are considering telling their partner to get counseling. Frequently when women would make this request as a condition of their returning home, they would be unclear as to what signs to look for when determining whether treatment was helping their partner. In addition, many women would make the false assumption that because he was in treatment, it was now safe to return home. We now give this form to all of the partners of the men in our program so that they can look for particular signs of positive change as well as clues to danger. We also believe that it is our moral obligation to not imbue false hope as to the length of time it takes to change as well as whether or not change is possible at all.

D. Intake/Assessment Form

One of the most important aspects of assessment is the determination of lethality. Each of the factors discussed earlier in the text is included in this form. In addition, a number of other questions are asked that facilitate the assessment process. The client is given this form at the first interview to complete by the second appointment. Although the form is lengthy, it serves as an introduction to treatment and discussing violence. In addition it serves as a tool for determining motivation for treatment based on whether or not the form is completed or how well it is completed. Clients unable to read the form adequately are interviewed in person over a period of three or four sessions.

E. Anger Inventory

This form may be filled out weekly or daily by each member of the group or each client. The purpose of this inventory is to help men become aware of the various ways in which people deal with anger. This inventory consists of four types of statements:

1. *Directing statements* that represent a person communicating anger directly to another or to themselves or channeling it in a constructive manner that is assertive and positive (Nos. 2, 7, 12, 16, 20, 24).
2. *Stuffing statements* that represent someone trying to deny, minimize, or not acknowledge their anger (Nos. 1, 5, 9, 13, 17, 21).
3. *Escalating statements* that represent someone actually increasing the level of anger as a result of thinking or behavioral patterns (Nos. 4, 6, 10, 15, 18, 22).
4. *Aggressive/psychological violence statements* that represent a person acting aggressively or intimidatingly. Frequently this type of violence continues long after the physical violence stops. When therapists are unaware of this type of violence, they develop a false sense of security as to the success of therapy (Nos. 3, 8, 11, 14, 19, 23).

When clients bring this form to a session, a discussion can develop as to how one can change subtle forms of control and intimidation as well as cope better with anger in general.

F. Violence Inventory

As discussed earlier, at the beginning of each session, clients will report any acts of violence they have committed during the past week. This inventory helps men reflect on this issue and commit to writing their assessment of themselves. A similar form is utilized with their partners over the phone or in person for corroboration of the man's report.

G. Sample Anger Journal

This journal is more fully explained in our book, *Learning to Live Without Violence: A Handbook for Men* (Sonkin & Durphy, 1982). Men are encouraged to fill out this journal at least twice a week, the results of which could be discussed in group.

H. Progress/Termination Reports

These reports are typically utilized with court-referred clients. Such a report includes an assessment of motivation, lethality, and prognosis of treatment. Each report also includes recommendations for future treatment/actions. We discuss the progress of each client routinely every 12 weeks or sooner if necessary. If a man drops out of treatment, probation and his partner are immediately notified by phone and letter.

A. Welcome to the Group

Welcome to Learning to Live Without Violence. The primary goal of this group is to prevent physical, sexual, property, and/or psychological violence in your life by helping you learn to cope with anger, stress, frustration, and anxiety in positive, constructive ways. We also hope to help you better understand yourself as well as your partner through your developing better communication skills and an understanding of what makes relationships work.

In order to reach these goals, we have found it necessary for participants to follow these guidelines:

_____ Your sessions will meet every _____ from _____
to _____ We will meet at _____
_____

_____ If you are more than 15 minutes late to your meeting, or if you need to leave early, *do not* come to the meeting. It is disruptive to the other members.

_____ Each participant is required to make a 12–week commitment to the program. You may miss one session for an emergency. If you miss more than two sessions during any 12–week period, you will be dropped from the program. At the completion of your 12–week commitment, if you want to stay in the group, you will be asked to make another 12–week commitment, and so on. From our experience it takes most men a minimum of six months to a year of counseling before they begin to feel in control of their anger and how they express themselves.

_____ If you are on diversion or probation and need a counseling update for the court, you are to notify us *two weeks* before you need this report. Both the therapists and the group members will discuss with you in person their recommendations to the court/probation. If you stop attending the group before you need this report, we will make our recommendations without discussing them with you first.

_____ If you plan to drop out of the group for any reason, please give two weeks notice before doing so. It is disruptive to the group when members drop out without any notice.

_____ In case of any problems during the week, don't forget to use your phone list of the other group members, as well as your counselors. Reach out if there is a crisis; that's what we're there for.

Once again, welcome to Learning to Live Without Violence. Should you have any questions or concerns, feel free to call us at any time at the numbers listed below.

                                                                    Good Luck!

I have read the above rules and agree to these conditions of treatment.

_____   _____
        Client Name   Signature

_____
        Date

Source: Michael Searle, M.A., (415–921–8506) and Daniel Sonkin, Ph.D., (415–332–9100).

B. Confidentiality Policy

_____ All statements that you make (both written and verbal) while in counseling are *confidential.* No information will be released to anyone without your written or verbal consent. This is your right.

_____ If you are on diversion or probation, you will be asked to sign a release
of information form so that your probation officer will be kept aware
of your progress in the program. Only the following information will be
released:

   1. Attendance
   2. Participation in treatment
   3. Additional acts of violence

If there are additional acts of violence, we will encourage *you* to notify your probation officer first. If you are unable or unavailable to do
so, we will contact that person.

_____ If you and your partner are seeing another counselor, we will ask you
and your partner for permission to speak to that counselor. Of course,
you have the right to refuse, but the more closely the counselors work
together, the more we will be able to help you. In some cases, this contact may be a condition of treatment.

_____ If you are seeing another counselor by yourself, we may also want to
speak to that person so that we are working together. Again, it is your
right to refuse this consent and it may also be a condition of treatment.

_____ If you continue to have letter, phone, or in-person contact with your
partner, or get involved in a new relationship, we will want to have
contact with that person(s). Through these conversations we will continue to respect your confidentiality by only discussing your progress
in the program with regard to taking time-outs, additional acts of violence, and the risk of continued violence. We will not discuss the spe-
cifics of what you say in session that are not relevant to these issues.

_____ If you are seeking treatment on your own, that is, not referred by the
courts, and there are additional acts of violence, we will inform and
encourage your partner (or the person you have been violent with) to
utilize the police and the courts for relief.

THERE ARE SEVERAL INSTANCES WHEN WE *WILL* VIOLATE CONFIDENTIALITY WITHOUT YOUR PERMISSION.

_____ 1. If it is assessed during your participation in this program that abuse
or neglect of children is occurring, we will report this to the Department of Social Services and the Police. We will make an attempt to
let you know when we are going to make such a report. We will also
encourage you to report yourself.

_____ 2. If you threaten to kill or harm another person in our presence, while you are in this program, we are obligated to warn the potential victim as well as notify the police. We will attempt to tell you if we are going to do this.

_____ 3. If you commit a criminal offense while you are in this program, we may report such information to the police and/or probation. We will encourage you to do the same. In such cases we may be subpoenaed by the court and have to violate confidentiality.

_____ 4. If at any time during the course of treatment we determine that you are a danger to yourself or another person, we will inform you of that opinion and in the case of the latter we will also inform that other person. In some cases this may also include notifying the police.

As it is your privilege to have guaranteed confidentiality, so it is your fellow group members'. Please respect their right to confidentiality. Always ask first before discussing someone else's thoughts outside the group.

Thanks!

I have read the above confidentiality policy and agree to these conditions of treatment.

_____   _____
            Client Name   Signature

_____
             Date

Source: Michael Searle, M.A., (415–921–8506) and Daniel Sonkin, Ph.D., (415–332–9100).

Release of Information

I authorize Daniel Jay Sonkin and/or Michael Searle to release the following
information to _____

_____

_____

_____   1. Attendance
_____   2. Participation in treatment
_____   3. Additional acts of violence
_____   4. Information relevant to enhancing treatment.

_____   _____
              Date   Signature

                                 _____
                                          Client Name

C. Facts Women Should Know about
Treatment for Male Batterers

For the past five years, treatment programs for male batterers have opened
across the country. Programs in the Bay Area have been leaders in this new field
of counseling. We are still learning new information on effective counseling
techniques; however, there are some facts we think you may find helpful.

- Over 50 percent of the men who come into treatment do so because
  the courts have told them to seek counseling. Many of the men whom
  we have worked with have said that they would not have been there
  had they not been forced by the criminal justice system.
- Forty percent of the men we have worked with were in treatment because their partner had left them and gone to a battered women's
  shelter and told them to either get help or she would not return to the
  relationship.
- A few men (less than 10 percent) will seek treatment on their own
  without the courts or their wife/partner telling them to do so.

Although we are making great progress in helping male batterers, it is important
for you to know that just because your partner is in treatment, that doesn't
mean that the violence will necessarily stop. We can give your partner tools and
techniques to stop the violence and manage his anger differently; however, he
has to *want* to stop the violence. In this way counseling will help only those men
who want to be helped.

Many women are disappointed when their partner does go to counseling but
still continues to batter them. For the majority of men who continue to be violent, it is not because they are sick or crazy; it's simply because there is a part of
them that really doesn't want to change. If he continues to batter you and/or
your children, you will need to ask yourself a question at some point. Am I willing to stay in a violent relationship? The answer to that question will be different for each woman.

If your partner is looking for a counselor, it is important that he look for
one with a particular philosophy and approach. Over the years we have found
that traditional counseling does not necessarily stop the violent behavior. Below
are a few points found to be effective in counseling these men:

- The first goal of counseling needs to be stopping the violence. This is
  best done through the use of anger–management techniques.
- Group and/or individual counseling for the man who is battering has
  been found to be the most effective means to stopping violence.

- Couples counseling should be undertaken only when the batterer is already in a program that focuses on stopping violent behavior and learning anger–management skills.
- Anger-management skills can take six months to a year to master. One cannot unlearn years of conditioning in a few weeks. If he drops out of counseling too soon, you may be at greater risk for being battered.
- Women need to view violence as the responsibility of the batterer. You don't make him violent. You may make him angry, just as he makes you angry sometimes; but what he does with that anger is his own choice.

When women come to shelters, their partners are frequently willing to do anything to get them back. This may include going to counseling. We want to caution women about returning too soon. When women return after their partner has been in counseling for only a few sessions, some men will interpret their returning as "Everything is okay now; I don't need any more counseling." At this point many men will drop out of counseling and the violence continues. We encourage women to stay away as long as possible to give the man the chance to be in counseling for himself, not because he wants to get his partner back. He has to want to stop the violence himself. Although it may be hard being away from home and he seems like he really means it when he says, "I'll never do it again," wait—give it some time.

Many women ask, "How can I tell if he is changing?" Here are a few ways.

- Is he trying to get you to come home, or does he understand that you are afraid of him and need some time away to become stronger and feel better about yourself?
- Does he blame you and call you names, or can he communicate his anger in direct nonintimidating ways?
- Does he just get himself more and more angry, or does he tell you he needs to cool off, calm down, and he will call you back when he does so?
- Does he get quiet and moody, or does he express his feelings clearly to you?
- Does he blame you for his violent behavior, or does he take responsibility for his actions?
- Is he only interested in when you are coming home, or does he talk about what he is learning in counseling?

These are but a few indications that a person is changing. It is important to take your time in deciding when to go back.

One of the most common anger–management techniques used today is the "time-out." Men are taught to identify their anger through physical (tension in the stomach, neck, etc.) and behavioral (yelling, getting quiet, etc.) signs. Whenever they feel these signs of anger, they tell their partner, "I am feeling angry and I'm going to take a time-out." They are then to leave the situation for an hour and cool off. When they come back they are to talk about what it was that made them angry. In this way they don't let the conversation get out of control to the point where violence is possible. Many women support the idea of a time-out, but find it difficult to stop talking when they are trying to make a point and let their partner leave. You may feel like you're left hanging. However, we need to remind you that the priority is to stop violence; therefore, some issues may have to be put on the back burner. For further information on this technique, or other ways of managing anger, read *Learning to Live Without Violence: A Handbook for Men,* by Daniel Sonkin and Michael Durphy, published by Volcano Press in San Francisco, California.

We hope these tips are helpful in your desire to live a life free of violence. Below are the names and phone numbers of domestic violence counseling programs for men in the Bay Area.

Bay Area Domestic Violence
Men's Programs/Services

San Francisco (City & County)

Center for
Special Problems   558-4801

Family Violence Project   552-6554

Learning to Live
Without Violence   332-9100

Men Overcoming
Violence (MOVE)   626-MOVE

Alameda County

Oak Knoll Naval
Hospital (Active
Duty Navy & Marines)   633-5392

Psychological Services
Center (Berkeley)   486-0840

San Leandro Community
Counseling (San Leandro)   352-5431

Violence Abatement
Training (Livermore)   229-3450

West Oakland Mental
Health (Oakland)   465-1800

Vet Center–Anger
Management Group   763-3904

Marin County

Marin Abused Women's
Services Men's Program   924-1070

Napa County

Effective Anger Resolution
Services (EARS)   707-253-1216

Contra Costa County

Battered Woman's
Alternatives (Concord)   676-2968

Sonoma County

Men Evolving Non-
violently (MEN)   707-528-2MEN

Santa Clara County

Mid Peninsula Support
Network Men's Program   964-2266

D. Intake/Assessment Form

The following form was developed to make the intake process easier for men entering our program. The questions are designed so that minimum writing is necessary; however, we ask you to elaborate on questions when requested. This form makes our work easier in that it standardizes the information we have on each of our clients. Hopefully it will begin to get you thinking about domestic violence and how it relates to your life. This form is a part of your confidential file and it is available for your review at any time.

Thank you.

Name _____

Address (home) _____ (work) _____

_____ _____

_____ _____

Company Name _____

Phone (home) _____ (work) _____ (message) _____

Age _____

Marital Status: _____ Married _____ Not Married _____ Separated _____

Living Situation: _____ Live with Partner _____ Live Alone _____

Race _____ Religion _____

Occupation _____

Presently Employed? _____ Yes _____ No

Income (monthly–approximate) _____

Dependants: _____ Children _____ (number)

_____ Spouse _____ Other

The following section pertains to you when you were a child up to the time you left home.

Parents' Marital Status: ____ Married ____ Divorced ____ Separated _____

If divorced or separated, at what age did it occur? _____

Father's Occupation: _____

Mother's Occupation: _____

How would you describe your relationship with your father? _____Close

_____Distant   How so? _____

_____

_____

How would you describe your relationship with your mother? _____Close

_____Distant   How so? _____

_____

_____

Number of *older* brothers _____

Number of *older* sisters _____

Number of *younger* brothers _____

Number of *younger* sisters _____

Were you ever physically punished as a child? _____ Yes _____No

If yes, please explain. _____

_____

_____

_____

Did you consider yourself physically or psychologically abused as a child?

_____ Yes _____ No   If yes, please explain. _____

_____

_____

_____

Did you ever know of or observe your father physically, sexually, or psychologically abuse your mother or destroy property in a fit of anger? _____ Yes

_____ No   If yes, please explain. _____

_____

_____

_____

_____

_____

Did you ever physically attack one of your parents? _____ Yes _____ No

If yes, please explain. _____

_____

_____

_____

Were any of your brothers or sisters physically, sexually, or psychologically abused as children? _____ Yes _____ No   If yes, please explain.

_____

_____

_____

_____

Who was the primary disciplinarian in your family? _____ Father

_____Mother   Comments _____

_____

_____

Have you ever been a victim of sexual assault by a member of your family or anyone outside your family? _____ Yes _____ No If yes, please

explain. _____

_____

_____

_____

Did you have any problems with violent behavior as a child or teenager?

_____Yes _____ No If yes, please explain. _____

_____

_____

_____

Did any of your brothers or sisters have problems with violent behavior while they were growing up? _____ Yes _____ No If yes, please explain.

_____

_____

_____

Briefly explain how you left home to live on your own. _____

_____

_____

_____

Were there any other events or circumstances regarding your childhood that may help us understand your particular counseling needs? _____ Yes _____ No

If yes, please explain. _____

_____

_____

_____

The following section pertains to your intimate relationships/marriages *prior to* your current or most recent relationship/marriage.

Have you ever been married before? _____ Yes _____ No If yes, how many times? _____

How many intimate relationships (other than marriages) have you had in your life prior to the current relationship (if applicable)? _____

Have you done any of the following in any of these relationships? Please check if it happened once, twice, three times, or more than three times.

	Once	Twice	Three Times	More Than Three Times
Slap				
Grab				
Punch				
Push				
Kick				
Push to ground				

	Once	Twice	Three Times	More Than Three Times
Choke				
Bite				
Pull hair				
Twist arm				
Pin to ground or wall				
Hold				
Hit with object				
Beat up				
Use gun				
Use knife				
Use other weapon				
Force to have sexual intercourse				
Force to have other sexual activity				
Force to have sex with other people, objects, animals				
Break objects				
Throw objects				
Break down door				
Throw food				

	Once	Twice	Three Times	More Than Three Times
Punch fist through wall				
Harm or neglect pet				
Threaten to hit or abuse				
Threaten to destroy property				
Threaten to sexually abuse				
Express intense jealousy				
Threaten to kill				
Threaten to commit suicide				
Force partner to do something against her will				
Tell her/him what she/he can and cannot do				
Be verbally aggressive				

Were any of these women pregnant when you did any of the above acts?

_____ Yes _____ No If yes, please explain. _____

_____

_____

Have you ever tried to control the violence in the past? _____ Yes _____ No

If yes, please explain. _____

_____

_____

_____

What kinds of injuries have your partners in the past sustained as a result of the above violence? _____ Knocked or choked unconscious _____ Bleeding _____ Swelling _____ Wounds from use of weapons _____ Broken nose _____ Broken bones _____ Scratches _____ Bruises _____ Black eye _____ Muscle sprains _____ Needed surgery _____ Other _____

Have you ever sought professional help in the past to stop the violence? _____ Yes _____ No If yes, please explain. _____

_____

_____

_____

The following questions refer to your present or most recent relationship or marriage.

Name of partner _____

Her address (home) _____ (work) _____

_____   _____

_____   _____

(Name of Company)   _____

Phone (home) _____ (work) _____ (message) _____

Occupation _____

Presently employed _____ Yes _____ No

Income (monthly–approximate) _____

Children (names, sex, and ages) _____

_____

_____

_____

Race _____ Religion _____

Length of marriage _____ Length living together _____

Length of relationship _____

_____

How many episodes of violence have there been in the last year of the relationship?

Physical _____ Property _____

Sexual _____ Psychological _____

How frequent have these incidents been, in the last six months? _____

_____

_____

_____

How soon after you met your current partner did the physical violence begin?

_____

_____

_____

Have you noticed that the violence is increasing in frequency over time?

_____ Yes _____ No   If yes, please explain. _____

_____

_____

_____

Have you noticed that the violence is increasing in severity over time? _____ Yes

_____ No   If yes, please explain. _____

_____

_____

_____

What do you and your partner argue over most? Rate in terms of frequency.

1—Very frequent   2—Frequent   3—Sometimes   4—Rarely   5—Never

_____   Housekeeping

_____   Sex

_____   Socializing

_____   Moncy

_____   Children

_____ Commitment to relationship

_____ Ways of talking to each other

Who has the final say on: (1—Wife   2—Husband   3—Both)

_____ Buying a car

_____ Having children

_____ What house or apartment to choose

_____ What job your wife/husband should take

_____ Whether you should go to work or quit work

_____ How much money a week to spend on food

_____ How much money to spend a week on entertainment

_____ Where to go out for an evening

_____ When to have sex

_____ How to discipline the children

_____ Whether or not your wife/husband can go out for the evening

_____ Whether or not to spend the holidays with relatives

Have any of your children been involved in or observed any violent episodes between you and your partner? _____ Yes _____ No If yes, please explain. _____

_____

_____

_____

Do any of your children have behavior problems at home? _____ Yes _____ No If yes, please explain. _____

_____

_____

_____

_____

Do any of your children have behavior problems at school? _____ Yes

_____ No   If yes, please explain. _____

_____

_____

_____

Do any of your children have problems relating to other children outside the

home? _____ Yes _____ No   If yes, please explain. _____

_____

_____

_____

Do any of your children have any ongoing medical or physical problems?

_____ Yes _____ No   If yes, please explain. _____

_____

_____

_____

Do any of your children act violently toward each other, you, or your partner?

_____ Yes _____ No   If yes, please explain. _____

_____

_____

_____

Do you ever physically punish the children in your household? _____ Yes

_____ No   If yes, please explain. _____

_____

_____

_____

Do you live in the same house with either your parents or your partner's parents?

_____ Yes _____ No   If yes, please explain. _____

_____

Are these parents able to take care of themselves?_____ Yes _____ No
If no, please explain. _____

_____

_____

_____

What kinds of problems do you encounter in this living situation?_____

_____

_____

_____

How do you deal with these problems? _____

_____

_____

Have you ever used physical force with these persons? _____ Yes _____ No
If yes, please explain. _____

_____

_____

_____

Do you own or have in your possession firearms, knives, or any other kinds of
weapons? _____ Yes _____ No If yes, please explain. _____

_____

_____

_____

Would you be willing to remove these weapons from the home while you are in
this program? _____ Yes _____ No Please explain. If no, state reason; if
yes, state how you will arrange for the removal of these weapons. _____

_____

_____

_____

Have you ever done any of the following to your current or most recent partner?
Check if the act has happened once, twice, three times or more than three times.

	Once	Twice	Three Times	More Than Three Times
Slap				
Grab				
Punch				
Push				
Kick				
Push to ground				
Choke				
Bite				
Pull hair				
Twist arm				
Pin to ground or wall				
Hold				
Hit with object				
Beat up				
Use gun				
Use knife				
Use other weapon				
Force to have sexual intercourse				

	Once	Twice	Three Times	More Than Three Times
Force to have other sexual activity				
Force to have sex with other people, objects, animals				
Break objects				
Throw objects				
Break down door				
Throw food				
Punch fist through wall				
Harm or neglect pet				
Threaten to hit or abuse				
Threaten to destroy property				
Threaten to sexually abuse				
Express intense jealousy				
Threaten to kill				
Threaten to commit suicide				
Force partner to do something against her will				
Tell her/him what she/he can and cannot do				
Be verbally aggressive				

Did any of these acts occur while your partner was pregnant? _____ Yes _____ No If yes, please explain. _____

_____

_____

_____

What kinds of injuries has your partner sustained as a result of these acts of violence? Knocked or choked unconscious _____ Bleeding _____

Swelling _____ Wounds from use of weapons _____ Broken nose _____

Broken bones _____ Scratches _____ Bruises _____ Black eye _____

Muscle sprains _____ Needed surgery _____ Other _____

To the best of your ability, we would like you to recount the last conflict situation when any of the above acts took place. Take your time to think about it and try to remember the details. If you can't remember the details, write down what you can remember.

What were the initiating circumstances? _____

_____

_____

_____

How did your anger escalate? _____

_____

_____

_____

Were there any weapons involved? _____ Yes _____ No If yes, please explain. _____

_____

_____

_____

_____

Describe the physical, sexual, property, or psychological violence that occurred.

_____

_____

_____

Were there any injuries? _____ Yes _____ No If yes, please explain.

_____

_____

_____

Did you or your partner use alcohol or other drugs prior to or during this incident? _____ Yes _____ No If yes, please explain. _____

_____

_____

_____

Was there any outside intervention during this episode? Did someone try to stop it (children, friends, neighbors, or the police)? _____ Yes _____ No If yes, please explain. _____

_____

_____

_____

Were the children involved in or did they observe this incident? _____ Yes _____ No If yes, please explain. _____

_____

_____

_____

Were the police called after this incident? _____ Yes _____ No If yes, please explain. _____

_____

_____

_____

Check off what acts of violence occurred in this incident. Check whether the act occurred once, twice, or repeatedly.

Acts of Violence	Once	Twice	Repeatedly
Slap			
Grab			
Punch			
Push			
Kick			
Push to ground			
Choke			
Bite			
Pull hair			
Twist arm			
Pin to ground or wall			
Hold			
Hit with object			
Beat up			
Use gun			
Use knife			
Other weapon			
Force to have sexual intercourse			
Force to have other sexual activity			

	Once	Twice	Repeatedly
Force to have sex with other people, objects, animals			
Break objects			
Throw objects			
Break down door			
Throw food			
Punch fist through wall			
Harm or neglect pet			
Threaten to hit or abuse			
Threaten to destroy property			
Threaten to sexually abuse			
Express intense jealousy			
Threaten to kill			
Threaten to commit suicide			
Force partner to do something against her will			
Tell her/him what she/he can and cannot do			
Be verbally aggressive			

Have you, your partner or any member of your families ever attempted suicide?

_____ Yes _____ No If yes, please explain. _____

_____

_____

Have you ever received counseling or psychotherapy? _____ Yes _____ No

If yes, please explain. _____

_____

_____

Are you currently seeing another counselor? _____ Yes _____ No If yes,

please explain. _____

_____

_____

Have you ever been hospitalized for mental health reasons? _____ Yes

_____ No If yes, please explain. _____

_____

_____

Do you have any ongoing physical health problems? _____ Yes _____ No

If yes, please explain. _____

_____

_____

Have you had any serious accidents or illnesses in the past? _____ Yes

_____ No If yes, please explain. _____

_____

_____

Do you drink alcohol? _____ Yes _____ No If yes, what kind do you

drink? _____

How often do you drink? _____

How much do you drink at a time? _____

How often do you get drunk or loaded? _____

_____

If you do not drink, did you ever drink? _____Yes _____No If yes, why
did you stop? _____

_____

_____

Do you use drugs? _____ Yes _____No If yes, what kind do you use?

_____

_____

How much do you use at a time? _____

_____

How often do you use these drugs? _____

_____

If you do not use drugs, have you ever used them? _____ Yes _____No
If yes, please explain why you stopped _____

_____

_____

Have you ever used violence while under the influence of alcohol or other
drugs? _____Yes _____ No

Have you ever used violence while *not* under the influence of alcohol or other
drugs? _____ Yes _____No

Have you or are you currently in the military? _____ Yes _____No If yes,
please explain _____

_____

_____

_____

Did you serve during a wartime situation? _____ Yes _____No If yes, please
explain _____

_____

_____ Combat duty or _____ Noncombat duty?

Were you a prisoner of war? _____ Yes _____ No If yes, please explain.

_____

_____

_____

Did you receive combat or noncombat injuries? _____ Yes _____ No If

yes, please explain. _____

_____

_____

_____

Did you receive an honorable discharge? _____ Yes _____ No If no, please

explain. _____

_____

_____

_____

Have you ever been violent in situations *not* involving your family?

_____ Yes _____ No If yes, please explain. _____

_____

_____

_____

Are you presently involved with the criminal justice system? _____ Yes

_____ No If yes, please explain. _____

_____

_____

_____

Have you ever been found guilty of a crime in the past? _____ Yes

_____ No If yes, please explain. _____

_____

_____

Have you ever been arrested in the past? _____ Yes _____ No If yes, please explain. _____

_____

_____

_____

Have you ever been in a diversion program before? _____ Yes _____ No If yes, please explain. _____

_____

_____

_____

Who are your current sources of support, understanding, and assistance (for example, family, friends, co-workers)? Please be specific. _____

_____

_____

_____

How often do you see these persons? _____

_____

_____

_____

Do you consider yourself isolated or a loner? _____ Yes _____ No If yes, please explain. _____

_____

_____

_____

Do you feel your use of violence is an acceptable way of solving conflict and/or disagreements? _____ Yes _____ No If yes, please explain. _____

_____

_____

_____

Please list three things you would like to learn from counseling. _____

_____

_____

Who referred you to this program?

Name: _____

Agency: _____

Address: _____

_____

_____

Phone: _____

This space is for any additional comments you would like to make about your

situation. _____

_____

_____

_____

_____

_____

_____

_____

E. Anger Inventory

Check off the statements that best describe the various ways you dealt with your anger in the past week. We want you to include low level anger such as annoyance, irritation; medium level feelings of anger; and high levels of anger such as rage, fury, or explosion. Check off as many of the statements as have applied to you during the past week.

_____ I pretended it didn't bother me when it really did bother me.
_____ I took a time-out.
_____ I was nonverbally threatening, frightening, or aggressive.
_____ I thought how he/she was against me.
_____ I decided not to show I was angry.
_____ I decided it was his/her fault that I got angry.
_____ I did some physical exercise.
_____ I tried to find something wrong with her/him.
_____ I thought that I was wrong for feeling angry.
_____ I thought how he/she was trying to make me seem wrong.
_____ I put her/him down verbally.
_____ I told her/him I was feeling angry.
_____ I got real quiet.
_____ I swore at her/him.
_____ I screamed at her/him.
_____ I told myself I was feeling angry at her/him.
_____ I told myself I shouldn't be feeling angry.
_____ I told her/him that *she/he* made me feel angry.
_____ I verbally threatened to hit her/him.
_____ I thought of ways I could control my temper.
_____ I thought that they wouldn't like me if I got angry.
_____ I gave her/him the third degree.
_____ I bossed her/him around.
_____ I took a deep breath and tried to relax.

_____   _____
              Your Name   Today's Date

F. Violence Inventory

Below is a list of physical, sexual, property, and psychological violence acts. Check off any of the acts that you have perpetrated during the last week or since you last attended counseling. Check off whether this act occurred once, twice, or three times or more during the week. Also indicate in the space provided who or what was the target of the violence.

	Once	Twice	Three or More	Person or Object
Slap				
Grab				
Punch				
Push				
Kick/knee				
Push to ground				
Choke				
Bite				
Stand or sit on				
Burn				
Try to drown				
Pull hair				
Twist arm				
Bang head or body against the wall				
Pin to ground				

	Once	Twice	Three or More	Person or Object
Pin against wall				
Hold				
Claw or scratch				
Drive over with vehicle				
Attack with knife				
Attack with gun				
Attack with other object or weapon				
Force to have sexual intercourse				
Force to have sex with objects				
Force to have sex with animals				
Force to have sex with other people				
Force into prostitution				
Break objects				
Throw objects				
Hit objects				
Punch fist through wall				
Pound fist on table				
Harm or neglect pet				

	Once	Twice	Three or More	Person or Object
Threaten to hit or abuse				
Threaten to sexually abuse				
Threaten to destroy property				
Express intense jealousy				
Act intimidating				
Try to frighten				
Be verbally aggressive				
Threaten to kill				
Threaten to commit suicide				
Try to control them				
Verbally insult or put down				

_____   _____
     Your Name   Today's Date

G. Sample Anger Journal

DATE	3/17/82	3/18/82
INTENSITY (1-10)	4	1
PHYSICAL SIGNS	Muscles tight arround forehead. Tense in chest & arms	STOMACH ACHED A little.
BEHAVIOR SIGNS	Raised voice; started pacing the floor. Making a fist.	STARTED MAKE FUN OF MY WIFE.
SITUATION	My wife came home late. It was my birthday and we were supposed to go out for dinner.	SHE WANTED ME TO TAKE SOME PAPERS TO BE XEROXED, WHEN I DION'T HAVE TIME TO DO IT.
Did you take a "Time-Out"?	✓Yes ___No **Comments** 1hour	✓Yes ___No **Comments** 1 hour
Did you Stuff it?	✓Yes ___No **Comments** AT FIRST—THEN DIRECTED IT	✓Yes ___No **Comments** AT FIRST, THEN TOOK A TIME-OUT
Did you Escalate it?	___Yes ✓No **Comments**	___Yes ✓No **Comments**
Did you Direct it?	✓Yes ___No **Comments**	✓Yes ___No **Comments** WHEN I TOOK MY TIME-OUT
"I" Statements	I'm feeling ANGRY that you CAME home lATE. I'M GOING TO TAKE A TIME-OUT	I'm feeling ANGRY. I NEED TO GET AWAY. I DON'T WANT TO GET VIOLENT.
Physical Activity	WALK THE DOG.	Bicycle to GROCERY STORE.
Alcohol or Drug use--6 hours before or after?	___Yes ✓No **Comments**	___Yes ✓No **Comments**

H. Progress Report

TO: _____
               _____
               _____
               _____

FROM: Daniel Sonkin/Michael Searle

RE: _____

DATE: _____

_____ has been in our domestic violence program for

(_____ 12; _____ 24; _____ 36; _____ 52; _____(____)) weeks. His

attendance has been (_____ Poor; _____ Fair; _____ Good; _____ Ex-

cellent). Comments: _____

_____

_____

_____

In our opinion the dangerousness/risk of this client in his/her present situation

is: (_____ Nonexistent; _____ Relatively Low; _____ Low to Moderate;

_____ Moderate; _____ High). Comments: _____

_____

_____

_____

Number of Reoffenses: _____ Physical; _____ Sexual; _____ Property;

_____ Psychological. Comments: _____

_____

_____

_____

We recommend the following action be taken on this case: _____ Continue group, individual, couple, family treatment; _____ Terminate group, individual, couple, family treatment; _____ Substance-abuse treatment needed; _____Continue substance-abuse treatment; _____Terminate substance-abuse treatment; _____ Refer for group, individual, couple, family treatment; Other: _____

Comments: _____

_____

_____

_____

Termination Report

TO: _____

           _____

           _____

           _____

FROM: Daniel Sonkin/Michael Searle

RE: _____

DATE: _____

This letter is to notify you that _____ is no longer
in our domestic violence treatment program. This client's termination was for
the following reasons: (_____ Program Completed; _____ Lack of Attendance; _____ Lack of Motivation; _____ Continual Reoffenses;
_____ Poor Participation; _____ Substance-Abuse Problem; _____ Lack
of Cooperation; Other: _____
It is our opinion that the dangerousness/risk of this client in his/her present
situation is: (_____ Nonexistent; _____ Relatively Low; _____ Low to
Moderate; _____ Moderate; _____ Moderate to High; _____ High) for
the following reasons: _____

_____

_____

_____

We recommend the following action be taken on this case: _____

_____

_____

_____

If you have any questions or need additional information, feel free to call us at
these numbers (below) at any time.

Source: Michael Searle, M.A., (415-921-8506) and Daniel Sonkin, Ph.D., (415-332-9100).

References

Adams, D. C., & McCormick, A. J. (1982). Men unlearning violence: A group approach. Based on the collective model. In Roy, M. (Ed.), *The abusing partner: An analysis of domestic battering*. New York: Van Nostrand Reinhold.

American Psychiatric Association. (1981). *Diagnostic and statistical manual of mental disorders* (3rd ed.). Washington, DC: Author.

Baker, R., & Ball, S. (1969). *Man, media and violence* (Vol. IX). Washington, DC: U.S. Government Printing Office.

Balsam, N., Ferry, M., & Przybeck, R. (1984). "Necessaries Doctrine" as possible source of shelter funding. *The Women's Advocate*, July.

Bandura, A. (1973). *Aggression: A social learning analysis*. Englewood Cliffs, NJ: Prentice-Hall.

Bandura, A., Ross, D., & Ross, S. (1963). Transmission of aggression through imitation of aggressive models. *Journal of Abnormal Social Psychology, 66*, 3–11.

Bard, M., & Zacker, J. (1974). Assaultiveness and alcohol use in family disputes. *Criminology, 12*(3), 283–292.

Barnard, G. W., Vera, H., Vera, M., & Newman, G. (1982). Til death do us part: A study of spouse murder. *Bulletin of the American Academy of Psychiatry, 10*(4), 270–280.

Barry, K. (1979). *Female sexual slavery*. Englewood Cliffs, NJ: Prentice-Hall.

Battered Women's Alternatives. (1984). Concord, California.

Bende, P. D. (1980). Prosecuting women who use force in self defense: Investigative considerations. *Peace Officers Law Report*, California Department of Justice, December, 8–14.

Blackstone, W. (1966). *Commentaries on the law of England*. Dobbs Ferry, NY: Oceana. (Originally published, 1765).

Bograd, M. (1983). *Excuses and justifications: How abusive couples under-*

stand violence. Presented at 91st Annual Convention of the American Psychological Association, Anaheim, CA.

Bourdouris, J. (1971). Homicide in the family. *Journal of Marriage and the Family, 33,* 667–676.

Bowen, G. L. (1983). Spouse abuse: Incidence and dynamics. *Military Family,* 3,(6) 4–6.

Broverman, I. K., Broverman, D. M., Clarkson, F. E., Rosenkrantz, P. S., & Vogel, S. (1970). Sex role stereotypes and clinical judgments of mental health. *Journal of Consulting and Clinical Psychology, 34*(1), 1–7.

Browne, A. (1984). Assault and homicide at home: When battered women kill. In M. J. Saks & Saxe, L. (Eds.), *Advances in Applied Social Psychology: Vol. 3.* Hillsdale, NJ: Lawrence Erlbaum Associates, Inc.

Carrillo, R. (1983). *The male batterer: A multivariate social learning analysis.* Doctoral dissertation, California School of Professional Psychology, Fresno, CA.

Carsenat, G. (1975). *Project interval house submission #1.* Toronto, Canada.

Check, J. V. P., & Malamuth, N. M. (1983). *The hostility toward women scale.* Paper presented at the 91st Annual Convention of the American Psychological Association, Anaheim, CA.

Chodorow, N. (1974). Family structure and feminine personality. In M. Rosaldo, and L. Lamphere (Eds.), *Woman, culture and society.* Palo Alto, CA: Stanford University Press.

Cline, V. B., Croft, R. G., & Courrier, S. (1973). Desensitization of children to television violence. *Journal of Personality and Social Psychology, 27,* 360–365.

Coleman, K. H. (1980). Conjugal violence: What 33 men report. *Journal of Marriage and Family Therapy, 6,* 207–213.

Cook, D. R., & Cook, A. F. (1984). A systemic treatment approach to wife battering. *Journal of Marriage and Family Therapy, 10*(1), 83–93.

C.S.A.T.P. (Child Sexual Abuse Treatment Program). (1982). San Rafael, CA.

DeCrow, K. (1974). *Sexist justice.* New York: Random House.

Deerings California Penal Code. (1983). San Francisco: Bancroft-Whitney.

Delacourt, T., Kinsey, J., & Halas, S. (1981). *How to get free press.* San Francisco: Harbor.

Deschner, J. (1984). The hitting habit: Anger control for battering couples. New York: Free Press.

Dinnerstein, D. (1976). *The mermaid and the minotaur.* New York: Harper & Row.

Dobash, R. E., & Dobash, R. (1978). Wives: The "Appropriate" victims. *Victimology, 2*(3-4), 426–442.

Dobash, R. E., & Dobash, R. (1979). *Violence against wives: A case against the patriarchy.* New York: Free Press.

Dolan, D. Personal communication. Family Service Agency of Marin County, California.

Douglas, C. A. (1983). MacKinnon on feminist theory. *Off Our Backs*, May.

Durbin, S., & Letko, C. (1977). Battered women: A social psychological perspective. In M. Roy (Ed.), *Battered women: A psychosocial study of domestic violence*. New York: Van Nostrand Reinhold.

Edleson, J. (1984). Working with men who batter. *Social Work, 3*, 237–242.

Eisenberg, S. E., & Micklow, P. (1979). The assaulted wife: "Catch-22" revisited. *Women's Rights Law Reporter, 3*, 138–161.

Erickson, M. H., & Rossi, E. L. (1979). *Hypnotherapy: An exploratory case book*. New York: Irvington.

Errington, G. (1977). *Family violence—Is it a woman's problem?* Paper presented at the United Way Symposium on Family Violence, Vancouver, BC.

Elbow, M. (1977). Theoretical considerations of violent marriages. *Social Casework*, Nov., 515–526.

Elliot, F. A. (1976). The neurology of explosive rage: The dyscontrol syndrome. *The Practitioner*, July, 217.

Evans, P. (1973). Do pugilists have more fun? *Cosmopolitan*, May.

Ewing, J. A. (1972). Addictions. II: Non-narcotic addictive agents. In A. M. Freeman & H. I. Kaplan (Eds.), *Comprehensive textbook of psychiatry*. Baltimore: Williams & Wilkins.

Fagan, J. A., Stewart, D. K., & Hansen, K. V. (1983). Violent men or violent husbands? In D. Finkelhor, R. J. Gelles, G. T. Hotaling, & M. A. Straus (Eds.), *The dark side of families: Current family violence research*. Beverly Hills: Sage.

Falk, M. (1977). Men who assault their wives. In M. Roy (Ed.), *Battered women: A psychosocial study of domestic violence*. New York: Van Nostrand Reinhold.

Feshback, S. (1976). Dynamics of morality of violence and aggression: Some psychological considerations. *American Psychologist, 26*, 281–291.

Feshback, S. (1978). *Sex, aggression and violence toward women*. Paper presented at the American Psychological Association, Toronto, Canada.

Fields, M., & Kirschner, R. (1978). Battered women are still in need: A reply to Steinmetz. *Victimology, 3*(1–2), 216–222.

Flanzer, J. P. (1982). Alcohol and family violence: Double trouble. In Roy, M. (Ed.), *The abusing partner: An analysis of domestic battering*. New York: Van Nostrand Reinhold.

Fleming, J. B. (1979). *Stopping wife abuse*. Garden City, NJ: Anchor/Doubleday.

Freud, S. (1905). Three essays on the theory of sexuality. *Complete psychological works of Sigmund Freud* (Standard Edition, Vol. 7).

Ganley, A. L. (1981). *Court-mandated counseling for men who batter (participants and trainer's manuals)*. Washington, DC: Center for Women's Policy Studies.

Ganley, A. L. & Harris, L. (1978). *Domestic violence: Issues in designing and implementing programs for male batterers.* Paper presented at the American Psychological Association, Toronto, Canada.

Garnet, S. & Moss, D. (1982). How to set up a counseling program for self-referred batterers: The AWAIC model. In M. Roy (Ed.), *The Abusive Partner: An Analysis of Domestic Battering,* New York: Van Nostrand Reinhold.

Gayford, J. J. (1975a). Wife battering: A preliminary survey of 100 cases. *British Medical Journal, 1,* 194-197.

Gayford, J. J. (1975b). Battered wives. *Medical Science Law, 15*(4), 243-244.

Gelles, J. A., & Walsh, J. C. (1977-78). A treatment model for the abused spouse. *Victimology: An International Journal, 2*(3-4), 627-632.

Gelles, R. J. (1974). *The violent home.* Beverly Hills: Sage.

Gelles, R. J. (1975). Violence and pregnancy: A note on the extent of the problem and needed services. *Family Coordinator, 24,* 81-86.

Gelles, R. J. (1979). *Family violence.* Beverly Hills: Sage.

Gelles, R. J. (1982). An exchange/social control approach to understanding intrafamily violence. *Behavior Therapist, 5*(1), 5-8.

Gil, D. G. (1970). *Violence against children: Physical child abuse in the United States.* Cambridge: Harvard University Press.

Giles-Sims, J. (1983). *Wife battering: A systems theory approach.* New York: Guilford.

Goffman, J. (1984). Batterers anonymous: Self help counseling for men who batter. San Bernadino, CA: B. A. Press.

Groth, N. (1979). *Men who rape: The psychology of the offender.* New York: Plenum.

Guttmacher, M. (1960). Assaultiveness and alcohol use in family disputes. *Criminology, 12,* 283-292.

Haley, J. (1976). *Problem solving therapy.* San Francisco: Jossey-Bass.

Harrison, B. W. (1981). Misogyny and homophobia: The unexplored connection. *Integrity Forum,* Lent Issue, 7-11.

Hathaaway, S. R., & Meehl, P. E. (1951). *An atlas for the clinical use of the MMPI.* Minneapolis: University of Minnesota Press.

Hilberman, E. (1978a). Response to Murray Straus. *Battered women: Issues of public policy,* Washington, DC: U.S. Commission on Civil Rights.

Hilberman, E., & Munson, K. (1978b). Sixty battered women. *Victimology: An International Journal, 3,* 460-471.

Hite, S. (1976). *The Hite report.* New York: Macmillan.

Holmes, T. H., & Rahe, A. H. (1967). The social readjustment rating scale. *Journal of Psychosomatic Research, 11,* 213-218.

Jefferson, B. S. (1982). *California Evidence Benchbook* (2nd ed., Vols. 1 and 2). Berkeley: Continuing Education of the Bar.

Johnson, D. L. (1974). *Child abuse: Some findings from the analysis of 1172 reported cases.* Paper presented to Southern Association of Agricultural Scientists, New Orleans, LA.

Jung, C. G. (1961). *Memories, dreams and reflections.* New York: Vintage Books.

Kinports, K., Bersoff, D., & Ennis, B. (1983). *Brief of amicus curiae.* American Psychological Association, *Hawthorne* v. *Florida,* No. AN-635.

Kinports, K., Bersoff, D., & Ennis, B. (1984). *Brief of amicus curiae.* American Psychological Association, *State* v. *Kelley,* No. A-99.

Kirkendall, L. (1958). Towards a clarification of the concept of the male sex drive. *Journal of Marriage and Family Living, 20,* 367–372.

Laws, J. L., & Schwartz, P. (1977). *Sexual scripts: The social construction of female sexuality.* Hinsdale, IL: Dryden.

Lefkowitz, M. M., Eron, L. D., Walder, L. O., & Hussman, L. R. (1977). *Growing Up to Be Violent.* New York: Pergamon.

Leghorn, L. (1978). Grass roots services for battered women: A model for long-term change. *A Newsletter of the Feminist Alliance Against Rape and the National Communication Network,* July/Aug.

Lehne, G. L. (1976). Homophobia among men. In D. S. David & R. Brannan, (Eds.) *The forty-nine percent majority: The male sex role.* Reading, MA: Addison-Wesley.

Leonard, L. (1983). *The wounded woman.* Athens, OH: Swallow Press.

Levinger, G. (1966). Sources of marital dissatisfaction among applicants for divorce. *American Journal of Orthopsychiatry, 36,* 803–807.

Lion, J. R. (1977). Clinical aspects of wife battering. In M. Roy (Ed.), *Battered women: A psychosocial study of domestic violence.* New York: Van Nostrand Reinhold.

Macoby, E. E., & Jacklin, A. N. (1974). *The psychology of sex differences.* California: Stanford University Press.

Malamuth, N. M., & Check, J. (1983a). Sexual arousal to rape depictions. *Journal of Abnormal Psychology, 92,* 55–67.

Malamuth, N. M., & Check, J. (1983b). Sexual role stereotyping and reactions to depictions of stranger versus acquaintance rape. *Journal of Personality and Social Psychology, 45,* 344–356.

Margolin, G. (1979). Conjoint marital therapy to enhance anger management and reduce spouse abuse. *American Journal of Family Therapy, 7(2),* 13–23.

Martin, D. (1981 rev.). *Battered wives.* San Francisco: Volcano Press.

Martin, D. (1982). Wife beating: A product of sociosexual development. In M. Kirkpatrick (Ed.), *Women's sexual experiences: Explorations of the dark continent,* New York: Plenum.

McCord, W., McCord, J., & Howard, A. (1961). Familial correlates of aggression in nondelinquent male children. *Journal of Abnormal and Social Psychology, 62,* 79–93.

McGlynn, F., Mealiea, W. L., & Landau, D. L. (1981). The current status of systematic desensitization. *Clinical Psychology Review, 1*(2), 149–179.

McNeil, M., (1984). *Domestic violence: The skeleton in Tarasoff's closet.* Unpublished paper. San Francisco.

Miller, J. B. (1976). *Toward a new psychology of women.* Boston: Beacon.

Monahan, J. (1981). *The clinical prediction of violent behavior.* Crime and Delinquency Issues Monograph. U.S. Department of Health and Human Services, Publication No. ADM 81-921. Washington, DC: U.S. Government Printing Office.

Morgan, E. (1975). *The erotization of male dominance/female submission.* Pittsburgh: Know.

Morlan, D. (1977). Why are men angry at women? *The Battered Women's Conference Report.* New York: American Friends Service Committee.

Moss, L. E. (1985). Feminist body psychotherapy. In L. B. Rosewater & L. E. Walker (Eds.), *Handbook of feminist therapy.* New York: Springer Publishing Company.

O'Faolin, J., & Martines, L. (Eds.) (1974). *Not in God's image: Women in history,* Glasgow: Fontana/Collins.

Pagelow, M. D. (1981). *Women battering: Victims and their experience.* Beverly Hills, CA: Sage.

Piercy, M. (1984). The turn-on of intimacy. *Ms.* February.

Pleck, E., Pleck, J., Grossman, M., & Bart, P. (1978). The battered data syndrome: A reply to Steinmetz. *Victimology, 2*(3–4), 680–683.

Pogrebin, L. C. (1980). *Growing up free: Raising your child in the 80's.* New York: Bantam Books.

Pollack, N. (1980). Battering husbands: A personality profile as perceived by their wives. *Dissertation Abstracts International, 41,* 51–1522D.

Post, R. M. (1975). Cocaine psychosis: A continuum model. *American Journal of Psychiatry, 132*(3), 225–231.

Prescott, J. W. (1975). Body pleasure and the origins of violence. *Bulletin of Atomic Sciences,* Nov., 10–20.

Proctor, S. (1968). *Duration of exposure to items and pre-treatment training as factors in systematic desensitization therapy.* Unpublished manuscript, Indiana University.

Ptacek, J. (1984). The clinical literature on men who batter: A review and critique. Paper presented at the Second National Conference for Family Violence Researchers, August 7–10, 1984, University of New Hampshire, Durham, NH.

Purdy, F., & Nickle, N. (1981). Practice principles for working with groups of men who batter. *Social Work with Groups, 4,* 111–122.

Raihan, N. (1982). Spouse abuse in the military community: Factors influencing incidence and treatment. In M. Roy (Ed.), *The abusing partner: An analysis of domestic battering.* New York: Van Nostrand Reinhold.

Rheingold, J. C. (1964). *The fear of being a woman.* New York: Grune & Stratton.

Rian, K. (1982). Sadomasochism and the social construction of desire. In R. L. Linden, D. R. Pagano, D. E. H. Russell, and S. L. Star (Eds.), *Against sadomasochism: A radical feminist analysis.* East Palo Alto, CA: Frog in the Well.

Ritchie, J. M. (1965). The aliphatic alcohols. In L. S. Goodman & A. Gilman, (Eds.), *The pharmacological basis of therapeutics.* New York: Macmillan.

Ritterman, M. (1983). *Using hypnosis in family therapy.* San Francisco: Jossey-Bass.

Roberts, A. R. (1981). *Sheltering battered women: A national study and service guide.* New York: Springer Publishing Company.

Roberts, A. R. (1982). A national survey of services for batterers. In M. Roy (Ed.), *The abusing partner: An analysis of domestic battering.* New York: Van Nostrand Reinhold.

Rosenbaum, A. (1979). Wife abuse: Characteristics of the participants and etiological considerations. *Dissertation Abstracts International, 40,* 1383–1388.

Rosenbaum, A., & O'Leary, D. K. (1981a). Marital violence: Characteristics of abusive couples. *Journal of Consulting and Clinical Psychology, 49,* 63–71.

Rosenbaum, A., & O'Leary, D. K. (1981b). Children: The unintended victims of marital violence. *American Journal of Orthopsychiatry, 51,* 692–699.

Rosenbaum, C. P., Adams, J. E., Scott, K. L., Renson, G. J., Tinkleberg, J. R., & Hanks, S. E. (1981). Alcohol and violence: A clinical study. In D. A. Hamberg & M. B. Trudeau (Eds.), *Behavioral aspects of aggression.* New York: Alan R. Liss.

Rosewater, L. B. (1982a). *The development of an MMPI profile for battered women.* Doctoral dissertation, Union Graduate School.

Rosewater, L. B. (1982b). Schizophrenic or battered? In *Feminist therapy: A coming of age.* Selected proceedings from Advanced Feminist Therapy Institute, Vail, CO, April. Manuscript in press.

Rosewater, L. B., & Walker, L. E. (1985). *Handbook of Feminist Therapy: Women's Issues in Psychotherapy.* New York: Springer Publishing Company.

Rounsaville, B. J., & Weissman, M. M. (1977). Battered women: A medical problem requiring detection. *International Journal of Psychiatry, 8,* 191–202.

Roy, M. (1982). Four thousand partners in violence: A trend analysis. In M. Roy (Ed.), *The abusing partner: An analysis of domestic battering.* New York: Van Nostrand Reinhold.

San Francisco Family Violence Project. (1982). *Domestic violence is a crime.*
    San Francisco, CA.
Santa Barbara County District Attorney's Office. (1981). *Family violence
    prosecution manual.*
Saunders, D. (1982). Counseling the violent husband. In P. A. Keller & L. G.
    Ritt (Eds.), *Innovations in clinical practice: A source book. Vol 1.*
    Sarasota, FL: Professional Resource Exchange.
Schechter, S. (1982). *Women and male violence.* Boston: South End.
Schneider, E. M., & Jordan, S. B. (1981). Representation of women who
    defend themselves in response to physical or sexual assault. In E. Boch-
    nak (Ed.), *Women's self defense cases: Theory and practice.* Charlottes-
    ville: The Michie Company.
Scott, P. D. (1974). Battered wives. *British Journal of Psychiatry, 125,* 443–
    451.
Searle, M. A. (1982). *Men who batter and isolation.* Unpublished paper.
Seligman, M. E. P. (1975). *Helplessness: On depression, development and
    death.* San Francisco: W. H. Freeman.
Singer, J. L., & Singer, D. G. (1975). A member of the family. *Yale Alumni
    Magazine, 38,* 10–15.
Smith, S. M., Hanson, R., & O'Noble, S. (1973). Parents of battered babies: A
    controlled study. *British Medical Journal, 4,* 388–391.
Snell, J. E., Rosenwald, R. J., & Robey, A. (1964). The wifebeater's wife.
    Archives of General Psychiatry, 11, 107–112.
Sonkin, D. J. (1983). *Legal and ethical issues in the treatment of court
    mandated male batterers.* Paper presented at the American Psychologi-
    cal Association, Anaheim, CA.
Sonkin, D. J., & Durphy, M. (1982). *Learning to live without violence: A
    handbook for men.* San Francisco: Volcano Press.
Sonkin, D. J., & Fazio, W. Men who kill: The role of the prosecution. In
    Sonkin, D. J. (Ed.), *Domestic Violence on Trial.* Manuscript in prepara-
    tion.
Star, B. (1978). Comparing battered and non-battered women. *Victimology:
    An International Journal, 3,* 32–44.
Star, B. (1983). *Helping the abuser: Intervening effectively in family vio-
    lence.* New York: Family Service Association of America.
Star, B., Clark, C. G., Goetz, K. M., & O'Hara, C. (1979). Psychosocial aspects
    of wife battering. *Social Casework, 41,* 479–487.
Steinmetz, S. K., & Straus, M. (1974). *Violence in the family.* New York:
    Harper & Row.
Steele, B. F. (1978). The child abuser. In I. L. Kutash, S. B. Kutash, L. B.
    Schlesinger, & Associates (Eds.), *Violence: Perspectives on murder and
    aggression.* San Francisco: Jossey-Bass.

Stephens, D. W. (1977). Domestic assault: The police response. In M. Roy (Ed.), *Battered women: A psychological study of domestic violence.* New York: Van Nostrand Reinhold.

Storr, A. (1970). *Human aggression.* New York: Bantam.

Straus, M. (1978). Wife beating: Causes, treatment, and research needs. *Battered women: Issues of public policy.* Washington, DC: U.S. Commission on Civil Rights.

Straus, M. A. (1980). Social stress and marital violence in a national sample of American families. In F. Wright, C. Bahn, & R. W. Rieber (Eds.), *Forensic psychology and psychiatry. Annals New York Academy of Sciences,* Vol. 347.

Straus, M. A., Gelles, R. J., & Steinmetz, S. K. (1980). *Behind closed doors: Violence in the American family.* New York: Anchor-Doubleday.

Symonds, M. (1978). The psychodynamics of violence-prone marriages. *The American Journal of Psychoanalysis, 32,* 213–222.

Tannenbaum, P. H., & Zillman (1975). Emotional arousal in the facilitation of aggression through communication. *Advances in Experimental Social Psychology, 8,* 149–192.

Thyfault, R. (1980). *Sexual abuse in the battering relationship.* Paper presented at Rocky Mountain Psychological Association, Tucson, Arizona.

Thyfault, R. (1984). Self defense: Battered woman syndrome on trial. *California Western Law Review, 20*(3).

Trevelyan, G. M. (1966). *History of England,* London: Longmans, Green.

Walker, L. E. (1977). Battered women and learned helplessness. *Victimology: An International Journal, 2*(3-4), 525–534.

Walker, L. E. (1979). *The Battered Woman.* New York: Harper and Row.

Walker, L. E. (1980). Battered women. In A. Brodsky & R. Hare-Muston (Eds.), *Women and psychotherapy.* New York: The Guilford Press.

Walker, L. E. (1981). Battered women: Sex roles and clinical issues. *Professional Psychology, 12*(1), 81–91.

Walker, L. E. (1983). The battered woman syndrome study. In D. Finkelhor, R. J. Gelles, G. Hotaling, & M. Straus, (Eds.), *The dark side of families: Current family violence research.* Beverly Hills, CA: Sage Publications.

Walker, L. E. (1984). *The battered woman syndrome.* New York: Springer Publishing Company.

Werner, P. D., Rose, T. L., & Yesavage, J. A. (1983). Reliability, accuracy and decision-making strategy in clinical prediction of imminent dangerousness. *Journal of Consulting and Clinical Psychology, 51*(6), 815–825.

West, L. A., Turner, W. M., & Dunwoody, E. (1981). *Wife abuse in the armed forces.* Washington, DC: Center for Women's Policy Studies.

Williams, T. (Ed.). (1980). *Post Traumatic Stress Disorders of the Vietnam Veteran.* Cincinnati, OH: Disabled American Veterans.

Williams, T. M., Zabrack, M. L., & Joy, L. A. (1982). The portrayal of aggression on North American T.V. *Journal of Applied Social Psychology, 12*(5), 360–380.

Wilson, G. T., & Davidson, H. C. (1971). Process of reduction in systematic desensitization. *Clinical Psychology Review, 1*(2), 149–179.

Wolfgang, M. E. (1958). *Patterns in criminal homicide.* New York: Wiley.

Wolfgang, M. E. (1967). A sociological analysis of criminal homicide. In M. E. Wolfgang, (Ed.), *Studies in homicide.* New York: Harper & Row.

Wolfgang, M. E. (1978). Violence in the family. In I. L. Kutash, (Ed.), *Perspectives on murder and aggression.* San Francisco: Jossey-Bass.

Wolpe, J., & Lazarus, A. A. (1966). *Behavior therapy techniques.* Oxford, England: Pergamon Press.

Woods, L. (1984). A status report on marriage license and dissolution surcharge laws. *The Women's Advocate,* March.

Wurr, A. (1983). Domestic violence is a crime. *Mid-peninsula support network for battered women newsletter,* Summer.

X, Laura (1984). Marital rape. (Letter to the editor.) *San Francisco Examiner,* Sept. 9.

Yalom, I. D. (1975). *The theory and practice of group psychotherapy.* New York: Basic Books.

Index

Group counseling
  client process-counselor process,
    107-109
  first sessions/last session, 101-103
  vs. individual counseling, 85-86
  problem areas, 103-106
Group leaders, 98-101, 105-106, 108
Group structure, 94-98

Harrison, B., 23
*Hedlund v. Superior Court of Orange
  County*, 134-136, 140
Hilberman, E., 3
Hite, S., 20
Homicide, domestic, 1-2, 72-73
  risk of, 72-73, 74, 80, 144
Homophobia, 22-23
Homosexual battering, 37
Hospital referrals, 174
Hostility Toward Women Scale, 46
Husband beating, 2-3

Identification stage of treatment, 66-70
Impotence, 21
Impulse disorder, 89
Incarceration of batterer to avoid
  violence, 32, 78, 82; *see also*
  Criminal justice system
Individual counseling, 85-86, 106-107
Intake stage of treatment program, 70-
  85, 196, 208-229 (forms)
Isolation
  decreasing, as goal, 90-91
  and dependency of batterers, 43
  and domestic violence, 78, 82
  and jealousy, 43
  as psychological violence, 39

*Jablonski v. Loma Linda Veterans
  Administration*, 134, 135, 136, 140
Jealousy, 38, 39, 43
Judeo-Christian tradition, 21, 23; *see
  also* Patriarchal system
Judicial system, *see* Criminal justice
  system

Kirkendall, L., 20-21

La Casa de las Madres, San Francisco, 4
Law Enforcement Assistance
  Administration, 25
Laws, J. L., 20
Learned behavior, violence as, 46-50
Learned helplessness, 12, 55, 158-160
Learning to Live Without Violence, 46-
  47, 93-94, 195-237 (forms)
  see also Treatment program
Legal issues
  case examples, 145-149
  child abuse, 130-131
  child sexual abuse, 131, 132
  in counseling batterers, 129-133
  of domestic violence, 24-30
  physician's report of victims or
    offenders of violent crime, 132-
    133
  see also Criminal justice system;
    Ethical issues
Leghorn, L., 5
Legislation
  and domestic violence, 54-58
  and marital rape, 17
Lehne, G. L., 22
Leonard, L., 185
Lethality, determination of, 70-71, 72-
  83, 144
  assaults on other family members,
    76-77, 81
  attitudes toward violence, 79, 82
  cycle/frequency of violence, 75, 81
  general mental functioning, 79, 82
  history of violence, 75-76, 81
  homicide risk, 72-73, 74, 80, 144
  isolation, 78, 82
  life stresses, 89, 82
  physical health, 79-80, 83
  previous criminal history, 77, 81-82
  proximity of victim/offender, 78, 82
  responsibility for violence, 144-149
  substance use/abuse, 76, 81
  suicide risk, 74-75, 80, 112-113, 144
  violence outside the home, 78, 82

Male batterers
  acknowledging and expressing